HOTEL MANAGEMENT
Diet and Nutrition

HOTEL MANAGEMENT
Diet and Nutrition

R.P. Saxena

CENTRUM PRESS
NEW DELHI-110002 (INDIA)

CENTRUM PRESS
H.O.: 4360/4, Ansari Road, Daryaganj,
New Delhi-110002 (India)
Tel: 23278000, 23261597, 23255577, 23286875
B.O.: No. 1015, Ist Main Road, BSK IIIrd Stage,
IIIrd Phase, IIIrd Block, Bangalore-560085 (INDIA)
Tel: 080-41723429
Email: centrumpress@gmail.com
Visit us at: www.centrumpress.com

Hotel Management: Diet and Nutrition

First Edition, 2010

ISBN 978-93-80540-90-0

Contents

Contents

Preface

Food is any substance, composed of carbohydrates, water, fats and/or proteins, that is either eaten or drunk by any animal, including humans, for nutrition or pleasure. Items considered food may be sourced from plants, animals or other categories such as fungus. Although many human cultures sought food items through hunting and gathering, today most cultures use farming, ranching, and fishing, with hunting, foraging and other methods of a local nature included but playing a minor role. Many traditions have a recognizable cuisine, a specific set of cooking traditions using various spices or combinations of flavours unique to that culture. Other differences include preferences (hot or cold, spicy etc.), and practices, the study of which is known as gastronomy. Many cultures have diversified their foods by means of preparation, cooking methods and manufacturing. This also includes a complex food trade which helps the cultures to economically survive by-way-of food, not just by consumption. Some popular types of ethnic foods include: Italian, French, Japanese, Chinese, American, Thai and Indian. Many cultures study the dietary analysis of food habits. While evolutionarily speaking, as opposed to culturally, humans are omnivores, religion and social constructs such as morality, activism or environmentalism will often affect which foods they will consume.

Nutrition is the provision, to cells and organisms, of the materials necessary (in the form of food) to support life. Many common health problems can be prevented or alleviated with a healthy diet. The diet of an organism is what it eats, and is largely determined by the perceived palatability of foods. Dietitians are health professionals who specialize in human nutrition, meal planning, economics, and preparation. They are trained to provide safe, evidence-based dietary advice and management to individuals (in health and disease), as well as to institutions. A poor diet can have an injurious impact on health, causing deficiency diseases such as scurvy, beriberi, and kwashiorkor; health-threatening conditions like obesity and metabolic syndrome, and such common chronic systemic diseases as cardiovascular disease, diabetes, and osteoporosis.

Food scientists at hotel may study more fundamental phenomena that are directly linked to the production of a particular food product and its properties. This book makes a thorough and comprehensive examination of all these details, giving insightful information to the readers on nearly every dimension of the subject. A careful selection of topics has been heeded on the basics of food and nutrition of greater interest like nutrients, food and food facts, food pyramid, healthy eating diet plan, vegetarianism, life span nutrition and raw food which would be extremely useful to the general readers, public as well as to the students and teachers of home science, nutrition and hotel management.

—*R.P. Saxena*

1

Introduction

The food industry, be it the processing industry or the catering industry, is one of the largest and most needed industry in the world today fulfilling one of our three basic needs, i.e., food. Its growth rate is phenomenal, growing by leaps and bounds to provide three square meals to our rapidly increasing population and keeping pace with the ever-changing demands of the population.

The developments in the food industry can be traced back to surplus food which needed to be preserved for a rainy day. Food preservation is not a new phenomenon. Our forefathers understood the basic principles underlying food preservation and practised them using natural ingredients and the forces of nature like sunlight and ultraviolet rays till newer and more scientific methods were developed.

Improvement in equipment and machinery has made it possible to increase the capacity of food processing plants greatly. The shelf life of perishable foods has increased dramatically with the invention of the refrigerator and the use of dry ice.

With the advent of the wheel, surplus food was transported several hundred miles. As early as in 1850, milk was transported by special milk trains and tank trucks over a distance of several hundred miles with negligible loss in quality. Food which was perishable was moved thousands of miles before it was processed, stored, and consumed.

Over the past few decades, the food industry has witnessed a significant change. The market has witnessed such a flood of food commodities, superior in quality and available all year round.

Ice cream filled cones and nuts in ice cream retaining their crunch, fresh milk stored on the shelf for months, and crisp croutons in a ready to serve cream soup are a few marvels of food science and technology. With these advances in science and technology, the consumer has an unlimited choice of meals to choose from all year round.

The aesthetic value of food is important. To be able to offer the consumer quality cuisine, basic knowledge of food science and its applications is necessary. Every food handler should know the composition, structure, and behaviour of food and the changes that take place during cooking, holding, and storage as well as what happens to food once it is consumed, i.e., its digestion, absorption, and metabolism in the human body.

The study of food is today accepted as a separate discipline called food science.

Definition: Food science is a systematic study of the nature of food materials and the scientific principles underlying their modification, preservation, and spoilage.

To understand food science, the basic concepts of physics, chemistry, mathematics, and biology and their applications, i.e., biochemistry, microbiology, and food technology, are necessary to prepare, package, store, and serve wholesome, high quality products.

All foods are chemical compounds which undergo various chemical reactions at all stages from production to consumption. These reactions are based on the laws of chemistry. Many processes used while preparing food involve physical changes apart from chemical changes.

Matter exists in three states-solid, liquid, gas.

In general, as the temperature is increased, a pure substance will change from solid to liquid and then to a gas, without change in chemical composition. However, many organic compounds will decompose, undergoing various chemical reactions, rather than a change of state when temperature is raised.

Many foods are complex mixtures of chemical substances. In processed foods, additives are added to improve colour, texture, flavour, etc., and these additives are also chemical compounds. It undergoes further chemical changes during storage, cooking, processing as well as in the human body during digestion of food by action of chemical substances.

Physical aspects of food such as the various food systems are of colloidal dimensions. Food is subjected to various physical conditions during preparation and storage which affect its quality such as temperature and pressure changes.

Food chemistry is the science that deals with the composition, structure, and properties of food, and with chemical changes that take place in food. It forms a major part of food science and is closely related to food microbiology. The chemical composition of food dictates which microorganisms can grow on it and the changes which take place in the food because of their growth. The changes may be planned and desirable or may result because of contamination, causing disease, i.e., causing food poisoning and food infection or just spoiling the food rendering it unfit for consumption. Microorganisms have basic growth requirements, namely, food, moisture, temperature, time, osmotic pressure, pH, and the presence or absence of oxygen.

Food chemistry and food microbiology are intimately related to food processing because the processes to which food needs to be subjected to improve its taste, texture, flavour, and aroma depend on its composition and ingredients. The time and temperature for food processing depend not only on the chemical composition of food but on its microbial load and the type of packaging to be used.

The growing public demand for meals away from home has made the problem of serving safe wholesome food more critical and challenging. This makes it imperative for food handlers to understand and implement the basic principles of the food science to enable them to prepare and serve high quality products over extended lunch hours.

The Need for Convenience Foods

Rapid urbanization and changes in social and cultural practices have modified the food habits of the community. Industrial development in Indian cities has compelled labour from villages to migrate to cities in search of employment. It is estimated that within the next ten years, half the world's population will be living and working in urban areas. Increase in buying power and long hours spent away from home commuting to work places, make convenience foods a necessity in every home. The ever-increasing market for convenience foods, be it tinned, canned, chilled, frozen, or preserved, presents a whole array of complex operations in food processing. This weaning away from the traditional fare of yesteryears provides a tremendous and urgent challenge to the food industry: serving safe, attractive, and nutritious food that is wholesome and bacteriologically safe and conforms with quality standards.

The urban workforce does not have the time or inclination to follow the traditional recipes and would rather pick up packed, clean, and reasonably priced meals rather than return home from work and do domestic chores.

Most food consumed in developed countries is in the form of *convenience foods.* Convenience foods are foods that require little labour and time to prepare. A pack-et of frozen green peas is a convenience food since it requires no shelling. A pack-et of whole wheat flour is also a convenience food as it has already been milled. A packet of instant idli mix is more of a convenience food, and 'ready to eat' or 'heat and eat' foods like chicken keema matar or canned palak paneer are most convenient since they need no further cooking.

Many different types of convenience foods are available in the market today. The speed and efficiency of cooking and service increases dramatically with the use of convenience foods, giving the caterer, homemaker, or working professional more time to devote to other activities. The convenience food revolution is possible because of a wide variety of chemicals which are added to food not only to preserve it but to enhance its overall quality. These numerous chemicals, tested and permitted by law to be added to food are called *food additives.*

Today, convenience foods are being specially packed for caterers and are avail-able in large catering packs. Manufacturers of specialized food supplies pack food so that it fits into standard catering equipment, e.g., catering packs that fit into vending machines. The caterer can choose between smaller packs and larger packs that are economical.

Convenience foods need to be handled with care because one source of infection can contaminate thousands of prepacked items. Take-away meals should not be kept for a long time, hygiene should be practised in processing plants, and time and temperature control should be observed during storage. Leftover contents in large catering packs should not be stored in the open.

Convenience foods help by saving considerable time and effort. However, the cost of convenience foods compared to home-prepared foods should be considered before purchase. Some foods may not be costlier while others may work out to be expensive. For people who have to rush home from work and prepare a meal, such foods purchased on the way home or stacked in the deep freezer are not only time-saving but also convenient.

Convenience foods vary widely in their palatability, nutrient content, and cost. The consumer can choose from a bewildering display of snacks, soups, sauces, fruit chunks and juices, desserts, meat, and vegetable preparations and gravies in the ready to eat and ready to cook form. They need to be warmed up in a microwave before they are served.

Canned foods, commercially prepared chappatis, snacks both sweet and savoury, main course, vegetable preparations, soups, gravies, sauces, breakfast cereals, bakery items, deep frozen foods, dry ready mixes, etc., are not only time saving but convenient to cook and store.

Thus, food science covers all aspects of food, from the properties of food materials and influences of all factors affecting food, beginning from growing the food to harvesting or slaughter, i.e., all stages from the farm to the table, from raw food till it is consumed like processing, nutritive value, shelf life, novel sources of food, fabricated food and food analogs, conservation and reuse of resources to make more food.

A study of food science and nutrition will be of benefit to all food professionals.

Summary

The food industry is a fast-growing industry that applies the principles of food science and technology to offer the consumer a wide array of fresh and processed foods to meet their nutritional needs, wants, and budget. These foods are available under different brand names, all year round in delectable flavours and assorted preparations. The aesthetic value of food is an important criterion in its acceptability. Every food handler should be aware of the composition, structure, and behaviour of food and what happens to it during processing and after consumption. The systematic study of food is called food science.

All foods are chemical compounds and under-go physical as well as chemical changes. The various food systems are of colloidal dimensions and various physical conditions such as temperature and pressure affect its quality.

Food science is intimately related to food chemistry, food microbiology, and food processing. To understand this, the basic concepts of physics, chemistry, mathematics, and biology are necessary.

The growing demand for meals away from home has made the problem of serving safe and wholesome food critical and challenging. With rapid urbanization and changes in food habits and lifestyles, and increase in the number of couples who have little time has caused a shift in focus from farm-grown fresh foods to partially or totally processed convenience foods.

These foods require little labour and time to prepare and are useful to both caterers and homemakers.

The shelf life and acceptability of these foods are enhanced by the use of permitted additives. The consumer can choose from a wide range of 'ready-to-cook' and 'ready-to-eat' foods.

Interactions in Food Technology, Agriculture, and Nutrition

The last 30 years have witnessed spectacular increases in food-grain production in India, from 51 million tonnes to more than 130 million tonnes. A sizeable buffer stock has also been built up to face the likely shortages arising out of uncertain production levels (DES 1975).

Table 1. Food-grain Production

Food grains	*1950/51*	*1966/67*	*1978/79*
Cereals	42.41	65.88	119.20
Pulses	8.41	8.34	12.16
Total	50.82	74.22	131.36

Source: DES 1975.

Various national projections indicate that food-grain production must be doubled to meet the needs of an estimated population of more than 950 million by the turn of this century. Since food grains constitute the principal source of calories, proteins, and other nutrients , careful efforts are necessary not only to conserve them against qualitative and quantitative losses but also to upgrade their nutritional and acceptability features. Thus, a systems approach has become crucial for integrating the production, conservation, and nutrition of food grains to get maximum benefits from national efforts.

Table 2 Daily Per Capita Food Consumption and Recommended Levels

		Recommended level (g)	
Food materials	***Consumption (g)***	***ICMR***[a]	***Task Force on***
Cereals	434	412	376
Pulses	34	60	64
Green leafy vegetables	21	125	116
Other vegetables	71	50	61
Roots and tubers	-	87	69
Fruits	10	30	40
Milk	69	100	189
Fats/oils	12	40	39
Meat and fish (and egg)	14	30	23
Eggs	-	30	15
Sugar/jaggery	19	35	38

a. Indian Council of Medical Research

Source: Gopalan et al 1971, Gopalan and Narasinga Rao 1971; NCST 1972.

Breeding of new food-grain varieties has been directed to increasing per hectare yields and resistance against field-borne microorganisms and insect pests. Advances in food technology and nutrition have, however, given some insight into the desirable features that need to be considered in breeding programmes. This paper attempts to highlight some salient features of the processing, storage, and nutritive value of food grains produced in India so as to understand the interphase linkages between production and post-harvest conservation.

Research and Development Efforts to Raise Food Production

The impressive growth in food-grain production during the last 30 years has resulted from increases in the area under food-grain crops; improvement of their per hectare yield; introduction of high-yielding varieties, particularly of wheat and rice; and an expansion of area under their cultivation, together with the provision of irrigation and other inputs.

Table 3. Total Cropped Area and Food-grain Production

	1960/61	*1965/66*	*1970/71*	*1971/72*	*1972/73*	*1973/74*
Area (in million hectares)	115.6	115.1	124.32	122.63	119.30	126.2
Production (in million tonnes)	82.3	72.3	108.43	105.17	97.02	103.6

Sources: DES 1975; Tata Services Ltd 1980.

Table 4. Yield of Important Food Grains (tonnes/hectares)

Crop	*1950/51*	*1970/71*	*1975/76*
Wheat	0.66	1.31	1.41
Rice	0.67	1.12	1.25
Jowar	0.35	0.47	0.59
Gram	0.48	0.66	0.71
Groundnut	0.77	0.83	0 95

Source: DES 1978 1980.

Table 5. Area under High-yielding Varieties (in million hectares)

Crop	*1966/67*	*1977/78*
Wheat	0 54 (4.2)	15.5 (73.1)
Rice	0.89 (2.5)	15.6 (39 0)
Jowar	0.19 (1.1)	3.1 (19.0)
Bajra	0.08 (0.5)	2.6 (23.6)
Maize	0.21 (041)	1.2 (21.1)
Total	1.91 (2.3)	38.0[a] (40.3)

a. Target for 1978/79, 42 million hectares. Figures in parentheses indicate the area under high-yielding varieties out of total area under the respective crop.

Source: Tata Services Ltd. 1980.

Despite these efforts, unstable production has been a conspicuous feature even in identical areas devoted to food-grain cultivation. Hence, research and developmental efforts have focused on bridging the gap between the proven yield potential and national yield average of food-grain crops.

Table 6. Gap between National Average Yields (NAY) and Yield in National Demonstrations (YND) in Farmer's Fields

Crop	*Ratio of NAY to YND*
Wheat	2:4
Rice	2:5
Gram, arhar, and groundout	40:70

Source: UNCSTD 1978.

Maximum productivity has been sought by judicious water-management practices, appropriate cropping systems (double, triple, and multiple) under dry and irrigated conditions, improved dryland agriculture (mulching, recycling of runoff water to provide supplementary irrigation, and choice of crop compatible with season), intercropping, multilevel cropping, and mixed farming practices (UNCSTD 1978).

Technological Considerations in Evolving Strategies for Varietal Development of Food Grains

About 70 per cent of food grains produced in India are retained for farm-level consumption and the rest moves along a chain of agencies before it reaches the consumption points. Post-harvest conservation by modern procedures is therefore a crucial need to prevent the dissipation of national efforts to raise food production levels. The incidence of bunt in wheat, chalky grains in rice, and Gibberella infection in maize, and the impairment of processing qualities as a result of pre-harvest infection have engaged the attention of scientists in recent years. The expertise in food conservation built up during the last 30 years has found increasing application, but basic information to evolve varieties with desirable storage, processing, and nutritional or organoleptic qualities is important in meeting future needs. Variable production levels in different years emphasize the need for varieties that give maximum yields during processing and suffer minimum losses during post-harvest handling and storage.

Processing

Food grains harvested from standing crops are dried and processed before cooking and consumption. Milling is used to obtain rice from paddy, dhals from pulses, and flours from wheat and millets. The wastages inherent in some traditional practices have been minimized through improved processing technology and equipment design. The physico-chemical features of food grains need attention in varietal development programmes.

Rice

About 50 per cent of all cereal production consists of rice, represented by numerous varieties exhibiting diverse per hectare yields and physico-chemical features. Research and developmental efforts have focused on the best utilization of paddy varieties grown in the country through:

a. minimizing qualitative and quantitative losses during harvest and post-harvest handling and drying stages;
b. improving the milling yields of rice by appropriate drying and milling procedures, and the development of milling equipment;
c. adapting processing procedures to improve nutrition and acceptability;
d. utilizing by-products; and
e. product development for diverse needs.

The investigations at the Central Food Technological Research Institute (CFTRI) have conclusively shown that inherent grain structure and harvest/post-harvest drying practices directly influence the milling behaviour of paddy.

Paddy is currently harvested at 16 to 18 per cent moisture level because of difficulties in getting labour, drying space, and other amenities during harvest periods. Harvesting at this stage results in shattering and sun-checking of grains ultimately reflected in heavy breakages and reduced milling yields. Harvesting at higher grain moisture levels of say 20 to 24 per cent (indicated by the presence of 1 per cent milky grains), and a controlled drying procedure with an intermediate conditioning stage, is suitable for farm level use, and also reduces milling breakages.

Breeding of crack-resistant varieties, the second approach, overcomes frequent process alterations and equipment designs.

Crack-resistant and low-shattering selections from pushpa, vani and madhu varieties have been identified, tested and released by the CFTRI for mini-test trials through the University of Agricultural Sciences, Bangalore, Further, a chalky variant of Alur sanna (a rice variety), which seems to cook into discrete, fluffy grains even without ageing, has also been identified by the CFTRI for further trials. The influence of physico-chemical characteristics on the storage, packing, and processing of rice has been examined as an aid in post-harvest conservation. For example, grains with low length: breadth ratio exhibit higher bulk density (and lower porosity), indicating that a given volume of round grains has a greater weight than slender grains. Similarly, the friction coefficient of grains increases with moisture level, contributing to handling and packing problems. Brown rice and highly milled rices, characterized by low friction coefficients, pack well, while intermediate milled rice, particularly from parboiled paddy, packs badly because of high friction and low bulk density (DES 1975). Yellow discoloration of rice preharvest has also been a problem in some parts of the country.

Varieties of rice with a high amylose content cook into dry and flaky products, while those with a low content into pasty products. The gelatinization temperature (GT) of starch has proved to be an important quality criterion and low-GT rices are preferred for puffed products (Bhattacharya 1979). Data such as these are extremely useful in developing varieties capable of yielding cooked products that suit the diverse food habits of Indian populations.

Breeding of varieties with a higher bran oil content, and weak or no bran-lipase activity, is also indicated in relation to the edible oil requirements of the country. Breeding for low husk content would lead to higher yields of edible material, but the storage qualities of such varieties would need scrutiny.

Coarse Grains

Coarse grains consisting of jowar, maize, bajra, and other millets account for about 25 per cent of total cereal production. They are dryland crops capable of withstanding variable climatic conditions. Recent years have witnessed the evolution and commercial cultivation of hybrids, new varieties, and composites characterized by good yields, disease resistance, and adaptability to different cropping systems.

Table 7. Some New Hybrids and Varieties of Millets Evolved or Recommended in Recent Years

Crop	*Hybrids and new varieties*
Jowar	CSH-1, CSH-4, CSH-5. CSH-6, CSH-7R, CSH-8R (all hybrids).CSV-3 (370), CSV-4 (CS 3541), CSV-2 (303), CSV-5 (168), CSV-6 (604) (kharif varieties).SPY-86, FR varieties (few) (rabi).
Maize	Deccan, Ganga Safed-2, Hi-Starch, Him-123, Ganga-5, Deccan-101 (all hybrids), Amber, Jawahar, Kisan, Vikram, Sona, Vijay (all composites), Shakthi, Rattan, Protima (nutritionally superior Opaque-2 composites).
Bajra	BJ-104, BK-560, NHB-5, PHB-10 and 14, CJ-104, CK-560 (stable hybrids resistant to downy mildew), VZM-composite (resistant to mildew).

Sources. Ganga Prasada Rao 1976; Joginder Singh 1976; Murthy 1976.

Coarse grains yield cooked products of harder texture than rice and wheat because of a fibrous bran layer that is relatively resistant to water permeability during the cooking process, and also of hard and horny subaleurone layers. Milling procedures and equipment (Desikachar 1976) have been evolved that remove 10 to 15 per cent of grain layers as bran to obtain grains and flours without serious impairment of nutritional qualities. Large-sized and damaged starch granules present in the grains of certain varieties of maize, jowar, and bajra are conductive to higher water uptake by flours and soft cooked products.

Wheat

Over 90 per cent of the wheat produced in the country is ground in chakkis to obtain flour of about 95 per cent extraction, used for making various unleavened breads such as chapati and poor). Only about 2 million tonnes pass through roller flour mills to yield maida and white flour used in bakery products. New varieties in various stages of development and cultivation are systematically screened for characteristics needed for the manufacture of bread and biscuits (Shankar and Amla 1979). Comprehensive data have become available from the Indian Agricultural Research Institute (IARI), the CFTRI, and the Food Grains Research Centre at Hapur. A programme has been undertaken at the CFTRI to gain an insight into the protein characteristics of wheat and their relationship to the quality of chapati, the most important means of utilizing wheat in this country. Some attempts have also been made to define chapati quality by sensory methods and to correlate the data with instrumental methods of analysis (CFTRI 1977-1981). Translation of these criteria into physico-chemical characteristics could help in evolving varieties specially suited for chapati.

Pulses

Pulses are the principal means of raising the protein quality of Indian cereal-based dietaries. Pulse production has not exceeded 12.5 million tonnes, although consumption requirements for 1980181 can be estimated at 15 million tonnes (at 60 9 per capita per day for a 684 million population). To minimize the wastages in traditional milling practices and hence nutrient losses, improved procedures and milling equipment have been evolved for commercial use. This technology has been used by industry for the milling of pigeon-pea almost throughout the year, independent of the climatic conditions, which play an important role in traditional practices (Kurien 1979).

Milling conditions are also being optimized for mung bean, chick-pea, urd bean, cow-pea, kidney bean, horse gram, winged bean, and peas by suitable adaptation or modification of the technology developed for pigeon-pea at the CFTRI.

Wide variations in physical properties and chemical composition of each of these pulses and their varieties are to be expected in different regions and cropping systems. These properties would influence the milling behaviour of pulses, necessitating expensive changes in technologies and equipment. Intra-and inter-varietal differences in physico-chemical properties should be exploited to upgrade the milling quality of the grain, without sacrifice of yield and duration.

Storage

Food grains in the hot and humid countries of Asia suffer qualitative and quantitative losses from insects, microorganisms and rodents during post-harvest handling and storage. Impairment of organoleptic and nutritional qualities and health hazards arising from insect and fungal metabolises, are well-known effects of inadequate grain protection measures and undesirable storage conditions. Food grains handled by government agencies benefit from improved storage practices, but not those remaining in farm storage.

To eliminate or minimize such losses, pesticidal chemicals and their formulations are used widely for prophylaxis or destruction of insect pests both pre- and post-harvest. Pesticide residues are monitored and regulated under Indian food laws to ensure safety to consumers. Increasing hazards from the pesticide residues on food grains accumulating in the human system either by direct consumption or through animal-based foods, have led to an intensification of research on non-toxic insecticides, biological methods of control, and breeding of varieties resistant to pre-harvest infestation.

A mass of experimental data on the varietal resistance of different food grains to storage pests has been put out from various parts of the world. More often than not, the susceptibility or resistance of high-yielding varieties to storage pests is tested just before release for commercial cultivation. Attention to pest resistance is important at all stages of the breeding programme. Maintaining desirable genetic characteristics on a national scale of cultivation is difficult and expensive.

Sixty-seven varieties of rice have been tested for field infestation by Angoumois paddy moth (Sitotroga cerealella) and graded for susceptibility (Kittur and Patel 1972).

Genetic resistance of certain rice varieties to this storage pest has also been reported from the United States (Cogburn 1977). Information on susceptibility or resistance of wheats grown in India to storage pests such as the rice weevil (Sitophilus oryzae), or khapra beetle (Trogoderma granarium), Rhizopertha dominica, and Tribolium castaneum have also been generated to help in breeding and cultivation.

In maize, Angoumois paddy moth is found to damage varieties with a high amylose content (Fergason et al. 1970). Reports from Africa indicate that local varieties are more resistant to insect infestation than improved varieties and hybrids, because of hard kernels and complete coverage of cobs by sheaths (Adams 1977; Dobie 1977). Resistance and susceptibility of India maize varieties to Trogoderma granarium and Rhizopertha dominica have also been tested. Six genotypes (M-25-1, CSH-1, CSH-2, CSH3, CSH-4, and CSH-5) of Indian jowar have also been tested and the degrees of resistance to storage pests ascertained (Krishnamurthy et al. 1976).

Varietal resistance of pulses to storage pests has also been indicated in India. Trials on chick-pea have shown that grains of indigenous varieties G-24 and G-30 are more tolerant than new varieties to the pulse beetle (Callosobruchus chinensis) because of a wrinkled surface and tough coat (Gupta and Mishra 1970).

Continuous efforts are necessary to develop and maintain pest-resistant germplasm of different food grains so as to economize on the costs of storage and infestation control.

Breeding for Improved Nutritional Quality

Breeding for nutritional quality has mainly been directed to improving the protein content, which may or may not be reflected in increased levels of specific essential amino acids. The dwarf wheats cultivated in India contain 12.5 - 16 per cent protein and 2.21 - 2.9 9 of lysine per 100 9 protein (Deosthale et al. 1969). The protein content of improved sorghum varies from 7 to 10 per cent, and that of lysine from 0.9 to 2.6 9 per 100 9 protein. Lysine is the amino acid that limits the nutritional quality of sorghum protein; however, there is overwhelming evidence to show that excess of dietary leucine (another essential amino acid) results in a conditioned nicotinic acid deficiency. More recent studies have shown that the leucine/isoleucine ratio may be as important as the leucine level in causing pellagra. Deficiency of lysine is also relevant in bajra and ragi as in other cereals (Srikantia 1976).

Tannin present in the testa of sorghum grains at about 1 per cent level is known to reduce protein digestibility and availability by binding some of its fractions. Most Indian varieties contain less than 0.1 per cent tannin and it may not be of much significance. However, recently the National Institute of Nutrition indicated that the big-availability of iron from a variety of jowar that contained 136 mg/100 9 of tannin was lower than in one containing 20 mg/ 100 g of tannin. Of the common cereals, the big-availability of iron from jowar is least and iron deficiency anaemia is common among poorer sections of the population. A low tannin content in jowar is therefore a desirable breeding feature (Srikantia 1976).

Very little attention seems to have been given to the carbohydrates of food grains be they cereals, millets, or pulses, although animal experiments indicate that flatulence can occur by feeding food grains containing stachyose (CFTRI Annual Report 1980/87), and that protein quality can be affected by the level of digestibility of dietary starches. For example, feeding the field bean and some of its carbohydrate fractions to rats affected the absorption of calcium and nitrogen. Detailed carbohydrate profiles of food-grain varieties appear relevant in breeding programmes in terms of nutrition, processing and culinary practice (Srikantia 1979).

Conclusions

The impact of scientific advances in raising food-grain production levels and building buffer stocks could in future years be diluted by agro-climatic uncertainties and population growth. Accordingly, efforts have been intensified to develop sturdy varieties capable of withstanding adverse conditions, resisting infestation, and giving high per hectare yields.

Research and development in post-harvest conservation of food grains have begun to provide a fund of information on physico-chemical characteristics that influence milling yields, cooking behaviour, and sensory qualities. Inherent crack-resistant feature of paddy for better milling yields and low breakage of rice, the influence of carbohydrate make-up and starch characteristics on cooking qualities and digestibility of rice and millets, imbalances in amino acid profiles causing nutritional deficiencies like pellagra, and hard texture coupled with a wrinkled surface in grain as a deterrent against pest infestation, are some specifics that merit consideration in breeding programmes.

Commendable advances in breeding, post-harvest conservation and nutrition have been made, but only through isolated efforts. Technologies and equipment have also been developed to process varieties under commercial cultivation, but may not cope with the diversities in physico-chemical characteristics of different food-grain varieties. Constant interaction among breeders, post-harvest technologists, nutritionists, and extension specialists is necessary to integrate the developments in various disciplines and evolve a systems approach that will result in raised production levels and optimal utilization without sacrifice of nutritional or sensory qualities.

While the evolution of varieties characterized by high productivity and disease resistance will continue to have a high place in breeding programmes, genetic translation of such desirable attributes as milling yield, cooking quality, acceptability, nutritive value, and post-harvest infestation is a challenge to the scientific community.

Coordination between the areas of agriculture, food technology, and nutrition needs to be reflected in practice (and not just as policy) in the evolution of food-grain varieties possessing the best possible attributes of production, utilization, and nutrition. Such interaction has a very crucial role to play in the food system.

Generating Multidisciplinary Action: The Importance of Interface Activity between Agriculture, Food Science, and Nutrition

The spectre of hunger, poverty, and malnutrition continues to stare at mankind. It represents a multidisciplinary challenge of no small magnitude and therefore requires a multidisciplinary approach to find a solution. Science and technology have been able to make meaningful contributions to socioeconomic development only when they have acted in an interdisciplinary manner to solve the problems. The United Nations University has therefore recognized the value of such an approach and has given special attention to organizing activities that would involve teams of scientists (both social and natural), technologists, policy-makers and planners (including development economists) and the implementers of programmes to collectively look into the major problems of mankind and find solutions for them through co-operative efforts. The United Nations University is doing this in the hope that the concerned disciplines will stimulate each other consciously and create a comprehensive and dynamic system capable of multidisciplinary action that could increase the pace of progress towards establishment of a more equitable and just social order in this world. This effort could convert the vicious circles in which we are caught at present into dynamic development cycles. What can agriculture, food science, and nutrition contribute towards this effort? And how can all three fields interact with each other and with other areas in order to benefit society? These questions need to be critically examined.

It is with this objective in mind that the UN University has supported the organization of interface workshops. It is hoped that the present workshop on the interfaces between agriculture nutrition, and food science will provide an opportunity for better understanding of the whole system in greater depth and in relation to actual problems, so that more meaningful multidisciplinary solutions can be sought through cooperation between the scientific communities concerned in other fields.

The world population, which at present stands at about 4,300 million, is expected to reach a figure of well over 6,000 million by the year 2000 (FAO 1979). Agricultural production has barely kept pace even with the present need. The requirement of food, even to meet minimum need, will be nearly twice the present production level by the turn of the century and the challenges for the next century would become much greater. Food losses continue to be high and take away from mankind a substantial amount of what is produced with a great deal of inputs and human effort. The consequent qualitative deterioration of food, resulting from infestation by rodents, insects, and microorganisms, adds to the problem of malnutrition. Prevention of these losses would increase and improve food supplies without additional demand on land, and raise nutritional standards.

The UN University looks to this workshop to provide multidisciplinary leadership, and for its recommendations that may be useful in moving forward more rapidly towards solving this global problem, which is among the greatest challenges facing mankind in the twenty-first century scientifically, socially, and politically. In this, the efforts of the organs, organizations and bodies of the United Nations system will have an important role to play, but the real efforts needed will have to come from the countries themselves where the problem really exists.

The Role of Science and Technology

The phenomenal rate at which science and technology continue to develop is clear from even one single indicator: 3,000 words of scientific literature are published every minute. Yet their impact on developing countries has been far from satisfactory. Only a few developing countries have benefited. These are the countries that have recognized the nature and magnitude of their problems, and have built capabilities in the form of human resources and institutions able to use the available knowledge, generate new knowledge, and further bring about its interaction with society to produce technologies that can be absorbed into the social system.

It must, however, be noted that the interaction that has taken place between science and society in advanced countries cannot always be the same as that required in the developing countries because of the fact that conditions are vastly different. There is a need in the developing countries to bring about more meaningful and deliberate interaction between science and society if technologies are to be generated that would be really useful to them. Trained human resources that can bring about the interaction must be created, that is, people who understand not only the disciplines of science and technology, but also the interfaces involved in ensuring a multidisciplinary effort. Only then will the results produced be such as to bring real benefit to the countries by triggering self-reliant and long-lasting processes of progress. The developing countries, which represent nearly 70 per cent of humankind, account for barely 5 per cent of the world expenditure on research and development in science and technology. If they have to achieve the desired results, every effort must be made to build their capabilities and optimize their impact through creation of multidisciplinary networks of cooperating institutes. The UN University is giving special attention to the need for this type of development in its Medium Term Perspective for 1982/87 (UNU 1981).

The present poverty and socioeconomic stagnation has resulted in creating a condition where 65 per cent* of the world population live on about 15 per cent of the world income (Parpia 1979). The economy of these countries is primarily based on agriculture; therefore, it is through agriculture and related fields of economic activity that resources have to be generated that would contribute to overcoming poverty and bringing nutritious food within the reach of the common man. To talk of nutrition in isolation from raising income levels and increasing food supplies would be like telling the poor that if they do not have bread they should eat cake.

The Approach for Developing Countries

When one considers the available potential, there is a great deal of hope for improving the situation. It is unfortunate that such negative aspects as the limitation of resources, population growth, and environment have received greater publicity than the positive aspects. To exploit fully the resources available. There is an urgent need for both the political will and the provision of financial resources to build scientific capabilities.

The Post-harvest Phases

Despite the emphasis on raising agricultural production, shortages of food continue, showing that such efforts must in future follow a different course. Some of these represent intelligent estimates and indicate the need for much more data to be collected. These losses are not only quantitative but qualitative in nature. Within four weeks of insect infestation, the protein efficiency ratio (PER) of wheat and legumes can come down substantially, while the food itself becomes unacceptable through development of undesirable metabolites.

Policy Planning and Management of an Integrated Agriculture and Nutrition Technology Network

Missing Link

Agriculture, nutrition, and food science have seldom been discussed together. Somehow, discussions on overall planning and policies for agriculture have remained isolated from food science and nutrition. However, taking the overall need as a working base, nutritional inputs and requirements are projected so as to work out per capita availability and consumption. Agricultural production will continue to remain short in relation to overall nutritional requirements.

Advances in food science and technology have been made, and various appropriate technologies applied. It is disheartening to observe that despite the existence of a very large fund of knowledge for bringing about technological changes, overall adoption of new technologies that involve agricultural produce has been slow, even when acceptance of the new technology is considered to be in national interests.

Policies and Planning

Is integrated management of agriculture policies and planning feasible in India? Agriculture is a state subject. No amount of policy planning at the central level can be effectively implemented uniformly on an all-India basis. This means, therefore, that policies will have to be broad-based and that implementation will occur according to the specific needs of the area, or, for that matter, the crop system. Coordination and integration at an all-India level have been attempted through well-devised interactions between policy-makers and the implementing agencies. Repeatedly over the years policymakers have recognized that planning should be at the base level, and, therefore, policies should be evolved at national level. Under the circumstances how do we go about planning an all-India crop pattern? For certain categories of production, such as those that are of a perennial nature, some planning is possible since one can estimate the areas under such plantations. But when it comes to general agricultural crops, the pattern of production would vary depending on many factors, primarily decision-making on the part of the individual farmer. Planning in agriculture therefore must establish linkages with the farmer, and some means will have to be found to involve him in the adoption of the plan: otherwise no worthwhile policy can be evolved. It will thus be necessary to know how the farmer will react to various policies in deciding his own plan. We will also have to determine what his options are, as well as his reactions to any new ideas, and how far he is convinced of the significance of things considered beneficial. So far no attempt has really been made to have the primary producer comprehend any cost-benefit ratios, or to know how he would benefit by adopting a policy strategy evolved at district, state, or central level. In the present socioeconomic and political system, it would indeed be important to establish full rapport with the primary producer. This can be achieved to a large extent by interacting first with selected farm leaders, and have these leaders transmit to the farmers the overall need for policies and planning in the total national context. Through such means, there could be widespread adoption of agricultural policies and planning.

However, it is recognized that even with the diverse nature of a subcontinent like India, considerable success has been achieved in improving the overall agricultural situation. The Green Revolution, with its significant adoption of high-yielding varieties all over India, has many lessons for us. Perhaps the techniques employed in extension need much wider appreciation and adoption. Although there may be shortcomings, agricultural development has in itself been epoch-making.

Inputs

With the high population growth rate in India, there would have to be continuous effort to improve food production. Agricultural production can be considerably increased in India because circumstances are favourable. It has been shown that a very high rate of crop productivity can be achieved, and from the achievement of the research stations one can visualize how much potential there still is to improve overall production. The lab-to-land programme can provide many examples of feasible adoption of high productivity.

The basic need for any human being is food, and in the Indian context, even shelter and clothes are less important. If we decide as a policy to have adequate food for everyone, an all-out attempt must be made to attain the needed production through agriculture by way of a plan that would match agricultural production with nutritional needs. This is feasible, but it does seem that our policy perhaps lacks this recognition of a need for a national nutritional uplift. Some of the policies adopted are discouraging, and do not seem to help the attainment of a higher rate of productivity.

Inputs like seed, irrigation, fertilizer, and pesticides are the basic requirements for attaining a high rate of production. Take for example the use and cost of fertilizer. Since fertilizer is essential to productivity, in the initial stages all encouragement was given to the use of fertilizer. However with the recent considerable escalation in cost, the overall demand for fertilizer has decreased, and this has substantially (10 per cent) lowered agricultural production. Is this in the national interest? would it not have been better to continue to encourage the use of fertilizer and help the farmer achieve higher rates of production? Similarly, for other inputs like pesticides, power, and fuel for irrigation, the policy should be to minimize their costs. It is a tragedy that whenever there is a shortage of power, the first restriction in most states falls on the rural feeders; this restricts use of irrigation, at a time when it is most required.

Certain advanced countries, and even developing countries, have helped achieve higher rates of productivity in agriculture by assuring a supply of inputs at very low cost. Even in India, if we were to produce much more of any foodstuff, it could be an export earner. Considering the overall potential of agricultural development, prospects for India becoming a net exporter of agricultural produce rather than having to depend on imports are very good.

The rate of productivity in agriculture can also be further increased by giving special incentives to those who attain a higher-than-average rate of productivity. Such incentives would attract many farmers, and might give the direction needed to attain specific production aims of any commodity. Many forms of incentive have been designed for industrial development and for export, but in the area of agriculture such forms are very few. In reality there is a negative approach to higher agricultural production, since urbanites and policy-makers continue to scoff at any successes made in agriculture.

Agricultural Prices Commission

The Agricultural Prices Commission (APC) is an important agency that can be effectively used as a mechanism of planning and of attaining some integration in agriculture. This role has not so far been fully visualized for the APC. It deals only with working out price support for selected agricultural commodities. To be used as an instrument in policy implementation, APC must broaden its mandate, since it is the prices of agricultural commodities that largely determine the decisions of the farmer. So far the APC has perhaps not given consideration to the nutritional aspect of agricultural commodities. No weightage seems to have been given directly to nutritional need in fixing prices, though in recognition of the overall shortfall in such agricultural commodities as oilseeds or pulses, higher incentive prices have been given. In recommending an overall "food basket" of balanced nutrition for the country, it may not be feasible to advise APC to encourage higher prices for any products that would improve the overall nutritional needs of the nation. As a matter of policy, however, a recommendation should be made that a nutritionist may be included as a member of the APC, with the intention of influencing pricing policies from the point of view of nutrition.

Integration of Policies

There is a serious lack of integration in the formulation of policies by various ministries. It would appear that often the exigency of the situation is overrated and the perspective plan is sacrificed. To give an example, the policy decision that has been made in regard to sugar price, levy excise duty, and export, in spite of integration at the highest level, suffers from lack of perspective, and has not taken into consideration the high potential for sugar production nor its effect on producers and consumers. Similarly, the decision to import 1.5 million tons of wheat as an expedient reaction to a particular situation may have a long-term effect on the production of wheat, in which India has attained an international record of productivity would it not be possible to evolve a long-term policy, by which the farmer would be assured of prices that are reasonable, which is linked with any escalation (such linkages are in operation for all dearness allowances) and which is guaranteed for a period of five years? This would enable the farmer to work out a plan of rotation according to his own feasibility.

Another example is the price of milk. Most urban areas in India now have public sector dairies. Milk prices of these dairies are artificially kept low, resulting in substantial losses to the exchequer and, of course, in no significant improvement in the purchase price of milk. There is therefore a lack of any incentive for a higher production of milk, and this would naturally reduce the overall availability of milk and milk products. Not only is the pricing policy affecting milk production, it is also affecting the nutrition of people.

Credit

Credit again is an instrument that can really help attain higher agricultural production, but this instrument has not been properly used. General availability of credit is based on the cost of specific crops. However, only a few banks have linked a higher rate of productivity to higher credit. Such linkages between credit and productivity would enable the farmer to use effectively more inputs and improved technology.

Apart from short-term credit for the crop, there is also a real need to organize better credit linkages for land development, irrigation and such post-harvest facilities as storage, handling, and marketing. This has not been recognized. Agricultural production would be diluted through large wastages for lack of post-harvest handling facilities. Damage to perishable commodities would be especially higher without proper post-harvest facilities at the farm level and all through the marketing chain.

The processing and marketing of various agricultural commodities deserve better terms of credit. With many of them, the producers' interest can be protected only if commodities are properly preprocessed, packaged, and marketed. However, credit is sometimes restricted and is now given at a lower rate of interest only towards production. But if full benefit of greater production is to be acquired, extension of credit to the later steps of handling, packaging, and transport would not only protect many food commodities from deterioration, not only in terms of quantity but of product quality and nutrition. Much could be done in preventing if easier terms of credit were made available for these purposes. Not only must credit be provided, but incentives may have to be designed to improve the overall handling of all commodities.

Marketing

Planners often consider agricultural production as a base for all policies. This is highly erroneous. A country that is predominently rural, with an obvious lack of rural development, suffers when the infrastructure needed for proper marketing of agricultural commodities is missing. Post-harvest handling, processing, and marketing of agricultural commodities influence individual nutrition. In other words, it is not sufficient to evaluate the availability of nutritional foodstuffs by considering just the overall production of agricultural commodities. It is necessary to understand how the marketing of food has been organized and how the needs of each consumer have been met.

A study of the public distribution system through ration shops, of the Food Corporation of India and of other agencies that are handling such programmes as Food-for-Work, shows how ineffective are the means to properly protect food and service the consumer. Not only are the costs high, but the deterioration of food in terms of quality and nutrient content is very evident. Surely there is a need for much better understanding of how post-harvest technology could be the means for improving substantially the quality of food.

It may also be relevant to ask whether it is necessary to continue a policy of rationing, recognizing that there is an overall significant reduction in the quality and nutrition of food. Why would it not be possible to replace the entire programme by one of Food-for-Work, which has relevance to the use of manpower and the employment of food as a resource? Extension of the Food-for-Work programme could also generate employment in the private and public sectors, or enhance a self-employed status. This programme could perhaps adopt nutritional criteria as a means for improving the nutritional status of the lower strata of the community.

Market yards and mandis could also be used in monitoring and evaluating standards and the quality of agricultural commodities. This would also help in improving handling, storage and processing of the trade commodities.

Agro-industries are on the threshold of an expansion programme. However, it is unfortunate that most agriculture commodities needed by these industries are not produced in accordance with the requirements of industry since there is hardly any link between industry and agriculture. An isolated exception is sugar, where productivity has been very effectively linked with the quality of sugar-cane. Establishing linkages between agriculture and agro-industry would help to improve the status of food technology and most likely nutrition. Vertical integration through use of an agricultural commodity would contribute substantially to overall economic progress.

Integrated Use of Agricultural Commodities

An important area affecting both nutrition and food technology lies in the utilization of agricultural produce to full potential. In developed countries, producers receive maximum benefit out of such total utilization of agricultural produce. This is achieved through vertical integration, utilizing each and every by-product of agriculture. Food science and technology could significantly contribute to this end of improving the status of agricultural commodities in terms of higher utilization. Moreover, many of these commodities could contribute greatly to nutrition. It is not necessary that all processes produce items for human use; there are many innovative technologies that could use agricultural commodities as cattlefeed, fertilizer, and fuel. Some studies have been made to prepare balance sheets of all inputs into agriculture and its outputs. Through such studies, one can perhaps evaluate, if not the cost-benefit at least the nutrition-benefit ratio for important agricultural commodities. If this were done, we could perhaps achieve a proper interphase of agriculture, nutrition, and food science.

2

Organic Foods in Relation to Nutrition and Health

Food, Nutrition, and Health

When I accepted the invitation of the Royal Society of Arts to deliver the Cantor Lectures — an invitation by which I was greatly honoured — it was my intention to speak on the more general aspects of nutrition in relation to public health.

But during the time that has elapsed since then I have seen, heard and read much both in the lay Press and elsewhere which leads me to believe that the significance of the term, 'nutrition', is not always fully understood.

It has seemed to me desirable, therefore, to attempt an explanation of it, for if its meaning be clearly comprehended, its importance to the national health will become self-evident. This explanation must of necessity deal with fundamentals, familiar possibly to many of you. But there may be others of my audience, or who may read these lectures in their published form, whose understanding of nutrition is less complete: to these I especially address myself.

It is not possible to comprehend the relationship of food to nutrition, and of both to health and disease without some understanding of the structure of the body, of the functions of food, of the processes involved in the function of nutrition, and of the pathological changes brought about in the organs and tissues of the body by derangements of nutrition consequent on faulty food.

The Cell

The human body, like the bodies of all plants and animals, excepting those of a very lowly order, is made up of countless millions of cells. Each cell is composed of a microscopic mass of protoplasm enclosed in a delicate membrane and having a differentiated part — the nucleus. Every cell is a perfect physico-chemical laboratory, doing specialized work and needing special materials, both for this work and for the maintenance of its structure and functions. The protoplasm, or essential substance of living cells, is the physical basis of organic life. Upon it depend all the vital functions: nutrition, secretion, growth, reproduction, irritability and motility. It is subject to change or differentiation of the most varied sort: forming epithelium, bone, muscle, nerves, glands, organs of special sense, etc. It is a viscid, colloidal material made up of water (hydrogen and oxygen), carbon, nitrogen, and a number of other elements in complex and unstable combinations. The nitrogenous substances, known as proteins, enter largely into its structure, as do a number of inorganic salts. In addition to these, the cells contain another indispensable component: a phosphorized fat called lecithin. This substance facilitates the absorption of nutriment by the cell, the discharge of such specific products as it may contribute to the processes of the body as a whole, and the elimination of the end-products of its chemical activities.

The nucleus is the directing centre of the functional activity of the cell. It consists of a network of filaments whose meshes are filled with a special kind of protein containing phosphorus (nucleo-protein). Along the course of these filaments there are granules formed of an iron-containing protein (chromatin). Upon the integrity of the nucleus and the normal structure of its proteins depend all the vital processes. Presently we shall see how important the specific proteins of the nucleus are, how important are the mineral elements — phosphorus and iron — entering into their composition, how important is the optimum supply to the cells of all elements and complexes needed for cellular activity. For the root of the whole matter of food and nutrition is the nourishment of the cell, whether it be of bone, epithelium, muscle, gland, nerve or special sense. The inevitable consequence of its faulty nourishment is depreciation of its structure and functions — the foundation upon which a vast edifice of disease is built.

Food

Man is made up of what he eats. The constituents of his food are those of which his body is composed. His foodstuffs, derived from the vegetable and the animal kingdoms, consist, for the most part, of matter that is living, that was formerly living or that is derived from matter that was formerly living. Man cannot himself build up living tissue from materials which have in themselves no necessary connection with living protoplasm. This, plants do for him. Out of the earth and air, and under the influence of the sun, they transmute certain inorganic substances — mineral salts, water and carbon dioxide — into organic foodstuffs suited to his use and to the use of the animals whose produce or whose flesh he uses as food. He is, indeed, created out of the earth; and according as the earth provides, by way of plant and animal life, the materials needed by his body, so is that body well, ill or indifferently made and sustained.

Food may be defined as anything which when taken into the alimentary tract provides on digestion materials for the nourishment of the body; materials wherewith its cells fashion themselves each after its kind; materials to sustain their structure and to co-ordinate and control their functions; materials wherewith tissues of specialized functions elaborate their products; and materials to provide energy for cellular work.

The substances wherewith these purposes are effected are oxygen, water and the digestion products of proteins, fats, carbohydrates, inorganic elements and vitamins. Apart from oxygen and water, those at present known to be indispensable to the performance of the body's functions are thirty-six in number. Of these eighteen are amino-acids, derived from the proteins of the food. Eleven are inorganic elements: sodium, potassium, calcium, magnesium, phosphorus, iron, copper, sulphur, manganese, chlorine and iodine. One is glucose, derived chiefly from carbohydrates (though the body can in certain circumstances convert proteins and fats into glucose). One is linoleic acid, derived from fats. And five are vitamins: called respectively vitamins A, B, C, D and E.

No single foodstuff contains all these essentials. A properly constituted diet is such a combination of foodstuffs as does provide them all in proper quantity and proportion one to another. Their proportion, or balance, is a matter of great importance. We may, indeed, conceive of a properly constituted diet as a system of mutually adapted parts working together; absence or inadequacy of one part deranging the whole system. It may be said of the essential constituents of food, as Marcus Aurelius has said of other things: 'Meditate often upon the connection of these things and upon the mutual relation that they have one unto another. For all are, after a sort, folded and involved one within another and by these means all agree well together.'

In addition to proteins, carbohydrates, fats, mineral salts and vitamins, there are in food blood-forming substances, extractives, flavouring matter and pigments that have parts of greater or lesser importance to play in the nourishment of the body. The food must also contain a certain amount of innocuous, indigestible material, or roughage as it is called, to stimulate intestinal movements. Besides all this, there is something in the freshness of food, especially vegetable food — some form of energy perhaps; it may be certain rays of light or electrical property — which gives to it a health-promoting influence. Certain it is that no synthetic diet that I have been able to devise has equalled in health-sustaining qualities one composed of the fresh foodstuffs as nature provides them.

Further, the quality of vegetable foods depends on the manner of their cultivation: on conditions of soil, manure, rainfall, irrigation. Thus, we found in India that foodstuffs grown on soil manured with farmyard manure were of higher nutritive quality than those grown on the same soil when manured with chemical manure. Rice grown in standing water — the common practice in India — was less nutritious than when grown on the same soil under conditions of natural rainfall. Spinach grown in a well-tended and manured kitchen-garden was richer in vitamin C than that grown in an ill-tended and inadequately manured one. Examples of this kind might be multiplied, but these suffice to indicate ways in which agricultural practice is linked with the quality of food, with nutrition and with health. If, indeed, man is to derive all the benefits that the soil is so ready to yield to him, he must employ his intelligence and his knowledge in rendering it fit to yield them to him. Impoverishment of the soil leads to a whole train of evils: pasture of poor quality; poor quality of the stock raised upon it; poor quality of the foodstuffs they provide for man; poor quality of the vegetable foods that he cultivates for himself; and, faulty nutrition with resultant disease in both man and beast. Out of the earth are we and the plants and animals that feed us created, and to the earth we must return the things whereof we and they are made if it is to yield again foods of a quality suited to our needs. Man's dependence on the earth is beautifully expressed by Robert Bridges when he says:

From Universal Mind the first-born atoms draw their function, whose rich chemistry the plants transmute to make organic life, whereon animals feed to fashion sight and sense and give service to man, who sprung from them is conscient in his last degree of ministry unto God, the Universal Mind, whither an effect returneth whence it first began.

Nutrition

Nutrition is the act or process — it is, in fact, the series of coordinated processes — whereby the nourishment of the body is effected. It consists in the taking-in and assimilation through chemical changes (metabolism) of materials with which the tissues of the body are built up and their waste repaired, by which the processes of the body are regulated, from which energy is liberated for the work the body has to do, and heat generated for the maintenance of its temperature. Nutrition is thus a fundamental function of the body. By the activity proper to it the structural integrity and functional efficiency of every cell is maintained. This, indeed, is its primary purpose; for if the mechanism of the body be perfect, and continue in perfection, it may be trusted to produce the energy needed for its work provided it be constantly supplied with suitable fuel. It is the mechanism that matters; the fuel (or Calories) is merely a question of the energy the body expends in the maintenance of vital processes — respiration, circulation, secretion, etc. — and in external (muscular) work.

The processes involved in the function of nutrition are mastication, deglutition, digestion, absorption, circulation, assimilation and excretion; the last including perspiration, exhalation, urinary excretion and defecation There are thus three stages in nutrition: the first, effected in and by the alimentary tract; the second, in or by the cells composing the body; and, the third by the organs of excretory function — skin, lungs, kidneys and bowel. It is of the utmost importance to realize that not only is the activity proper to the function of nutrition dependent on the efficient performance of all these acts, but their efficient performance is dependent on the adequate nourishment and functional efficiency of the organs and tissues performing them.

At this point, and to maintain the sequence of our story, reference might be made to the implications of these acts: mastication, digestion, absorption, assimilation, and so on. But it may be enough to remind you that they include the ordered operation of involuntary muscular action, the production of various digestive and other juices, the elaboration of ferments, or enzymes, and of catalytic agents needed for the speeding-up of chemical processes, the production of blood-forming substances, the interchange of body fluids, the transport of nutrients to the remotest recesses of the body, the removal of end-products of chemical action and of waste products from the body, and many other vital processes, all of which are influenced favourably or unfavourably by the constitution of the food. The alimentary tract and the organs (including the teeth) associated with it are of particular importance in this connection. They form a highly specialized mechanism designed for the nourishment of the body. The efficiency of the function of nutrition depends primary on the functional efficiency of this mechanism and this, in its turn, on the constitution of the food.

Let me here draw your attention to some of the tasks which this mechanism has to perform. It splits up, by digestion, the foodstuffs in such a way that the essential nutrients are readily absorbed and made available to the cells in forms best suited to their use. Thus, the many and differing kinds of proteins, present in the plant and animal tissues we use as food, are all decomposed into fragments: the amino-acids to which previous reference has been made. From these fragments, on their absorption, the body builds up the proteins suited to it and to its different parts; for each part its special kind. Mark then, how important it is that the ingested proteins are of kinds that will furnish all the fragments needed. Similarly, the many kinds of carbohydrates – starches, sugars, cellulose – in food are all converted into glucose which is the chief fuel needed for the production of energy, muscular work and the maintenance of the temperature of the body. Likewise, the many kinds of fats, each containing different fatty acids, are converted by digestive processes into soluble soaps which pass readily through the intestinal wall and in their passage are reconverted into the fats needed by the body. The mineral ingredients of food are not only made available for use by the body but the intestinal canal itself regulates to a considerable extent their absorption and excretion. Each part of this mechanism has its own contribution to make to the furtherance of the function of nutrition. Thus, the stomach, in normal conditions, not only produces the acid and enzymes needed for gastric digestion but, by its normal contractions, it sustains the appetite for food. It produces, too, a substance which, by its combination with a material or materials of unknown nature contained in certain foodstuffs, gives rise to a product having the specific property of ensuring the normal formation of the red cells of the blood. Absence of one or other of the component parts of this product — that produced in the stomach or that provided in certain foodstuffs — leads to the occurrence of pernicious anaemia. This product is stored in the liver for use as required by the bone-marrow — the birthplace of the red blood cells — hence the use of liver extract for the cure of this disease. The stomach produces yet another substance which is necessary for the normal nutrition of the central nervous system. Thus early in the process of digestion is the welfare of these two most important tissues — blood and nerve — taken care of, and by the stomach.

Beyond the stomach, in the duodenum, there are glands that not only secrete digestive juices but some that produce protective substances lest the acid contents of the stomach should, after they leave it, erode the mucous membrane of the bowel. The continued production of these alkaline and other protective substances is an important factor in the prevention of duodenal ulcer; and the continued functional efficiency of the glandular cells producing them is dependent on the quality of the food. There is no stage in the whole process of digestion, absorption and passage of the gastro-intestinal contents along their appointed way which is not regulated and controlled by some substance or substances derived from food. Even the timetable of events, which normally proceeds with clockwork regularity, is under such control. It cannot be too insistently stated that disturbance of these processes, disturbance of this timetable, and alterations in form or consistency of the faecal residues are signs that something is going wrong or has gone wrong with the function of nutrition.

The alimentary tract is very prone to suffer both structurally and functionally in consequence of faulty food and to become the prey of pathogenic agents of disease or the harbourer of parasites. Further, states of ill health of this tract often provide conditions precedent to the development of diseases of faulty nutrition. In such circumstances essential constituents of food may not be absorbed in sufficient quantity for the needs of organs and parts of the body, and disease due to their deficiency may arise. Many years ago (1918), when the newer knowledge of nutrition was in its infancy, I obtained some dozens of healthy monkeys from the jungles of Madras. Some I fed on faulty and ill-balanced food deficient in vitamins and mineral elements, others on perfectly constituted food. The latter remained in good health; the former developed gastro-intestinal ailments, ranging from gastritis and ulcer to colitis and dysentery, while one amongst them had a commencing cancer of the stomach. The passage of years has not dimmed the recollection of this crucial experiment nor detracted from the far-reaching importance of the results yielded by it. Indeed, there is, perhaps, no more significant fact in regard to the function of nutrition than that this highly specialized alimentary mechanism on which the nourishment of the body depends is itself amongst the most susceptible of the structures of the body to faulty nutrition.

Nutrition is affected adversely by a number of factors: imperfect oxygenation of the blood and tissues, as from faulty breathing, lack of fresh air, bad ventilation, overcrowding and lack of exercise; insufficient rest and want of sleep; overwork and fatigue; worry and emotional excitement; lack of sunshine; insufficient Calories for the work the body has to do; excessive consumption of alcohol; indigestible food; gastro-intestinal disorder; and many conditions of ill health. But by far the most important factor is food of improper constitution. The determination of the constitution of the food is the first essential in the assessment of the efficiency or lack of efficiency of the function of nutrition; the correction of food-faults is the first essential in the restoration of this function to normal.

Disorder of the function of nutrition, brought about by faulty food, causes the body to react in a variety of ways, depending on the nature of the food-faults that give rise to it, the part or parts of the body effected by it, and the intervention or the nonintervention of toxic or microbic agents of disease. These reactions, involving as they do disturbance in structure or in functions of various parts of the body, manifest themselves as subnormal states of health or as actual disease in great variety of form.

It will be realized from these considerations how far-reaching are the aspects of nutrition. They include the chemistry of food, the chemical changes (metabolism) whereby the function of nutrition is effected, the activity of the various organs and tissues in response to food conditions, the structural and functional changes induced in organs and tissues by faulty food, and the conditions of the body that result from faulty nutrition.

Nutrition touches upon, indeed embraces in its compass, many subdivisions of biology — biochemistry, biophysics, morphology, physiology, pathology and medicine. Knowledge of it helps to bridge the gulf between physiology and pathology — a gulf in need of bridging — it is, indeed, an essential foundation of rational medicine.

Nutrition is commonly spoken of as a condition of body -- excellent, normal or subnormal, as the case may be — when, in truth it is a function of the body on which condition of body — i.e. health — depends. For a proper comprehension of nutrition and of the processes involved in it this distinction has to be borne in mind. Such terms as undernutrition and malnutrition are nowadays in common use, often without a clear conception of their meaning. Sometimes they are used to signify a condition of body which under-nourished would more fittingly describe; sometimes to signify under-feeding. 'Malnutrition', we are reminded by Fowler in his Modern English Usage, 'is a term to be avoided as often as under-feeding will do the work', for malnutrition is not merely underfeeding but disorder of the processes of nutrition brought about, as a rule, by the habitual use of food of improper quality.

Nutrition is, also, commonly defined as 'food', 'nourishment', 'that which nourishes'. But, as we have just seen, it is something much more than this. Food is the instrument, nutrition is the act of using it. To employ the term 'nutrition' as an alternative one for 'food' is to miss its true meaning, to fail in comprehending not only that in which nutrition consists, but all that is meant by its derangements.

Health

Health is variously defined as 'soundness of body', 'state of bodily or mental well-being', 'freedom from disease, disorder, pain or weakness'. It is, in fact, a variable condition of body as in good, bad, poor or ill health. At its best it is 'that state of being in which all the parts and organs are sound and in proper condition; that condition of the body and its various parts and functions which conduces to efficient and prolonged life. It implies, moreover, the ability to produce and rear offspring fitted to live and efficiently to perform the ordinary functions of their species'. (Century Dictionary.) This optimum state of being can be attained when — but only when — the animal organism is adequately nourished. Further, it is possible to produce at will in animals under experimental conditions every grade of health — good, bad or indifferent — by alterations in the composition of their diets. Specific diseases of many kinds can be produced by feeding them on diets having specific food-faults or prevented by the correction of these faults. The interaction of faulty food, faulty nutrition and microbic or toxic agents leads to the spontaneous appearance of many others or to their controlled appearance at the will of the experimenter. I know of nothing so potent in maintaining good health in laboratory animals as perfectly constituted food; I know of nothing so potent in producing ill health as improperly constituted food. This, too, is the experience of stockbreeders. Is man an exception to a rule so universally applicable to the higher animals? It seems most unlikely that he can be, although it is to be recognized that his requirements for adequate nutrition, and the effects upon him of deficiencies of various food-essentials, are not necessarily the same as in animals. Indeed, these effects are known to differ in different species of animals. Nevertheless, the principles of nutrition are fundamentally the same in man and in animals. It may, therefore, be taken as a law of life, infringement of which will surely bring its own penalties, that the greatest single factor in the acquisition and maintenance of good health is perfectly constituted food. It is this thesis that I have to sustain in these lectures.

The Experimental Method in Research on Nutrition

As you are probably aware, it is customary in the investigation of nutritional problems in the laboratory to use the experimental method and to feed animals — rats, as a rule — on synthetic diets composed of purified food-materials, but lacking this or that essential according to the nature of the inquiry in hand. The results of such experiments, though of great value in the ascertainment of the function of a given essential of food, and in the precise determination of the biochemical and pathological changes resulting from its want, are open to the objections that the observations made in rats are not necessarily applicable to human beings, that synthetic diets such as are used in these experiments are never eaten by human beings, that human diets are rarely or never wholly lacking in any single food-essential, that their deficiencies are usually multiple, and, that the diets of mankind are often unbalanced in other regards, such, for instance, as in their high content of carbohydrates relative to other food-essentials.

The validity of these objections cannot be gainsaid; nevertheless, it may be remarked in passing that the frequency with which results observed in rats are applicable to man is remarkable — a fact which will be the better appreciated from the examples I am about to place before you. Further, without such experiments on animals the vast amount of knowledge revealed by them within recent years would, for the most part, be hidden from us, and we would still be in ignorance of the kind of consequences to expect in man from his continued use of food of faulty constitution. We would, moreover, be in ignorance of what a properly constituted diet is.

But when in such investigations, diets composed of food-materials in common use by man or diets in actual use by human beings are used in the feeding of our animals, most of these objections do not arise, and the results observed have a more direct application to man, provided the faulty combinations of the food-materials entering into the diets are such as uninstructed man himself commonly employs. It has seemed to me necessary, therefore, to use in my experimental work diets composed of the actual materials that human beings eat; and it is with such diets that most of my work has been done.

Before giving examples of the effects of such faulty diets on the animal organism, let me draw your attention to the relation of the national diets of India to the physical efficiency of the races using them.

Food and Physical Efficiency

Nowhere in the world is the profound effect of food on physical efficiency more strikingly exemplified than in India. As you know, India has some 350 million inhabitants, made up of many races presenting great diversity in their characteristics, manner of life, customs, religion, food and food-habits. The tribes of the Indian Frontier, and of Himalayan regions, the Peoples of the Plains — Sikhs, Rajputs, Mahrattas, Bengalis, Ooriyas, Madrassis, Kanarese and many others — exhibit, in general, the greatest diversity of physique. And as each race is wedded to its own manner of living, to its own national diet, comparison between them is easy.

The level of physical efficiency of Indian races is, above all else, a matter of food. No other single factor — race, climate, endemic disease, etc. — has so profound an influence on their physique, and on their capacity to sustain arduous labour and prolonged muscular exertion. 'As we pass from the North-West region of the Punjab down the Gangetic Plain to the coast of Bengal, there is a gradual fall in the stature, bodyweight, stamina and efficiency of the people. In accordance with this decline in manly characteristics it is of the utmost significance that there is an accompanying gradual fall in the nutritive value of the dietaries.' So wrote McCay, as a result of his investigations, a quarter of a century ago. My own observations have served to confirm his conclusions, though I find other causes in addition to protein-insufficiency — to which he attached chief importance — for the decline he refers to. This decline extends also to the peoples of the south and west of India, being especially apparent in certain parts of the Madras Presidency. This is not to say that in these parts there are not many people of good physique nor that in the north of India there are not many whose physique is poor. But speaking of the generality of the people, it is true that the physique of northern races of India is strikingly superior to that of the southern, eastern, and western races. This difference depends almost entirely on the gradually diminishing value of the food, from the north to the east, south and west of India, with respect to the amount and quality of its proteins, the quality of the cereal grains forming the staple article of the diet, the quality and quantity of the fats, the mineral and vitamin contents, and the balance of the food as a whole. In addition to these questions of quality there is the further one of quantity. In regard to the latter little need be said;

for it is obvious that if a man is not getting enough to eat he cannot be physically efficient. Unfortunately, the numbers in India who do not get enough to eat may be counted by the hundred thousand.

In general the races of northern India are wheat-eaters, though they make use also of certain other whole cereal grains. Now the biological value of the proteins of whole wheat is relatively high; and the wheat is eaten whole, after being freshly ground into a coarse flour (*atta*) and made into cakes called *chapattis.* It thus preserves all the nutrients with which Nature has endowed it, particularly its proteins, its vitamins and its mineral salts. The second most important ingredient of their diet is milk, and the products of milk (clarified butter or ghee, curds, buttermilk); the third is *dhal* (pulse); the fourth, vegetables and fruit. Some eat meat sparingly, if at all; others, such as the Pathans, use it in considerable quantity. Their food thus contains — when they can get the food they want, which they do not always do — all elements and complexes needed for normal nutrition (with the possible exception of iodine in some Himalayan regions) and abundance of those things that matter from the point of view of the structural and functional efficiency of the body.

In conformity with the constitution of their dietaries they are the finest races of India, so far as physique is concerned, and amongst the finest races of mankind. Familiar as I am with the chapatti-fed races of northern India, I have little patience with those who would have us believe that 'white flour' is as good an article of diet as 'whole wheat flour'. White flour, when used as the staple article of diet, places its users on the same level as the rice-eaters of the south and east of India. They are faced with the same problem; they start to build up their dietaries with a staple of relatively low nutritive value. If their health and physical fitness are not to suffer, they must spend more money on supplementary articles of diet in order to make good the deficiencies of white flour than if they had begun to build on the surer foundation of whole wheat flour. So it is with rice, which is the staple article of diet of about ninety millions of India's inhabitants.

The rice — a relatively poor cereal at best — is subjected to a number of processes before use by the consumer; all of which reduce — some to a dangerous degree — its already sparse supply of certain essential nutrients. It is parboiled, milled or polished; often all three. It is washed in many changes of water and, finally, it is boiled. It is thus deprived of much of its proteins and mineral salts and of almost all its vitamins.

Add to this that the average Bengali or Madrassi uses relatively little milk or milk-products, that by religion he is often a non-meat-eater, that his consumption of protein, whether of vegetable or of animal origin, is, in general, very low, that fresh vegetable and fruit enter into his dietary but sparingly, and we have not far to seek for the poor physique that, in general, characterizes him. In short, it may be said that according as the quality of the diet diminishes with respect to proteins, fats, minerals and vitamins, so do physical efficiency and health; a rule which applies with equal force to the European as to the Indian.

Relative Values of National Diets of India

This truth will probably be best appreciated by a reference to an experiment carried out in my laboratory some years ago, with the object of determining the relative values of certain national diets of India: Albino rats were employed in this test. The cycle of development in the rat takes place about thirty times as quickly as in man, so that the experiment about to be described, which lasted 140 days, would correspond to the observation of human beings, under the same experimental conditions, for a period of nearly twelve years.

Seven groups of twenty young rats, of the same age, sex-distribution and bodyweight, were confined in large, roomy cages under precisely similar conditions of life. To one group the diet as prepared and cooked by the Sikhs, was given; to another that of the Pathans; to a third that of the Mahrattas; and so on through Goorkhas, Bengalis, and Kanarese to Madrassis. At the end of 140 days the animals in each group were weighed and an average taken of their aggregate weight. The rat which conformed most closely to the average for its particular group was photographed side by side with the average rats from other groups. In brief, the best diet — that of the Sikhs — contains in abundance every element and complex needed for normal nutrition, the worst diet— that of the Madrassi — has many faults: it is excessively rich in carbohydrates, and deficient in suitable protein, mineral salts and vitamins. Presently we shall see that this difference in the nutritive value of these diets is reflected in the diseases from which the people of the north and south of India suffer.

Freedom of Well-Fed Animals from Disease

So impressed was I by the adequacy of the northern Indian's diet that during the later years of my experimental work I used it as the diet of my stock rats. These numbered about 1,000. Their food consisted of *chapattis* lightly smeared with fresh butter, sprouted Bengal *gram* (pulse), *raw, fresh* vegetables (cabbage and carrots) *ad libitum*, milk, the hard crusts of bread (to keep their teeth in order), a small ration of meat with bone once a week, and water. They were kept in stock for about two years — a period approximately equal to the first fifty years in the life of a human being — the young being taken as required for experimental purposes, and the remainder used for breeding. During the five years prior to my leaving India there was in this stock no case of illness, no death from natural causes, no maternal mortality, no infantile mortality. It is true that the hygienic conditions under which they lived were ideal, that they were comfortably bedded in clean straw, that they enjoyed dally exposures to the sun practically the whole year round, and that the care bestowed upon them was great; but the same care was bestowed during these years on several thousand deficiently-fed rats, which developed a wide variety of ailments (*vide infra*) while the well-fed animals enjoyed a remarkable freedom from disease. It is clear, therefore, that it was to their food that this freedom was due. If man himself did not provide in his own person the proof that a diet composed of whole cereal grains, or a mixture of cereal grains, milk, milk-products, pulses and vegetables, with meat occasionally, sufficed for optimum phys:cal efficiency, this experience in rats would do so. It is not, therefore, unreasonable to conclude that if by minute attention to three things — cleanliness, comfort and food — it is possible to exclude disease from a colony of cloistered rats, it is possible greatly to reduce its incidence by the same means in human beings and to produce a race whose physique is as nearly perfect as nature intended it to be.

Supposing now we cut out the milk component of this diet or reduce it to a minimum, we find that disease soon begins to make its appearance, especially if at the same time we limit the consumption of fresh vegetable foods. I have repeatedly made these restrictions with the result that respiratory diseases, gastro-intestinal diseases and maladies consequent on degenerative changes in mucous membranes and other structures of the body become frequent. It is apparent, therefore, that the diet of the Sikhs is only health-promoting so long as it is consumed in its entirety. Indeed, we know that those of this race who, for whatever reason, do not consume adequate quantities of milk, milk products and fresh vegetables, do not long retain the fine physique for which the Sikhs are famous. These food-materials are for them and in their own parlance, *takatwar khurak* (foods that give strength); nowadays we speak of them as 'the protective foods', since they make good the deficiencies of muscle meat, refined cereals, etc., which enter so largely into the diets of western peoples.

Before leaving this experience, let me emphasize two things: the first, that all things needful for adequate nourishment of the body and for physical efficiency are present in whole cereal grains, milk, milk-products, legumes, root and leafy vegetables and fruits, with egg or meat occasionally. What is eaten besides these is more a matter of taste than of necessity. And the second: that the diet must be complete in every essential. It is not to be expected that by substituting, for instance, wholemeal bread for white bread, health will benefit greatly unless the substitution completely restores the balance of an ill-balanced diet, nor that by adding bottled vitamins or mineral elements to a faulty diet its faults will be remedied, unless they be confined to vitamins or mineral elements. The correction of food faults lies first in their computation and thereafter in the construction of a diet so balanced and complete as to satisfy all physiological needs. Fortunately, the layman need not concern himself with such computations, though in institutions they may be necessary. It suffices for him to know that in whole cereal grains, milk, milk products, eggs and fresh vegetables he has foods that, when used in adequate quantities, will maintain the structural integrity and functional efficiency of his body.

A Good Diet and a Bad One: A Comparative Study

Consider now another experiment, also in rats. Two identical groups, twenty in each, from the above-mentioned stock were used in it. They were housed in colonies: both in large cages of the same dimensions. One group was fed on a diet similar to that used by the Sikhs; the other on a diet such as is commonly used by the poorer classes in England. The latter diet consisted of white bread, margarine, over-sweetened tea with a little milk (of which the rats consumed large quantities) boiled cabbage and boiled potato, tinned meat and tinned jam of the cheaper sorts. It has many faults, of which vitamin and mineral deficiencies are the chief. The first thing one noticed, as this experiment progressed, was that the members of the former, and well-fed, group lived happily together.

They increased in weight and flourished. The other group did not increase in weight; their growth was stunted; they were badly proportioned; their coats were staring and lacking in gloss; they were nervous and apt to bite the attendants; they lived unhappily together and by the sixtieth day of the experiment they began to kill and eat the weaker ones amongst them. When they had disposed of three in this way I was compelled to segregate the remainder. The experiment was continued for 187 days, or for a period which would correspond to about sixteen years in man. During this period three animals in the former group died — one (a pregnant animal) from an abdominal injury, one from an undiscovered cause, and one from pneumonia. In the latter group six died of pneumonia and three were killed by their fellows. The survivors in both groups were killed and subjected to post-mortem examination.

The outstanding differences in the incidence of disease in the two groups were these: disease of the lungs was much commoner in the group fed on the poorer class Britisher's diet; gastro-intestinal disease (gastritis, gastric congestion, outgrowths of epithelium in the stomach, and intestinal stasis) was frequent in this group, while that receiving the Sikh diet was free from it. Indeed, the animals fed on the poorer class Britisher's diet fared little or no better than those, in another experiment, that were fed on a diet in common use in Madras, and the maladies from which they suffered were much the same. The results of this experiment indicated clearly that a diet, such as is commonly used by the poorer classes in England, gives rise in rats to two chief classes of ailment — pulmonary and gastrointestinal — while a more perfectly constituted diet, such as is commonly used by northern Indian races, affords a considerable measure of protection against both. It is not unreasonable, therefore, to expect that, other things being equal, similar results will arise in man from the use of these diets. We do, in fact, find that these two classes of ailment are amongst the most frequent of the maladies afflicting the poorer class Britisher as well as the poorer class Madrassi.

Food and Peptic Ulcer

Another example may be provided by peptic ulcer (gastric and duodenal). This malady is very common in the south of India, rare in the north. It is, in fact, fifty-eight times more common in the latter part of India; it is particularly so in Travancore. In order to determine whether or not it was related in its genesis to diet the following experiment was undertaken.

Three groups of young rats, from the healthy stock above referred to, were fed as follows: one on the well-constituted diet as used by the Sikhs, but reinforced with additional milk; one on the carbohydrate-rich, protein-poor, vitamin-poor and mineral-poor diet in common use by the poorer class Madrassi; and the third on the diet — largely made up of tapioca — in common use by the poorer classes in Travancore, amongst whom peptic ulcer is so common. This diet has many faults, of which protein, mineral and vitamin deficiencies are the chief. The experiment was continued for close on 700 days, a period which would correspond to about fifty years in man. Many animals in the last two groups died during its course, from the usual respiratory and gastrointestinal diseases. The results revealed at post-mortem examination of all the animals were, as far as peptic ulcer was concerned, as follows: first group (Sikh diet), nil, second group (Madrassi diet), 11 per cent; third group (Travancore diet), 29 per cent incidence of peptic ulcer.

Here, again, we see that a disease common in certain parts of India (as it is in this country) can be produced in rats by feeding them on the faulty diets in common use by the people of these parts, while other animals, fed on a perfectly constituted diet in common use by human beings, amongst whom peptic ulcer is rare, remain free from it. Surely, if we are to place any reliance on animal experiments of this kind, we must regard faulty and ill-balanced food as a cause of gastric and duodenal ulcer in human beings? How it causes it, whether by direct or indirect action or want of action, or because of want of this or that essential of food or excess of this or that one, is a matter of little consequence— though of much scientific interest. What is of consequence, not only to the people of India, but, I venture to affirm, to the people of this country, is that by the continued use of a perfectly constituted diet they are unlikely to develop gastric or duodenal ulcer.

Experimental Beri-Beri and 'Stone'

Examples of this kind, occurring in my own experience, might be multiplied to an extent that would occupy many hours in their narration. I must, therefore, limit their numbers. Two will suffice: As no doubt you all know there is a disease called beri-beri, which is prevalent in certain parts of the tropics, chiefly amongst rice-eaters. It is not prevalent amongst rice-eaters in other parts of India, nor is it so prevalent in its endemic homes as a comparatively recent broadcast by the B.B.C. may have led some of you to suppose: every other woman in the south of India does *not* suffer from beri-beri. About forty years ago Eijkman noticed that if fowls were fed on an exclusive diet of polished rice they developed a type of polyneuritis which had certain likenesses to beri-beri — a malady in which polyneuritis is a prominent symptom.

He found, moreover, that they did not develop this 'nutritional polyneuritis' — as he rightly called it — when they were fed on unpolished rice or on polished rice to which the rice-polishings were added. So he, and his colleague, Grijns, concluded that there was something — vitamin B1 as it ultimately proved to be — in the rice-polishings which prevented the nutritional polyneuritis in birds, a something that might possibly prevent beri-beri in man, as indeed it (vitamin B1) is now known to do. But to prevent is one thing, to cause, if the preventive be removed, is, or may be, another. It is nowadays an almost universal belief that on a diet of polished rice or on a diet devoid of vitamin B1 beri-beri develops after a few months. Theoretically, this is possible, in practice it is a rare occurrence. For no one, even in localities where beri-beri is endemic, ever does live on an exclusive diet of polished rice or on a diet devoid of vitamin B1; always the diet contains some of this factor, however little that may be.

Further, only a relatively small proportion of persons subsisting on diets deficient in vitamin B1 do develop beri-beri, even in endemic areas of the disease. If one feeds pigeons on a diet almost devoid of this vitamin they develop polyneuritis, but polyneuritis is only one of the symptoms of human beri-beri; there are two others, equally important — grave disorder of the heart and oedema. Now supposing one does, as I have often done, feed pigeons on diets similar to those in actual use by human sufferers from beri-beri, then we find that a disease having all the pathological characters of true beri-beri does develop in a proportion of the birds, just as it does in a proportion of human beings. But this diet is not devoid of vitamin B1, although it is low in it.

It does not contain enough of it to prevent the disease, or enough of some other factor in addition to vitamin B1, to prevent the development of the complete syndrome, or, alternatively, to prevent the development or operation of the ultimate causal agents of the malady. Now if in such a diet one substitutes whole wheat flour for a part of the rice and at the same time we add to it fresh vegetables, such as tomatoes, then the disease does not arise, either in birds or in man. I have, myself, so prevented human beri-beri in a certain gaol in the East where it was wont to break out year after year; and many others, since the days of Takaki — who first prevented it in the Japanese Navy as long ago as 1882 — have by similar means prevented it. This is another example of the control that the use, in animal experiments, of human diets may exercise over results reached by the use of a single component of them, such as polished rice.

We have seen that if rats be fed on the perfectly constituted diet of the Sikhs they remain in good health: they do not, for instance, develop stone in the urinary tract. But if one removes from this diet the milk and milk products and cuts down the fresh vegetable foods to a minimum, then many of them do develop this condition. They develop also a wide variety of other ailments, but it is with 'stone' that I am here concerned. If we replace the milk or butter they do not develop this condition. This is an observation of great importance to the wheat-eating races of northern India, amongst whom 'stone' is so common. For it is precisely these articles of diet — milk, milk products and fresh vegetables — which the poorer classes amongst them have to cut out when times are hard. There are, no doubt, other factors concerned in the causation of 'stone'; but the broad fact remains that a perfectly constituted diet rich in milk, milk products and fresh vegetable foods affords a high degree of protection against it.

Variety of Disease in Improperly Fed Animals

I have mentioned the freedom from disease enjoyed by well-fed and hygienically housed albino rats. During the last eighteen years of my experimental work in India I used many thousands of animals — rats, pigeons, fowls, rabbits, guinea-pigs and monkeys— feeding them on diets not synthetically prepared from purified foodstuffs but from foodstuffs in common use by the people of India; my purpose, as previously hinted, being to learn what relation the food used by the people had to the diseases from which they suffered. At the risk of being tedious I shall now enumerate the maladies I have encountered in these improperly-fed animals, leaving out of count such manifestations of ill health as weakness, lassitude, irritability and the like, which are commonly met with in malnourished animals. Here is the list. *Skin diseases:* loss of hair, gangrene of the feet and tail, dermatitis, ulcers, abscesses, oedema. *Diseases of the eye:* conjunctivitis, corneal ulceration, xerophthalmia, panophthalmitis, cataract.

Diseases of the ear: otitis media, pus in the middle ear. *Diseases of the nose:* rhinitis, sinusitis. *Diseases of the lungs and respiratory passages:* adenoids, pneumonia, broncho-pneumonia, bronchiectasis, pleurisy, pyothorax, haemothorax. *Diseases of the alimentary tract:* dental disease, dilatation of the stomach, gastric ulcer, epithelial new growths in the stomach (two cases of cancer), duodenal ulcer, duodenitis, enteritis, colitis, stasis, intussusception and a condition of the lower bowel suggestive of a pre-cancerous state. *Diseases of the urinary tract:* pyonephrosis, hydronephrosis, pyelitis, renal calculus, nephritis, urethral calculus, dilated ureters, vesical calculus, cystitis, incrusted cystitis. *Diseases of the reproductive system:* endometritis, ovaritis, death of the foetus in utero, premature birth, uterine haemorrhage, testicular disease. *Diseases of the blood:* anaemia, a pernicious type of anaemia, *Bartonella muris* anaemia. *Diseases of the lymph and other glands:* cysts, abscesses, enlarged glands. *Disease of the endocrine glands:* goitre, lymph-adenoid goitre, adrenal hypertrophy, atrophy of the thymus, haemorrhagic pancreatitis (very occasionally). *Diseases of the heart:* cardiac atrophy, cardiac hypertrophy, myocarditis, pericarditis, hydropericardium. *Diseases of the nervous system:* polyneuritis, beri-beri, degenerative lesions. *Diseases of bone:* crooked spine, distorted vertebrae (no work was done on rickets — a known 'deficiency disease'). *General diseases:* malnutritional oedema, scurvy, prescorbutic states.

All these conditions of body, these states of ill health, had a common causation: faulty nutrition, with or without infection. They are the clinical evidence — the signs and symptoms — of the structural and functional changes in organs or parts of the body that result directly or indirectly from faulty nutrition. It will be noted that local infections and maladies of a chronic and degenerative kind are conspicuous amongst them. These maladies are, in short, the symptoms of malnutrition as observed in animals fed on faulty diets — some of them admittedly very faulty — in use by human beings, or on food-materials in use by them. It is reasonable, then, to expect that maladies of a similar order are likely to result from malnutrition in human beings. In my next lecture I shall endeavour to make clear how it is that food of improper constitution leads to that disturbance of structure or function of organs or parts of the body which is 'disease'.

National Health and Nutrition

To one whose work has lain in India, and who for more than twenty years has been engaged in a study of the relation of faulty food to disease, the belief that such food is of paramount importance in the causation of disease amounts to certainty. For there he meets with 'deficiency diseases' of every kind: xerophthalmia, night-blindness, beri-beri, malnutritional oedema, scurvy, rickets, osteomalacia, pellagra, angular stomatitis and certain skin diseases that are of this order. There, too, he encounters many maladies, not usually regarded as of malnutritional origin, which experience, both in the laboratory and the field, teaches him to regard as wholly or in part of this nature: gastro-intestinal diseases of various kinds, including nonspecific colitis and peptic ulcer, certain respiratory diseases often found in association with xerophthalmia, urinary calculus, some ulcers and cardiac disorders, pyorrhoea and a number of others. Further, he soon becomes aware — if he had not available for his enlightenment the testimony of many shrewd observers who have gone before him — that malnutrition is a chief cause of the lowered resistance to infection exhibited by so many of the Indian people; the chief reason why they succumb by hundreds of thousands to the ravages of such scourges as malaria, kala-azar, cholera, dysentery, leprosy and tuberculosis. For him the soil assumes an importance even greater than the seed, and he becomes impressed by the urgent necessity to render it inhospitable to the growth of the seeds of disease by adequate nourishment of the body.

If we look upon 'infection' of whatever kind, be it due to microbe, protozoa, metazoa, or invisible virus, or to the intervention of vectors of pathogenic agents, as the evidence of personal or environmental uncleanliness, then it may be said that the two chief causes of disease are faulty food and dirt. These two are the senior partners in the criminal business of disease-production — each the coadjutor of the other. It is along lines of improved cleanliness, both personal and environmental, that the triumphs of modern medicine have lain; it is along lines of improved nutrition that greater triumphs still remain to be achieved. Some years ago I made the statement that 'the newer knowledge of nutrition is the greatest advance in medical science since the days of Lister. When physicians, medical officers of health and the lay public learn to apply the principles which this newer knowledge has to impart... then will it do for medicine what asepsis has done for surgery.' I see no reason, in these later days, to detract from this view; on the contrary, there is every reason to emphasize it the more, particularly in regard to preventive medicine.

In this country the conviction that faulty food, and the faulty nutrition resulting from it, is a principal cause of ill health, does not appear to be acquired so readily as it is in the tropics. Perhaps it is that as an island race we have no others, at close range, with whom to compare ourselves. The tribes of the Indian Frontier are far removed from the slums of our great cities; and it would be as difficult for the slum dweller to realize the perfection of physique to which these tribes attain, though nourished on the simplest and least varied kinds of foods, as it would be for the Frontier tribesman to understand that the physical imperfections of so many of the dwellers in the slums are largely due to the imperfections of the foods on which they are reared. Nevertheless, things nutritional are not, in essence, so different in India and in England as they may seem.

Diet and Incidence of Disease

Let me remind you of the experimental contrast to which I drew your attention in my first lecture. You may remember that the great majority of the rats in that experiment enjoyed good health when fed on a well-constituted diet such as is used by Sikhs of the better class, while the great majority of those fed on an ill-constituted diet, such as is commonly used by the poorer classes in this country, developed two chief kinds of disease: respiratory and gastro-intestinal. You may remember also that the majority of rats fed on a diet in common use by the people of Madras also suffered from disease of these two systems of the body. The diet of the poorer class Britisher was, in fact, little or no better, so far as disease prevention was concerned, than that of the Madrassi. Here, now, is a diagram prepared from the material provided in the Annual Report of the Chief Medical Officer of the Ministry of Health for the year 1933. You will observe that amongst every 1,000 sick persons of the insured classes in England and Wales no less than 250 suffered from diseases of the respiratory system, and no less than 110 from diseases of the digestive system. Diseases of these two systems of the body accounted for more than one-third of all illness in these classes of the community. A similar diagram, prepared from the Report (1933) of the Surgeon-General with the Government of Madras, reveals that amongst sick persons of the hospital class in Madras, no less than 183 out of every 1,000 suffered from diseases of the digestive system and 76 from diseases of the respiratory system; or more than one-quarter of the total sick. If from the calculation we remove the sufferers from purely tropical ailments, then in Madras also disease of these two systems of the body would account for approximately one-third of all sickness. I submit that if these diseases be, as they are, a chief consequence of feeding rats — living in an equable climate and as far as possible protected against infection or influences favouring it — on a diet in common use by the poorer class Britisher and, also, a chief consequence of feeding them on a diet in common use by the poorer class Madrassi, then these diets *per se* are likely to be favourable to the production of such maladies in human beings. I say these diets *per se,* for I am well aware that other influences — climatic conditions, cold, and factors favourable to the spread of infection -- play their part in the production of these illnesses, especially those of the respiratory system. Indeed, it is apparent, from the difference in incidence of respiratory disease amongst insured persons in this country and amongst Madrassis, that this must be so; for this incidence was more than three times greater in the former that in the latter, due, no doubt, to the differing climatic conditions. But, in general, the mal-effects of the poorer class Britisher's diet, as exhibited by rats, are similar in kind to those of the Madrassi diet.

It will be of interest now to consider the difference in incidence of certain diseases in Madras and the Punjab — having in mind that the diet of the poorer classes in this country affords as little protection against disease as that of the Madrassi, and that the diet of the people of the Punjab is, in general, of better constitution than either — though that of the poorer class Punjabi may lack a sufficiency of vitamins A and C. In the first place, we find that tuberculosis is nearly twice as common in Madras, and one is reminded, in this connection, of how closely the incidence of this disease is related to malnourishment in England. Next, we find that leprosy, a malady from which this country is happily free — but one allied in some ways to tuberculosis — is much more common in Madras than in the Punjab. We find, too, that other diseases of a chronic and degenerative kind are more common in the south than in the north of India: peptic ulcer (gastric and duodenal) is fifty-eight times more common, rheumatism is nearly five times as common, cancer is 3.5 times as common, anaemia and malnutritional diseases generally (excluding beri-beri, which rarely occurs in the Punjab) are more than twice as common; rickets is four times as common. Diabetes and mental disease are three times as common, disorders of the heart four times, nephritis ten times, and infestation by round worms twenty times as common in Madras, while ulcers, skin diseases and various other local ailments are all more common in Madras. These differences in the incidence of disease can, I think, be accounted for in large part by the difference in the nutritive quality of the diets of the two peoples, and in view of the poor quality of the diet of many of our own people, they are, to say the least of it, suggestive. They suggest that a similar relation of food of poor quality to the incidence of human ailments may be expected in other countries and in other peoples. That such a relation actually does exist elsewhere is exemplified by the studies made by Drs. Orr and Gilks of two African tribes whose diseases could be correlated with the defects of their diets and the incidence of these diseases with differences in these defects. Indeed, the experiences of a number of skilled observers in Africa provide abundant evidence that, there also, improper quality of human food is a factor of fundamental importance in the causation of disease.

Partial Degrees of Vitamin Insufficiency

In a book — *Studies in Deficiency Disease* — which I published as long ago as 1921, I provided experimental evidence which appeared to me to warrant the conclusion that food of improper constitution is responsible for a large proportion of ill health in this country. I emphasized then, and I have continued to do so on every convenient occasion since, that the less obvious manifestations of 'deficiency disease' were of vastly greater practical importance than the more obvious but less common diseases, such as scurvy, beri-beri, rickets, etc., to which the term 'deficiency disease' was usually restricted. I pointed out that the milder grades of deficiency of certain food-essentials — particularly of vitamins and mineral elements — were much more widespread among the people than the severer grades; and that they led as surely, though more slowly, to a lowering of vital processes, to impaired resistance to microbic and other pathogenic agents of disease and to the development of maladies of many kinds. At that time (1921) I laid emphasis, as I still do, on the consequences of the inadequate ingestion of vitamin B1, which appeared to me to be a conspicuous fault of the diet of the British people, a fault due to the extensive use of vitamin-poor white flour and to the inordinate use of vitamin-less sugar.

Excessive richness of the average Britisher's diet in these two carbohydrates gives rise to insufficiency of vitamin B1 for two reasons: the first, that the food as a whole does not contain enough of it, and the second, that relative to the richness of the diet in carbohydrates this vitamin is rendered still more deficient; for we now know that the greater the consumption of carbohydrates the more vitamin B1 is needed. Consider, in this connection, the chart which I now show you. It is self-explanatory and I need not, therefore, amplify its description. It illustrates, however, two things to which I would draw your attention: first, the inadequacy of white flour as compared with freshly-ground whole wheat flour; and second, the striking difference in appearance of rats fed properly from infancy as compared with those who in earlier life have been improperly fed and have to make up for lost time when properly fed at a later age.

In this connection, also, let me draw your attention to the results of a large-scale experiment, carried out by Professor J. C. Drummond and his colleagues, to which he made reference in his Harben Lectures for 1933. This experiment was designed with the object of learning whether or not mild degrees of vitamin B1 deficiency gave rise to disease, when animals (rats) were fed for long periods on food having this fault but otherwise satisfactory. Speaking of the results of this experiment, and of the kinds of disease from which the animals suffered, he said: 'He (McCarrison) is unquestionably right in insisting that vitamin-deficiency — and it must be remembered that he stresses at every turn the importance of recognizing the widespread occurrence of mild deficiency — is directly or indirectly responsible for a very large proportion of ill health today.' And in his Lane Medical Lectures, a year later, he repeats with even greater emphasis the same assertion.

It is not only amongst the poorer classes in this country, but also amongst those who are better off, that the diet is commonly excessively rich in vitamin-poor, mineral-poor starchy foods and in protein-less, vitamin-less, mineral-less sugar. It is impossible for people subsisting on such diets to remain in good health. 'It is only being gradually realized,' says Dr. Friend, whose recently published book, *The Schoolboy,* is so valuable a contribution to the problems of food and nutrition, 'that the deficiency of white bread in vitamin B1 is one of the most serious dietary deficiencies to which our populations are being subjected at the present time.' To this I would add that the inordinate use of refined sugar is one of the most serious addictions of the day. That the insufficient ingestion of Vitamin B1 is an important and widespread cause of ill health — especially of gastro-intestinal ill health — is now recognized in America, where 'the bread-meat-potato-sugar' diet of many American people has recently been shown to be dangerously low in this important factor, unless it is supplemented with a sufficiency of milk, eggs, fruits, nuts and vegetables (Sure, 1933).

And if in America, why not in this country also, where the average diet is of the same 'bread-meat-potato-sugar' sort? According to American observers the mal-effects of such a diet are chiefly to be observed in children who exhibit poor appetites, poor growth, nervousness, constipation and other digestive disorders: effects which I observed, and recorded, in monkeys eighteen years ago. For many years past I have advised European mothers in India to supplement the feeds of their infants with a watery extract of yeast in order to ensure an abundant supply of vitamin B1, which cows' milk certainly does not provide in that country. A similar recommendation is now widely made in America, following the finding that not only cow's milk but the pooled breast milk of nursing women is relatively poor in vitamin B1 — poor because the women's own diets are poor in it. Many experiments have been made within the last few years on American children, the results of which show the good effect of the supplementary provision of vitamin B1: better growth, better appetite, better assimilation of food and greater freedom from digestive disorders. Some clinicians in that country have come to the conclusion that a large proportion of the infantile mortality during the first year of life which is associated with gastro-intestinal disturbances may be due to vitamin B1 deficiency consequent on the relative poverty of mother's milk and of cow's milk in this vitamin; a conclusion that has also been reached recently by certain observers in the Near East.

National Ill Health

What evidence is there of physical inefficiency in this country? And what that such as may exist is related in its origin to faulty nutrition? For answer to the first of these questions I must turn to certain authoritative publications. From the first of these — the Report of the Adjutant-General for the year 1934 — I quote the following passage: 'What was disconcerting to any citizen with a care for the good of his country was that over 52 per cent of the men who went to the recruiting office did not come up to the physical standard laid down. In the big industrial areas of the north the percentage of rejections rose to sixty-eight.' The opinion of a high military medical authority was that the chief cause of the men's rejection was malnutrition during childhood. These figures are in themselves sufficiently disconcerting, but more so perhaps when it seems likely that the men who did present themselves for recruitment were not so physically impaired as many who did not. And if so high a percentage of men failed to come up to the by no means exacting physical standard laid down by the Army authorities, how many of their womenkind were likely to be physically inefficient?

Another example, also of recent date, is still more disturbing: Not long ago the Pioneer Health Centre in Peckham carried out a survey of families of the artisan class, for whom the centre is intended. This survey revealed that 90 per cent of those over twenty-five years of age had some physical defect. From another source I glean the following statement: 'Among the insured population there were lost in 1933 a total of 29,000,000 weeks of work. To this staggering loss must be added the cost of replacement of labour and the expense entailed in the care of the sick during the period of incapacity. These figures represent a heavy burden upon the community which is largely unnecessary.' It is a burden however, that the community must continue to bear until it has learned that to be physically efficient the individuals comprising it must not only be taught to practice the principles of nutrition, but be provided with the means to practice them. It is to be noted in connection with this enormous amount of certified sickness that it was not of the killing kind — 'the people were sick but not mortally sick.'

There is, too, the very high incidence of anaemia, due to deficiency of iron, in working-class women, to which attention has recently been drawn by Professor Davidson of Aberdeen. 'If', he says, 'the percentage of anaemic women found in Aberdeen is present in the industrial areas of the South (and we believe that anaemia may be even more serious there, since economic conditions are worse and the cost of living higher) then the loss of economic efficiency of the working-class mothers in this country must be enormous.'

The still very high incidence of tuberculosis, especially in adolescence, is another outstanding evidence of national ill health: 'During the last completed decade, 1921-30, there were, roughly speaking, forty-five thousand deaths of males and an equal number of females at ages 15-30. Amongst the males very nearly one-third of this mortality was due to tuberculosis while amongst the females the proportion was as high as one-half.' (Report of the Chief Medical Officer of Health, 1933.) It seems probable that a principal, if not a paramount, cause of this high incidence of, and mortality from, tuberculosis at this particular period of life is faulty food deficient in vitamin A, involving a low content of this vitamin in lung tissue and consequent susceptibility of the lung to infection.

As a final example of the prevalence of physical inefficiency, malnutrition in childhood may be cited. 'In his Annual Report for the year 1934, the Chief Medical Officer of the Board of Education repeats the emphasis of former reports on the necessity for satisfactory nutrition. During the routine medical examination 12 children per 1,000 were found to be malnourished and 14 per 1,000 undernourished' (I quote from the British Medical Journal). It may be taken as certain that a major proportion of this faulty nutrition was due to food of improper quality or to insufficient food or to both. Believing, as I do, that sickness is more often the result of malnutrition than malnutrition the result of sickness, I venture to think that the evidences of malnutrition in schoolchildren are likely to be more widespread than these figures indicate. For it is not only that children suffering from malnutrition are underweight or under-grown; that there is a disproportion between their weight and height; that their posture is poor; that they are often round-shouldered and have protruding bellies, winged scapulae and lordosis; that they are of poor muscular development and easily fatigued; that they are irritable, haggard, anxious and, perhaps, mentally slow if not precocious; that they are wakeful, restless, and often troubled with unpleasant dreams; that they have headache and fleeting pains, sometimes in one part of the body, sometimes in another; although all these are signs of malnutrition.

But there are others, indicating disturbances in structure or in function of organs or parts of the body: the circulation is poor; the skin is mottled or dry and hot, or moist, cold and clammy; there is usually anaemia; the digestive system is quite commonly unstable or disordered, constipation is frequent or may alternate with diarrhoea, the appetite is capricious — the desire for 'sweets' is often inordinate — dental caries is the rule — and susceptibility to infection is very marked, especially infection of the upper respiratory passages. It is well enough to say that malnutrition may be brought about by faulty health habits or by physical defects, such as dental decay or gastro-intestinal disorder; it may. But these physical defects, this bad or capricious appetite, this constipation or digestive disturbance, this anaemia, this poor circulation, this faulty function of the skin — these are themselves consequences of faulty nutrition and, as a rule, it is this that gives rise to them, not they that give rise to the faulty nutrition.

If we take this view of 'mal-nutrition' in schoolchildren — and for my own part I believe it to be the correct one — then it will be found that there are in this country not 12 per 1,000 who are suffering from it, but several times that number; nor will it be found to be confined exclusively to the poorer classes. Indeed, the widespread incidence of dental caries and of minor rickets is, in itself, sufficient evidence that this is so. There is one certain means of detecting dietetic malnutrition and that is by the assessment of the nutritive value of the diet that is actually being consumed; and in making this assessment attention must be paid as much to such essentials as calcium, phosphorus, iron and iodine as to vitamins, proteins and energy-bearing foods. If the diet does not contain in adequate amounts all elements and complexes needed for normal nutrition, then the user of it is suffering from, or will suffer from, malnutrition. It seems probable that a cause of malnutrition which may be overlooked is the non-provision of sufficient energy-bearing foods to meet the enormous expenditure of energy by growing children consequent of their bodily activities in sports and games.

The Death-rate and National Health

It is commonly stated that because the death-rate in this country is falling the national health is improving. Recently a writer in *The Listener* (20th November, 1935) voiced his dissent with this statement so pertinently that I am prompted to quote the major part of his letter, though recognizing that the falling death-rate is an achievement of which the public health services have every reason to be proud. This writer says, 'Again and again this fallacy appears in the Press. Why is it assumed that a falling death-rate connotes a higher standard of health? To save a man's life by drugs or surgery does not necessarily make a healthy man of him. The national health is the sum total of the healths of individuals; it can be nothing else. If the reasoning "low death-rate, therefore good health" is sound, then if in an institution filled with incurables there is no death during the year, the death-rate becomes nil, and consequently the institution the healthiest place in England, though there is not a single healthy person in it.' The same writer goes on to say: 'What we should like to know is the number of semi-invalids carried by the nation; why all hospitals and nursing homes, etc., are full.... Why, under National Health Insurance, the increase between 1920 and 1930 of short-term (not exceeding six months) sickness was 109 per cent, of long-term (exceeding six months) 230 per cent; why the enormous decline in quality of eyes and teeth.' I am convinced that faulty nutrition due to the long-continued use of food of improper quality provides a not inconsiderable part of the answer to these questions.

Effects of Improved Diet

What evidence is there that by the provision of properly-constituted food, and of the hygienic amenities that should go with it, the physical condition of the people can be improved and disease prevented? There is, to begin with, the evidence provided by Dr. Cory Mann, at the instance of the Ministry of Health and the Medical Research Council, which demonstrated the unique value of milk as a food and the great improvement brought about in the physical condition of children by its adequate provision. Similar results have within recent years been obtained by investigators in Scotland. There is abundant evidence of the value of the free meals now issued, in increasing numbers, to poorer class schoolchildren, and of the value of the cheap milk made available by the Ministry of Agriculture. In a private communication which Miss Joan Fry made to me some time ago she spoke of the improvement in the health of the children of the unemployed allotment holders, under the beneficent scheme of the Society of Friends, consequent on their greater use of fresh vegetable foods. But perhaps the most valuable, because the most extensive and complete amongst investigations of the kind, is that recorded by Dr. G. E. Friend, Medical Officer of Christ's Hospital, Horsham. In his book, to which I have previously referred, he recounts the dietetic history of the school and the results of his physical and clinical surveys. These show that during the period for which reliable data have been collected there is a continuous upward trend both of weight and height of the boys consequent on improvements effected in the school dietary. Further, there is a definite decline in certain classes of illness, particularly of septic conditions, a diminution in the amount of dental caries, and a remarkable drop in the incidence of fractures and bone injuries. It cannot be doubted but that these results are in great part due to dietetic improvements, though improvement in hygienic conditions generally no doubt contributed its share to them. Nor have I any doubt in my own mind that had the dietetic improvements approached nearer to the provision of a perfectly-constituted diet, their beneficial effects would, with respect to the health of the boys, have been still more striking.

Chief Faults of British Diets

If now we turn to the Report of the Chief Medical Officer of Health for the year 1933, we find therein a certain uneasiness that all is not so well with the nutrition of the British people as it might be. It is affirmed that the evidences of malnutrition are not widespread. This is no doubt true of its grosser evidences. But is it true of the less obvious manifestations of faulty nutrition? If, as I maintain, the latter include many forms of subnormal health, not all of which are scheduled in the Nomenclature of Disease, and of chronic ill health — many, in short, of the commoner degenerative ailments from which the people suffer: digestive, respiratory, osseous, arthritic, cardiac, haemic, glandular, inflammatory, etc. — then are the evidences of malnutrition, indeed, widespread.

We may read in this Report that the food-essentials most likely to be deficient in the diets of the people of this country are proteins of high biological value, calcium, iron and vitamins A and D; and we may, perhaps, conclude from the use of the words 'most likely' that the diets of our people are not uncommonly deficient in one or more or all of these essentials. If you are inclined to accept my own opinion, after what I have told you, there may be added to these likely deficiencies that of vitamin B1. I was assured recently by one who labours in the East End of London that such 'fresh' vegetable foods as ultimately penetrate into that locality are usually many days old; and I am reminded, in this connection, of certain interesting observations made some time ago by one of my Indian assistants. He found that within seventy-two hours of gathering green vegetables from my well-tended kitchen garden in Coonoor, they lost the major part of their vitamin C content.

I do not know whether the rapidity of this loss would be as great in England, where climatic conditions are so different; but it seems safe to assume that by the time their sparse supply of leafy vegetables reaches the dwellers in the East End of London the vitamin C content is considerably reduced. From which assumption I would be inclined to expect an inadequate intake of vitamin C by relatively large numbers of people in the slums of our great cities. But it is no longer necessary to make such assumptions, for in the 'Report on the Physiological Bases of Nutrition', recently submitted by a committee of experts to the Assembly of the League of Nations, it is stated that 'deficiencies in important nutrients are a common feature in modern diets, and these deficiencies usually occur in the protective foods (foods rich in minerals and vitamins) rather than in the energy-giving foods.' [The comment may, however, be made that the deficiencies do not occur in the protective foods themselves, but in modern diets because of the scanty use of the protective foods.] We have, too, the authority of the Committee on Nutrition set up by the British Medical Association

(1933) that 'a shortage of calcium, phosphorus and iron is not uncommon' in the diets of the people of this country. Let us, for a moment, refer back to my second lecture and see again what this not uncommon shortage means. It means, or may mean according to the degree of shortage, impairment of every vital function, stunting of growth, poor physique, poor bone formation, softening of bone, rickets (not necessarily of the florid type), tooth decay, crooked spines, impairment of muscular efficiency, including that of the gastro-intestinal tract and heart, abnormal response of the nerves to stimuli, tetany, disturbance of menstruation and lactation, disturbance of the neutrality of the body and of the interchange of body fluids, anaemia and all its attendant consequences. This is what a shortage of calcium, phosphorus and iron means. And if with these we are to include a shortage of vitamins A and D, as the Report of the Chief Medical Officer of Health suggests we may, and of vitamins B and C — as there is good reason to believe we should — then to these consequences of mineral shortage there are to be added those of vitamin shortage, in themselves a formidable array and not the least important of which is lowered resistance to local infections. To those who do not know what the shortage of these essentials means, the mere statement that it commonly exists is not impressive. But to those who do — and you are now amongst that number, if you were not so before — it must be obvious that faulty food is directly or indirectly responsible for a very large proportion of ill health today. If it be not, what then is its cause? You may search in vain for a more satisfying explanation of it.

Prevention of Disease by Diet

Concerning the matter of disease prevention and of the part which properly constituted food may play therein, I need give only three examples: the first provided by Miss Margaret in her book *The Nursery School* — which should be an obligatory text-book for every student of medicine; the second by the Papworth Village Settlement for sufferers from tuberculosis; and the third by the antenatal work now being done in Dublin. Many others could, of course, be given. Hear what Miss McMillan had to say of the weakly and ill-conditioned children who came from the slums of Deptford to her nursery school; children, rickety and bronchitic; children with adenoids and dental caries; children with inflammatory states of eyes nose, ear and throat. After they have been nurtured and properly fed for three or four years they are, she tells us, almost all cured of any ailments they may have had, 'they are all straight and well grown, the average child is a well-made child, with clean skin, alert, sociable, eager for life and new experiences'. He does not need, she says, to see the doctor or the dentist, and he has none of the minor ailments that affect the children of the slums. Surely this is an achievement of the highest order, an answer to the question how best to deal with 'the minor ailments that affect the children of the slums', and a cogent reason for the establishment throughout the length and breadth of the land of nursery schools of the McMillan type. It is a heartening sign of the times that the present Government intends actively to encourage their establishment.

And at the Papworth Village Settlement for the subjects of tuberculosis, what do we find? That in this village of 400 persons no child born there during the twenty years of its existence has, while a member of the community, contracted tuberculosis of the lungs, bones, joints, cerebral membranes, nor indeed any clinical form of the disease. Yet these children are the offspring of parents who suffer from tuberculosis and are in constant contact with them. How has this remarkable achievement been brought about? Sir Pendrill Varrier-Jones, to whose endeavours it is due, explains it as follows:

1. Adequate food supply. Ignorance as to dietetic values is dispelled by advice at the clinic, by lectures and by the village nurse. Also by actual demonstration by food supplied from the Central Institution at small cost.
2. Adequate food supply is possible because there is an adequate and prolonged parental income, maintained by means of assured employment.
3. Freedom from anxiety as to loss of employment; therefore expenditure can be budgeted in advance.
4. No risk of unemployment after breakdown; the income being maintained meanwhile *(a)* in the case of pensioners, by a pension, and *(b)* in the case of non-pensioners, by the Friendly Societies' contributions supplemented by the Welfare Fund.
5. Proper housing, which allows medical advice to be put into immediate practice; such as through thorough

ventilation in living rooms; isolation of infected persons in bedrooms or verandas. That is to say, avoidance of mass dose.

6. Public opinion, which makes it possible to live with windows open without being jeered at; to use sputum pots in the house, and pocket flasks out of doors, without being shunned or made conspicuous.

'To sum up — economic conditions determine the spread or otherwise of disease. To prevent disease it is necessary to create an environment rather than to give a dole where there is no opportunity for money to modify the condition of its recipient. The child's resistance to disease is maintained by *(a)* adequate nutrition, and *(b)* the absence of mass dose of infection.'

The antenatal work which I was privileged to see when in Dublin a few years ago is another activity that is yielding remarkable results, because it is based on the sound foundation of improving the nutrition of expectant and nursing mothers. Three months before the expected birth of their babies the poorer class women come daily to certain centres, where they receive an excellent midday meal. They are cared for during their confinement and a fortnight thereafter they continue their visits to these dinner-centres for another three months. I am told that the infantile mortality amongst the children of these women is approximately one-third of that in women of the same class who cannot or do not avail themselves of these facilities or for whom there are, for lack of funds, not sufficient centres.

Maternal Mortality

There is much talk at the present time of the high rate of maternal mortality in this country, and much argument in regard to factors that may or may not be concerned in its causation. Amongst these faulty nutrition has come in for its share of blame. How far it is to blame we do not yet know, since the matter has never been thoroughly investigated. But it is a false argument which would maintain that because in some places maternal mortality is higher in well-to-do women than in women of the poorer classes, faulty nutrition can have nothing to do with it. For some women amongst the better classes have no idea how to feed themselves properly during or after pregnancy. There is abundant evidence, derived from experiments on animals, that the activity proper to the function of reproduction and to the health of the reproductive tract is influenced unfavourably by faulty nutrition. Of particular importance in this connection is insufficiency of vitamin A. It has recently been found (Mason) that levels of vitamin A-deficiency which are insufficient to produce xerophthalmia result in marked disturbances of the reproductive function in female rats. These include difficult labour, often associated with uterine bleeding and infection. Observations such as these may have an important bearing on maternal mortality in human beings; for of this we may be certain, that unless the diet of the expectant mother conforms in every detail to the physiological requirements of pregnancy her chance of surviving the ordeal of childbirth will be lessened. In my second lecture I mentioned, under the various food-essentials there discussed, the amounts of some of them that are needed during pregnancy. These may be enumerated again: a well-balanced diet containing 70 grammes of protein, of which one-third must be derived from animal sources; an abundance of all vitamins, including vitamin D, which, however, should be provided in the form of cod liver oil so as to avoid the risk of overdosage and as an additional source of iodine; 2 grammes of calcium; 1.6 grammes of phosphorus; 0.3 gramme of magnesium; and 20 milligrammes of iron. Personally, I believe that the best diet for expectant mothers is one made up of whole cereal grains, milk, milk products and eggs, with fresh green vegetable foods and fruit in abundance.

Mention has already been made of the part which antecedent rickets and osteomalacia may play in increasing the risks of childbirth by causing alterations in shape of the female pelvis.

'Building of an Al Nation'

If I have convinced you of the fundamental importance of food in relation to public health, it will have become obvious that one of the most urgent problems of our time is how to ensure that each member of the community shall receive a diet that will satisfy his or her physiological needs. It is clear that to achieve this much-to-be-desired end many barriers — poverty, unemployment, apathy, ignorance, prejudice, habit — must be surmounted, and many interests — agricultural, industrial and economic — readjusted. To do so is, in the main, a primary function of Government. For, as Carlyle expresses it: 'Wherever the health of the citizens is concerned... all governments that are not chimerical make haste to interfere.' During the recent election campaign one read of plans for 'the building of an A1 nation'; antenatal, child-welfare and maternity services were to be improved and extended; nursery schools for children under school age were to be actively encouraged; increased facilities for treatment, particularly dental treatment, were to be provided, orthopaedic centres and open-air schools were to be formed; the medical insurance scheme was to be extended to include persons of younger age; physical education was to be undertaken.

All these are well enough — and laudable; they are, indeed, essential parts of a properly organized policy of health. But without measures that will ensure the better feeding of the people they cannot, like a diet inadequate in vitamins though complete in other regards, achieve the end in view — 'the building of an Al nation'. But while the main burden of achieving this end must rest on Government — and a heavy burden it is — there is much that individuals can do for themselves, much that the medical profession and the professions allied to it can do, much that the teaching profession can do, much that all people of education can do. For they can make it their business thoroughly to acquaint themselves with the principles of nutrition, to practice these principles and to inculcate them in others.

These principles are not difficult of comprehension, their practice is simple, and the benefits to be derived from their practice are sure. Fifteen years ago, in a book from which I have ventured to quote already, I wrote as follows: 'With increasing knowledge of nutritional problems, it has become apparent that our dietetic habits need remodelling, and that education of the people as to what to eat and why they eat it is urgently necessary. It is clear that green vegetables, milk and eggs should form a far higher proportion of the food of the nation than is now customary.

So far from curtailing the beneficent scheme whereby portions of land were made available during the war for cultivation by allotment holders, this scheme should be extended and facilities given to allotment holders for the keeping of fowls. Municipalities and other public bodies should concentrate on the provision of an abundance of milk, eggs and vegetables, for there is no measure that could be devised for improving the health and well-being of the people at the present time that surpasses this either in excellence or in urgency.' Today, fifteen years later, there is little I can add to this exhortation. Its truth is now generally admitted. It is, indeed, the essence of the 'Report on the Physiological Bases of Nutrition' submitted by a special committee two months ago to the Assembly of the League of Nations. It emphasizes two needs, as urgent today as when these words were written: the need for education in the principles of nutrition and the need for the employment of many of our 'unemployed' in the production of more milk, more eggs and more vegetable foods. Concerning this matter of the employment of the unemployed, I need only point to the splendid efforts of the Society of Friends; efforts which provided assistance for 120,000 unemployed men in 1934, and enabled them to produce fresh foods to the value of £600,000. I understand that the sole barrier to its further extension is want of funds. In a letter to *The Times*, about ten months ago, I appealed, in this connection, for the more prudent expenditure of public funds. I repeat the appeal here: 'Year by year we import vast quantities of vegetables all or most of which could be produced in our own country and by our own people. Long before these vegetables reach consumers of the poorer classes they have lost, especially those of the green leafy kinds, much of their health-promoting properties.... Surely it is prudent to provide our people with these important foodstuffs in a state as fresh as possible. Their production should therefore be greatly extended and their speedy distribution ensured.

'It is schemes such as that of the Society of Friends for the provision of allotments for the unemployed and for settlement on the land that deserve generous financial support rather than the expenditure of vast sums on the production of a food-material (sugar) whose consumption by the nation as a whole is vastly in excess of the nation's need for it. The need of our people for fresh vegetable foods, procurable at a cheap rate, is great — as great as their need for clean, cheap milk. Thousands of our people stand idle in the market place who would be well employed in the production and distribution of these health-giving foods. It should not be beyond the organizing capacity of a nation that produced a vast citizen army to meet the curse of war to organize a citizen army to meet, by the adequate production and distribution of fresh vegetable foods, dairy produce and eggs, the curse of preventable disease'. To this last phrase I can add nothing except to say that it envisages what England needs, and needs most urgently; for in this way there lies a solution of some of the problems of agriculture, unemployment, and improvement of national health.

It may, perhaps, be objected that, as it is, we produce more milk than our people can, under present conditions, buy. But the greater consumption of milk is now a national necessity and means must be found to ensure it. Coming from a country where, perforce, all milk must be sterilized by heating, the objections to its sterilization do not appear to me to be so great as some appear to think. It is true that this treatment does deprive it of some of its nutritive quality, but of little that cannot be made good by the adequate use of fresh vegetable foods; while even in its sterilized state, it remains one of the best and cheapest of all foodstuffs. Would it not be possible to sterilize milk in large centres of its production and distribute it in suitably sized sealed tins? Means have been found for the safe distribution of inflammable petrol — a cheaper fluid than milk — can none be found more efficient than the bottle for the house-to-house distribution of contaminable milk? At present the housewife in the slums of our great cities has often no place suitable in which to keep a reasonable supply of milk; the sealed tin might help to solve her difficulty, and a little knowledge help her to keep her supply untainted. However this may be, sterilized milk is vastly better than no milk, or than too little milk however pure it be. This also must be said: the provision of fresh vegetables is complemental to the provision of milk — the one is as much a national necessity as the other.

A notable attempt has recently been made in Bombay to improve the diet of the common people, and, after much trial in schoolchildren, a balanced and very inexpensive diet has been evolved that appears to satisfy physiological needs. This has been achieved by the inclusion in it of whole cereal grains, dried skim milk, soya bean, groundnut, pulses and green-leaf vegetables. So long as we in England insist on including in our dietaries the more expensive, though not necessarily the most nutritious foodstuffs, so long will a balanced diet be beyond the reach of many whose means are limited. In a recent authoritative report it is stated that meat is among the 'protective foods'. It is probably so included because it is a rich source of 'good protein' and of vitamin B2. But it is poor in certain other essentials, and is, indeed, one of the foodstuffs whose defects are made good by milk and green-leaf vegetables, to which McCollum originally applied the term 'protective'. As recently as 1934 he writes: 'There are available only two types of protective foods, or foods which are so constituted as to make good the defects of a white bread, meat, sugar and potato type of diet. These are milk and leafy vegetables.' It is, to my mind, inadvisable to include in the category of 'protective foods' a wide range of expensive foodstuffs, some of which may be beyond the reach of many of our people. By naming meat 'protective', the impression is created that health depends on its inclusion in the diet, which it does not. Far better is it to encourage the use of inexpensive but none the less nutritious foodstuffs (milk, cheese, herrings, wholemeal bread, vegetables, etc.), from which satisfying and well-balanced meals can readily be made at a relatively low cost. It is here that education is called for: education not only in food-values but in the correct and inexpensive selection and combination of foodstuffs.

Education

In this matter of education in the principles of nutrition two of the great professions — the medical and the scholastic — are in a position greatly to aid the endeavours of Government in 'the building of an Al nation'. In regard to my own profession I may repeat what I wrote fifteen years ago: 'It is for us so to instruct ourselves that we may... use our newer knowledge to the end that customs and prejudices may be broken and a more adequate dietary secured for those under our care.' 'There can be no doubt', said the *British Medical Journal,* in a leading article last year, 'but that this newer knowledge of nutrition has placed in the hands of our profession a potent weapon against disease — a potent instrument in the promotion of physical efficiency and well-being. It behoves us, therefore, to become proficient in this knowledge, to apply it in the daily course of our work, and to spread it by every means in our power.' A special responsibility attaches to our medical schools in this respect. 'At present medical students during the early years of their course are given a few lectures and demonstrations dealing with the physiology of nutrition, and perhaps carry out a little laboratory work in this field; the subject is presented as a chapter of physiology, and not as an integral part of preventive medicine.' The authors of the League of Nations Report (*Nutrition and Public Health,* 1935) from which we here quote, are 'far from suggesting that yet another speciality should be added to the already congested medical curriculum'. But surely a subject that is 'an integral part of preventive medicine' must in the future be given a place in the medical curriculum commensurate with its importance. In its teaching we must be content with no half-measures. The student must have the opportunity to see with his own eyes the havoc that is wrought in the various organs and tissues of animals subjected to faulty nutrition of various kinds and degrees. Only when the medical profession is itself so instructed, can it play its proper part in the instruction of the public.

The next most important direction in which educational effort is required is in the teaching of the elements of nutrition to schoolchildren: 'We spend millions', said Lord Bledisloe in a letter to *The Times* (6th November, 1935), 'on feeding the minds of the youth of the nation. Is it not time that we spent a little (as an essential part of all school curricula) on showing those young people how rationally and sensibly to feed their bodies and those of their prospective progeny?' Here he goes to the root of the matter, for it is only by the instruction of youth that the faulty food habits of the people can ultimately be altered and the desire created for those things that be good from the nutritional point of view.

This desire will lead to the demand for them, may be translated into the greater production of them and, perhaps, lead also to the return of many more people to the land — a thing greatly to be desired. But to teach the children the teachers must themselves be taught, and this requires the adequate provision in all training colleges for prospective entrants into the scholastic profession of facilities for the acquisition of a thorough knowledge of the subject. These facilities do not, so far as I can learn, now exist, or if existing they are not adequate. Their provision is an urgent matter. It 'should set the Board of Education thinking more deeply on a question which vitally affects our national physique'.

We have the assurance of Dr. Mary Swartz Rose, Professor of Nutrition, Teachers' College, Columbia University, than whom there is no greater authority on the teaching of nutrition to boys and girls, that it is a subject to which they take readily when it is properly taught. Her own book is a model of how such instruction should be given. An essential part of this instruction, as advocated by Professor Rose, is to give children the actual experience of feeding animals (rats, guinea-pigs) on different diets and to let them see for themselves the influence of food on health and growth.

There are many other directions in which organized effort is needed in regard to education in nutrition: the employment of public health nutrition workers and of 'nutritionists' and 'dieticians', as is now so largely done in America; the teaching of nutrition in schools of domestic science; education work among rural populations; publications and propaganda. These matters are all dealt with at length in a recent publication by the health organization of the League of Nations. (*Nutrition and Public Health,* IV, February, 1935.) But behind all such effort there is the dark cloud of economic conditions that make it difficult, if not impossible, for large numbers of our people to procure diets that will satisfy their physiological needs. Happily there are signs that this cloud is lifting, and there is no lack of evidence both of desire and of effort to ensure a better way of life for the less fortunate amongst us. Until this cloud is dispelled the distribution of relief in kind might well be resorted to. Collective feeding has much to recommend it, both for workers and for unemployed.

In dealing with a subject so vast as nutrition, the lecturer, perforce, confines himself to certain aspects of it — usually those that have come within his own experience. For my own part, my interests have lain in the direction of learning what I could of the relation of faulty food to nutrition and of both to health and disease; and out of this desire to learn there has come the desire to spread such knowledge of the subject as we already possess. It has been my endeavour, during these lectures, to convey this knowledge to you, in the hope that with understanding there may come belief. Belief that the continued use of properly-constituted food, from the earliest period of development onwards throughout life, is the surest means we have of acquiring and maintaining that condition of body — good health — which is 'the vital principle of bliss':

This Life-joy, like the breath-kiss of the all-ambient air unnoticed till the lack of it bring pain and death, is coefficient with the untrammel'd energy of native faculty, and the autometric scale of all functions and motions,... it is the lordly heraldry of the banner'd flower, in brutes the vaunt of vigour and the pose of pride, their wild impersonation of majesty; and in man the grace and ease of health alike in body and mind, that right congruity of his parts, for lack whereof his sanity is disabled, maim'd and compromised.

Diet, Nutrition, and Health

The biological process of aging begins at conception. Up to the age of reproduction, the changes in physical appearance and metabolic function that accompany aging can be viewed as a genetically guided developmental process. Senescence is the changes in cells, tissues, organs, and their respective functions that continue to occur after midlife. The capacity for physiological functions—from glucose regulation to digestion and absorption to renal function—decreases progressively as an individual ages. The immune system changes, enhancing susceptibility to infections, autoimmune diseases, and neoplasia.

Aging and communicable disease. Given the diversity of environments, nature of social changes, involvement in globalization, and the genetic and evolutionary experience across regions, it is difficult to generalize about the health of the growing elderly population. What is certain, however, is that the increasing number of elderly people in developing countries will be susceptible to the health problems associated with low-income societies, including infections and accidents, and that their diet and nutritional status will interact with these conditions.

Infections that traditionally produce mortality in early life, such as malaria, tuberculosis, respiratory infections, and diarrhea, may reemerge in later life if the individuals survive. Those who survive the lifelong risk from these infections might have constitutional resistance. However, for other elderly individuals the emergence of widespread drug resistance among the pathogens of malaria, tuberculosis, and respiratory infections, as well as less tolerance to dehydration and hypovolemia for infectious gastroenteritis, could mean an increased risk for these communicable diseases.

The appearance of HIV/AIDS in those over 60 years also may become an issue in the next two decades. The elderly traditionally are at lower risk of contracting sexually transmitted diseases, but as antiviral medications begin to become available in Asia and Africa, increased survival will project many chronic HIV cases from midlife into old age. Because of limited experience, the natural history of HIV infection in the elderly is not well understood. Imbalanced intake and chronic disease. New combinations of nutrition and health interactions with aging, namely, that of noncommunicable (chronic) diseases and dietary imbalances, are now emerging. That these diseases—obesity, diabetes, cardiovascular disease, and cancer—are becoming more common with aging is irrefutable. Equally undeniable is the fact that diet and lifestyle throughout life condition an individual's susceptibility to the eventual onset of chronic diseases.

The traditional rural diets of many tropical developing countries encompass characteristics associated with protection against chronic diseases: high intake of dietary fiber, such as coarse seeds or legumes; low intake of fat and cholesterol; high intake of herbs, fruits, and vegetables rich in carotenoids and phytochemicals; and modest consumption of red meat that comes from game and lean livestock and constitutes a small fraction of dietary protein and lower fat load than meat consumption in developed countries. To the extent that this pattern is maintained, developing-country populations may continue to be spared high rates of some chronic illnesses.

Cataracts and senile macular degeneration also are diet-related. Fresh green, yellow, and red fruits and vegetables, presumably their carotenoids content, delay the occurrence of these two diseases of the aged eye.

Sarcopenia, the progressive loss of lean tissue—especially skeletal muscle—with advancing years, presents an obvious interactive role with osteoporotic bone loss insofar as the risk of fracturing a hip or wrist depends not only on the mineralization of the bone but also on the chance of suffering a fall.

The Need for Research

In theory, elderly individuals are vulnerable to both undernutrition and its associated nutritional deficiencies and infectious diseases as well as to imbalanced intakes and the concomitant risk of chronic diseases. Because no empirical evidence of such links exists, however, the major challenge and opportunity in developing countries over the next two decades will be to establish a gerontology and a gerontological nutrition presence and to acquire the evidence necessary to address the policy and program issues represented by the burgeoning population of elderly. The research agenda for the next two decades should focus on the following issues related to nutrition, health, and aging:

Osteoporotic fractures. Developing-country populations appear to be more resistant to osteoporosis than people in developed societies. Research should be conducted to determine (1) if meeting the calcium requirements is essential to preventing bone mineral loss; (2) whether increasing vitamin K intake and decreasing preformed vitamin A can retard the epidemic of osteoporosis; and (3) if a lifelong consumption of dietary sources of phytoestrogens, as by the soy-eating populations of East Asia or where legumes are staples in south Asia and Latin America, helps reduce menopausal bone loss.

Dementias. Because Alzheimer's and multiple-infarct dementias are less common (on an age-adjusted basis) in developing countries, centenarian studies and epidemiology are required to identify persons at risk of dementias.

Depression. In order to determine whether stronger extended-family bonds in developing societies would limit loneliness, enhance feelings of self-worth, and reduce the risk of depression, culturally sensitive and adapted diagnostic instruments, such as rating scales for depression adopted for developing societies, are required. The role of pharmacological antidepressive medications also should be considered.

Undernutrition and food insecurity. The elderly are thought to be intrinsically at greater risk of dietary and nutritional deprivation. Therefore, the implications of rapid weight loss or low body mass among community-dwelling elderly (as opposed to those who are hospitalized or under other institutional care) need to be assessed. Scientists must also determine if "wasting" in elderly persons who live independently is reversible and how prudent and beneficial it is to reverse low weight. Research is also needed to determine whether the risks of having an underlying malignancy are the same at a given weight deficit in developing countries as they are in western geriatric practice.

Overweight and obesity. Poverty has been thought to protect against obesity. Now, however, persons can be poor, and still have access to abundant calories from poor quality foods. In low-income families, however, obesity and underweight occur simultaneously in the same households as shown in Brazil, China, and Russia.

Research is needed to determine whether ethnicity affects the tendency to obesity, the risk of obesity-related morbidity, and the consequences of having more body fat deposited in the abdominal cavity in relation to risk of obesity-related morbidity.

During the last decade, the international nutrition community has focused on eliminating or reducing three micro-nutrient deficiencies. At the World Summit for Children in 1990, followed by the Ending Hidden Hunger conference in 1991 and the International Conference on Nutrition in 1992, agencies and governments pledged to eliminate iodine and vitamin A deficiencies by 2000 and to substantially reduce iron deficiency anemia. As a result, about 70 percent of all salt is now iodized and half the countries in the world have vitamin A capsule distribution programs reaching a high percentage of women and children under 5 years. Efforts to reduce anemia have been less successful, but iron-folic-acid supplements are available to millions of pregnant women.

The international nutrition community focused on these three micronutrient deficiencies for logical reasons—they allowed relatively simple, inexpensive solutions with far-reaching health benefits. Iodine deficiency adversely affects intelligence, motor development, and pregnancy outcomes. Common in both industrialized and developing countries, this deficiency can be prevented by salt iodization. Interest in alleviating vitamin A deficiency increased in the 1980s, when researchers found that periodic high doses of vitamin A to young children in developing countries substantially reduced their risk of dying from measles. Iron deficiency is thought to be the most common nutrient deficiency in the world, and iron deficiency anemia slows mental and motor development and reduces work performance and physical activity. Progress in combating iron deficiency has been hindered by technological limits on iron fortification of staple foods and the need to supply iron supplements on an almost daily basis for them to be effective.

Focusing on other Micronutrient Deficiencies

The focus on these three micronutrients partly explains why relatively little attention has been paid to other, "neglected" micronutrients. Poorer populations, however, usually suffer also from inadequate intakes of zinc, riboflavin, vitamin B-12, vitamin

B-6, and calcium because they consume few animal products (meat, fish, poultry, eggs, or dairy products). Poor diets may also contain few fruits and a limited variety of vegetables and, therefore, low amounts of B-carotene (provitamin A), folic acid, and vitamin C. Surveys show that many individuals—especially women and children—are consuming lower than recommended amounts of the neglected micronutrients. But there have been relatively few studies of the prevalence of these micronutrient deficiencies or of how they cluster in specific populations. Limited data show that zinc, riboflavin, and vitamin B-12 deficiencies tend to cluster with vitamin A and iron deficiencies.

Zinc. No good indicators of zinc status exist, although plasma zinc concentrations fall if deficiency is sufficiently severe and/or prolonged. Interest in zinc was stimulated when zinc supplements given to short children and failure-to-thrive infants in the U.S. city of Denver improved growth. Many investigators then mounted zinc intervention trials with children, because intakes of absorbable zinc are often low and growth-stunting occurs nearly universally during the first two years of life in underprivileged populations. Diarrhea also causes the body to lose zinc. An analysis of 27 such trials concluded that zinc supplements are likely to improve the height gain of the most stunted children and to improve the weight gain of those with low plasma zinc concentrations. In recent intervention trials, zinc supplements reduced the prevalence of pneumonia and malaria in children, shortened the duration of acute and persistent diarrhea, and improved neuropsychological performance. Zinc supplements improved birth weight in one U.S. study, although in Bangladesh and Peru they did not.

Riboflavin. In the relatively few studies of riboflavin the prevalence of deficiency has been alarmingly high. Almost all the pregnant and lactating women studied in The Gambia, the majority of lactating women and elderly in Guatemala, and most Chinese adults were reported to be deficient. A high seasonal prevalence of clinical symptoms of deficiency has been reported in Iran. The adverse consequences of riboflavin deficiency are not yet well understood, although the reduced absorption and use of iron for hemoglobin synthesis reported in several studies suggests that riboflavin deficiency may contribute to the global prevalence of anemia. Riboflavin deficiency also may cause night blindness and muscle weakness.

Vitamin B-12. Because vitamin B-12 is found only in animal products, many poor populations, or those that avoid animal products for religious or other reasons, consume little or no vitamin B-12. Low serum B-12 concentration is associated with a higher risk of potentially irreversible harm to memory, cognitive function, and nerve conduction, as well as a higher risk of megaloblastic anemia. Studies among low-income people in Guatemala, Mexico, Nepal, Venezuela, and other countries show that 25 to 50 percent of individuals are deficient. Inadequate B-12 during pregnancy and/or lactation can cause breast milk to have such a low concentration of the vitamin that the infant grows too slowly and is developmentally delayed.

In addition to a diet low in animal products, risk factors for vitamin B-12 deficiency include infection with the bacteria Helicobacter pylori (a very common infection in populations living in poor sanitary conditions) or the parasite Giardia, and an overgrowth of bacteria in the upper intestine. Given that about 25 percent of the elderly in the United States have vitamin B-12 deficiency, a very high percentage of the elderly in developing countries must be deficient in this vitamin.

Other B vitamins. The prevalence of other B-vitamin deficiencies is unknown. Due to thiamin (vitamin B-1) fortification programs, this vitamin deficiency is no longer common in populations whose staple food is polished white rice. Poor vitamin B-6 status has been reported among Indonesian schoolchildren and in the Vietnamese population. In an Egyptian study, breast-milk concentrations of this vitamin were low, indicating that lactating women were deficient; mothers and infants both had abnormal behaviors associated with B-6 deficiency. In general, mothers with low stores or intakes of the B vitamins secrete inadequate amounts of these vitamins in their milk to support optimal child health and development.

Folic acid. The global prevalence of folic acid deficiency is uncertain. Folate consumption by the poor in developing countries actually may be better than in industrialized countries because legumes and many leaves are rich sources of this nutrient. Folic acid has long been included in iron supplements for pregnant women in developing countries, based on limited evidence that folic acid improved hemoglobin response to iron in Africa and India. Subsequent trials, however, failed to show that adding folic acid improved anemia more than iron alone. Folic acid supplements for pregnant women can reduce the risk of infants' having neural tube defects, but only if the supplements are taken by susceptible women around the time of conception. Recent evidence suggests that poor maternal folate status is also associated with a higher risk of abnormal pregnancy outcomes, including eclampsia, premature delivery, and birth defects such as club foot and cleft palate. Consuming more folic acid from supplements or folate from foods can also lower plasma homocysteine and potentially lower the risk of cardiovascular disease in adults and dementia in the elderly.

Calcium, vitamin D, and selenium. The extent of calcium, vitamin D, and selenium deficiency in developing countries is uncertain. Calcium consumption is extremely low in many locations where dairy products and fish are not eaten, but humans have the capacity to absorb calcium more efficiently in these situations. Very low calcium consumption does not seem to impair children's growth, but may reduce their bone mineralization. Low dietary calcium may be the explanation for non-vitamin D rickets in Nigeria, South Africa, and several other countries. Calcium deficiency is certainly a risk factor for osteoporosis in later life. Vitamin D deficiency, which is caused primarily by low exposure to ultraviolet light, is common in more northern and southern latitudes and in regions where infants and women are heavily clothed for cultural or religious reasons. In Europe and China, where few foods are fortified with vitamin D, infants born at the end of winter commonly show evidence of vitamin D deficiency. Selenium deficiency is localized in specific but large geographic regions, including China and parts of Africa, where it can exacerbate the symptoms of iodine deficiency and interfere with the anti-goiter benefits of iodine supplements.

Focusing on the elimination or reduction of iodine, vitamin A, and iron deficiencies has motivated many agencies and governments to work together and has demonstrated the benefits of intervention programs. Clearly, efforts are also needed to assess the prevalence of other micronutrient deficiencies. Several ongoing trials will evaluate the impact of providing multiple micronutrients to children and women in developing countries. The addition of other micronutrients adds relatively little to a supplement's price, most of which reflects the cost of packaging and distribution. The same obstacles to lowering the prevalence of iron deficiency, however, will plague the effectiveness of multiple-micronutrient programs.

Sustainable Solutions

The sustainable solution to multiple micronutrient deficiencies must be the discovery and implementation of innovative, affordable ways to improve poor people's diets. This probably will require consumption of more animal products, where these are culturally acceptable. Fortified foods are another logical strategy. Even in the United States, flours and cereal products are enriched with iron, riboflavin, niacin, folic acid, and sometimes calcium. The importance of food-based strategies to reduce micronutrient malnutrition is recognized by agencies and governments; however, there has been little effective communication between the nutrition community and agricultural producers. The latter group tends to believe that the answer to good nutrition is to produce more income-generating crops, when it would be more effective to consider the impact of agricultural products themselves on the nutritional needs of populations. Additional interaction is needed to bridge the gap between food production and nutrition security.

Failure to address the problem of these neglected nutrients will mean that a high proportion of the world's population—especially infants, children, women of reproductive age, and the elderly—will continue to suffer the consequences of micronutrient deficiencies. When the potential improvement in human capital is considered, investing in the prevention of micronutrient deficiencies is indeed cost-effective.

Significant progress in human development will not be made during the next two decades unless the nutrition and health issues discussed in this collection of policy briefs are addressed head-on. As described in the overview by Rafael Flores, some of these issues are emerging (HIV/AIDS, obesity, chronic disease, and neglected micronutrients) and others are reemerging (malaria and tuberculosis [TB]). These nutrition and health issues may cluster in populations, particularly among the poor and marginalized. And many of these issues interact with regard to risk, causation, and consequence.

Such interaction often is embedded within the "malnutrition-infection complex" that accounts for much of the preventable mortality in the developing world. In this vicious circle, underlying risk factors such as gender discrimination and poverty can be both determinants and outcomes.

Consider the interaction between HIV/AIDS and poverty, for example: Poverty increases people's exposure to HIV and heightens the disease's impact. At the same time, HIV/AIDS impoverishes households and communities.

Policy Themes

Many of these nutrition and health issues must be considered as fundamental development problems—not just the domain of the health sector. Such a shift in perception seems to be occurring with HIV/AIDS. The issue of HIV/AIDS, a disease that threatens the survival and well-being of entire populations, is slowly being mainstreamed into development-policy discourse, as agencies like the World Bank begin to retrofit ongoing projects with AIDS prevention or mitigation components.

Just as the determinants and effects of these health and nutrition problems often interact, so too there are potentially synergistic approaches to solving them. The following cross-cutting themes should be considered when selecting and implementing appropriate policies and programs.

Integration and collaboration. When problems interact and coexist among certain populations, integrated solutions can achieve multiple benefits and be more cost-effective. For example, to prevent intrauterine growth retardation (IUGR), food supplements for nutritionally vulnerable pregnant women may be linked to prenatal care at community health centers. There is evidence, moreover, to justify multiple, as opposed to single, micronutrient supplementation, which has potential not only for combating micronutrient deficiency, but also for preventing IUGR and even protecting against malaria. Food-based strategies to control micronutrient deficiency also should be pursued within agricultural development and extension programs.

Integration is best promoted through collaborative approaches. Collaboration does not refer to multisectoral coordination by any one organization; it means bringing concerned organizations together to consider how best to use their resources to meet common goals. Collaboration might involve different sectors of the government, civil society, the private sector, and the media;

governments and international organizations; or regional and international alliances.

Information, education, and communication. More and better information is required at many levels. There is a need for improved diagnosis of some illnesses (for example, TB). More information is needed about the prevalence and distribution of various health and nutrition outcomes, including the "neglected" micronutrient deficiencies, IUGR, overweight/obesity, and chronic diseases. A database on the nutritional problems of the elderly will help provide evidence for policy and programmatic changes. Better nutritional labeling of foods will increase consumer awareness of the effect of diets.

More effective communication is needed between the nutrition and agriculture communities regarding micronutrients; between those who are coping with HIV/AIDS and people more recently affected; and between health care providers and TB patients on patients' need to complete drug treatment and thus avoid building resistance to drugs. One often-overlooked result of premature adult death is the loss of the patient's knowledge and skills. Teaching survivors, particularly orphans, how to manage households and farm resources is critical in AIDS-affected communities.

Advocacy and social mobilization. Advocacy is a communication strategy aimed at convincing decisionmakers to give a higher priority to combating a certain problem or to adopting a particular approach. Advocacy efforts should be based on an assessment of the values, beliefs, and interests of decisionmakers that—along with information—will determine their choices. Within the set of health and nutrition issues addressed in this series of briefs are clear areas for greater advocacy. The need to raise the status of low birthweight as a critical indicator of human development and the need to ensure gender-equitable land tenure arrangements for widows of AIDS victims are just two examples.

Social mobilization is a process of generating bottom-up demand for action and ownership of solutions. Through social mobilization, the advantages of local diversity and existing capacity are maximized and sustainability is enhanced.

Capacity development. The capacity to achieve a sustained impact must be assessed at the early stages of program planning.

What level of effort will be required? Over what period of time will such efforts be expended? The capacity to measure the dimensions of these nutrition and health issues, assess trends, analyze causes, and act with appropriate levels of resources may be significantly lacking, particularly in areas and among populations that are most affected. Capacity development should be a priority for external agencies and donors as well as governments, and it should be pursued proactively.

Research. Research into ways of diagnosing disease, combating drug resistance, and developing vaccines must run parallel with research into improving approaches to disease control. The Multilateral Initiative on Malaria is an alliance of African organizations and individuals that aims (1) to strengthen and sustain the capability of malaria-endemic African countries to carry out research for developing and improving tools to control malaria and (2) to strengthen the research-control interface. With operational research, priorities should flow from management information systems built into programs. Evaluation must be made a priority and funds must be budgeted for this process. The results of evaluations need to be proactively fed into advocacy strategies to ultimately improve action.

Policy Actions

Policy actions governing these nutrition and health issues vary widely. Malaria, TB, and HIV/AIDS are currently the subjects of major campaigns backed by international organizations, including the World Health Organization and UNAIDS (Joint United Nations Programme on HIV/AIDS). By contrast, the dual agendas for undernutrition (IUGR and micronutrient deficiencies) and overnutrition (obesity and related chronic disease), where these two problems coexist, have been given little attention—though there are some signs of positive developments.

During the next two decades, the major strategic areas for action are clear: (1) prevention and promotion, (2) treatment, and (3) care and mitigation.

Prevention and promotion. Prevention will require accelerated efforts to develop vaccines (HIV, malaria, and TB), to increase access to effective antimalarial drugs and insecticide-impregnated bed nets (malaria), to make quality prenatal care more widely available (IUGR), and to expand use of recreational facilities (obesity and chronic disease). To prevent or forestall the emergence of many of these problems, various promotional efforts will be required. People must be made more aware of the need to maintain a healthy diet, use preventive health services, increase physical activity, and adopt safe sexual practices. Such behavioural changes should be facilitated through appropriate channels—from interpersonal communication between a community-based worker and a mother to mass-media messages on television and radio. Adults are not the only target group; children should be targeted directly by these methods and through school curricula.

Treatment. The availability and affordability of effective drugs (for malaria, TB, HIV/AIDS, and adult chronic disease) must be a priority. The importance of this issue is starkly evident in the easy access to retroviral drugs by HIV patients in industrialized countries compared with the inability of patients in Sub-Saharan Africa to obtain such drugs. Public-private partnerships are key: Private multinational drug companies have an ethical responsibility in regard to pricing, and the public sector must improve distribution and access. In addition, the search for new drugs must be intensified to counteract increasingly drug-resistant diseases, particularly TB and malaria.

Care and mitigation. Care and mitigation efforts need to focus on buffering individuals, families, communities, and countries from the impact of these nutrition and health problems. The care of adolescent girls and pregnant women must be emphasized, to protect their own health and that of their future children. Nutrition interventions in particular need to adopt such a life-cycle approach to targeting. Care for the elderly also will become increasingly important. The most urgent need is care for Africa's hundreds of thousands of "double orphans"—children who have lost both parents to AIDS. Widows of AIDS victims also need to be protected and supported. In several countries in Latin America, such buffers are institutionalized in the form of social safety nets designed to protect the most vulnerable.

Mitigation efforts initially should focus on strengthening local strategies for coping with premature adult deaths due to TB, malaria, and HIV/AIDS, rather than externally pre-packaging solutions. This will require more action research on livelihoods, with the aim of understanding such strategies.

Conclusions

Progress in human and economic development over the next 20 years will be determined largely by the manner in which households, communities, governments, and the international community react to the emerging and reemerging nutrition and health issues described in these policy briefs. Many of these problems affect public health, but they also demand larger, development solutions from the public and private sectors. In many cases, large-scale improvements will take time. But if the appropriate foundations are laid now, the gains will be wide-ranging and sustainable.

3

Carbohydrates and Proteins

Carbohydrates

Carbohydrates are a major source of energy for humans, providing approximately 45% to 80% of the total caloric intake in different income groups. Since they are a relatively inexpensive source of energy compared to fats and proteins, they form the bulk of the diet of humans throughout the world.

They are mainly present in food in the form of sugars, starches, and fibres. A study of the various types of carbohydrates is necessary because the kind and pro-portion of different forms of carbohydrate present in food have a direct bearing on our health.

Three groups of carbohydrates are of importance in our diet from the nutritional point of view, namely, sugars, starches, and fibres. The sugar and starch that we consume is ultimately broken down to glucose in the digestive tract and absorbed into the blood circulation. In the human body, glucose is removed from blood by the tissue cells and used as a source of energy. Some glucose is converted to glycogen, also called animal starch, and stored in the musicle and liver as a reserve store of energy.

Classification of Carbohydrates

Carbohydrates which are of importance in the diet are classified on the basis of the number of sugar units present in them. They may also be classified as:

Available carbohydrates Carbohydrates which can be digested in the human body and yield energy when they are oxidized in the body.

Unavailable carbohydrates Carbohydrates which cannot be digested because the human body does not contain the enzymes necessary for their breakdown. Unavailable carbohydrates do not provide any energy to the body but are necessary as they perform some important functions in the body such as regular elimination of faecal waste.

Digestion, Absorption, and Metabolism

Complex carbohydrates and sugars are too large to be absorbed through the intestinal wall. They need to be broken down into their constituent monosaccharides so that they can be absorbed. Only monosaccharides can be absorbed into the blood stream. The mechanical and chemical digestion of starch begins in the mouth.

Ptyalin or salivary amylase in saliva acts on cooked starch and partially breaks it down into dextrin. If ptyalin acts on starch long enough, i.e., if food is chewed well, some maltose may be formed. The stomach does not secrete any starch-splitting enzyme, hence no digestion takes place in the stomach. In the small intestine, pancreatic amylase acts on starch and dextrin breaking it down into maltose.

The intestinal wall secretes maltase, lactase, and sucrase which acts on maltose, lactose, and sucrose, reducing them to their respective monosaccharides. Some fructose may be converted to glucose. The monosaccharides are absorbed into the blood vessels lining the small intestine and carried to the liver for their further metabolism.

The absorbed monosaccharides, i.e., glucose, fructose, and galactose may be converted into glycogen and stored in the liver, or converted into glucose and released into the blood stream to be oxidized as a source of energy for various tissue cells.

In human metabolism, all sugars are converted into glucose. In the muscle cells, some glucose may be stored as glycogen. The fasting level of glucose in blood is maintained at 70-100 mg/100 ml blood. After consuming a meal rich in carbohydrates, it increases to 140-150 mg/100 ml blood. Glucose is taken up from blood by the body cells and oxidized as a source of energy.

In the cells, glucose is first oxidized to form pyruvic acid, and ultimately through the various metabolic cycles, energy is released in the form of adenosine triphosphate (ATP). The waste products of carbohydrate metabolism, i.e., carbon dioxide and water are released from the cell and excreted by the body. The energy released is used by the body for its various voluntary and involuntary processes and to maintains body temperature.

If the level exceeds 170 mg glucose/100 ml blood, it crosses the renal threshold and glucose is excreted in the urine. This condition is observed in diabetic patients. A fasting blood glucose level above 140 mg is called hyperglycaemia and below 70 mg is called hypoglycaemia.

The body tries to maintain the normal fasting level by remov-ing glucose from blood when the level is high and adding glucose to blood when the level falls, e.g., when a person is fasting. The hormone insulin, secreted by the cells of the islets of Langerhans in the pancreas, helps in regulating the blood glucose level.

Insulin is required for glucose utilization by the cells and synthesis of glycogen from glucose. If insulin is deficient, glucose is not utilized by the cells and blood level of glucose increases. Insulin is the only hormone which lowers blood sugar levels, other hormones, such as the thyroid hormone, increase blood sugar levels.

Sources

Daily diet should provide up to 50-70% kcal of energy from carbohydrate, which means that the diet of an individual who needs 2,400 kcal should consume 60% of 2,400, i.e., 1,440 kcal or 360 g of carbohydrates/day. Carbohydrates are not only an economical source of energy but are also readily available and easy to store as they have a long shelf life.

All foods of plant origin contain carbohydrates in varying amounts. With the exception of milk, animal foods do not contain carbohydrate. Although milk is not consumed as a source of carbohydrate, some milk products, such as khoa and milk powder, contain significant amount of carbohydrate lactose.

The important sources of carbohydrates in the diets of Indians are cereals and millets, roots, tubers, pulses, sugar, and jaggery.

All sugars provide 4 kcal/g of energy. The carbohydrate and calorie content of a food can be reduced by using sugars which are sweeter than sucrose so that the quantity of sugar required will be less.

Functions

Carbohydrates have many functions in the human body.

1. The chief function of carbohydrate is to provide energy to the body so that it can carry out day-to-day work and maintain body temperature. All carbohy-drates except fibre provide 4 kcal/g of energy. It is the cheapest source of energy available.
2. Glucose is the only form of energy used by the central nervous system. When blood glucose levels fall, the brain does not receive energy and convulsions may occur.
3. Carbohydrates spare proteins from being broken down for energy and are used for bodybuilding and repair. In carbohydrate deficient diets, proteins meant for bodybuilding and repair are oxidized to meet the most important and first need of the body, i.e., energy.
4. They are required for complete oxidation of fat. In a deficiency, fats are broken down rapidly for energy and intermediate products such as ketones are formed in large amounts resulting in a condition called ketosis.
5. Carbohydrates can be converted into non-essential amino acids, provided a source of nitrogen is available.
6. The sugar lactose helps in the absorption of the minerals calcium and phosphorus.
7. Lactose helps certain bacteria to grow in the intestine. This bacterial flora is capable of synthesizing B-complex vitamins in the gut.
8. Dietary fibre plays an important role of increasing faecal mass by absorbing and holding water, stimulating peristalsis, and eliminating faecal waste.
9. Fibre also helps in lowering blood cholesterol levels by binding bile acids and cholesterol.

Deficiency

The daily diet should not contain less than 100 g of carbohydrate. Carbohydrate deficiency is uncommon in our country as diets are cereal based. A deficiency of carbohydrate in the diet results in utilization of fat for energy. In severe deficiency, incomplete oxidation of fats causes ketone bodies to accumulate in the blood.

Excess Carbohydrates

1. Excessive consumption of refined sugars could be one of the causes of den-tal caries or tooth decay.
2. Excessive sugar depresses the appetite, provides hollow calories, and could result in malnutrition.
3. High intake of sugar and refined carbohydrates increase the blood triglyceride levels leading to heart diseases.
4. When excessive carbohydrates are consumed they are converted into fat and deposited in the adipose tissue, which could lead to obesity, i.e., body weight of 20% or more than desirable weight.
5. Excessive fibre could irritate the intestinal lining causing cramps or bloating due to gas formation.
6. Excessive fibre interferes with the absorption and availability of mineral elements such as iron and calcium.

Role of Dietary Fibre in Prevention and Treatment of Disease

Dietary fibre refers to the total amount of naturally occurring material in plant foods, which is not digested. The terms roughage, bulk, and unavailable polysaccharides are synonymous with fibre. Fibres cannot be digested by human enzymes.

Dietary fibre or roughage does not provide humans with energy but performs many important functions in the body. Fibre can absorb and hold water thereby increasing faecal bulk. This acts as a laxative and reduces intraluminal pressure in the colon preventing diverticulosis. Insoluble fibre prevents constipation by stimulating peristalsis in the large intestine. The contraction of muscular walls of the digestive tract is stimulated by fibre. Fibre increases water absorption, forming a larger, softer stool that rapidly passes through the colon. Soluble fibre binds bile acids and cholesterol and is beneficial to people suffering from coronary heart disease. Fibre reduces the triglyceride and cholesterol levels in blood.

Fibre is beneficial to people on weight reduction regime. It provides satiety value to the meal because of more chewing required and at the same time does not add to the calorific value of the meal. It helps in lowering blood sugar levels in diabetic individuals by slowing down carbohydrate absorption and lowers the insulin requirement. Regular intake of fibre may prevent cancers of the colon and rectum.

Although fibre is not a true nutrient, because it cannot be digested by humans, it is nutritionally important. Foods such as whole grain cereals, fruits, and vegetables, specially when the peel and seeds are edible, are rich sources of fibre.

Artificial Sweeteners

These are also known as non-nutritive sweeteners. Artificial sweeteners are 100-350 times as sweet as sucrose and provide no or very negligible calories. A wide variety of sweetening agents are available in the market and are used for low-calorie products such as diet coke. These processed products are specially manufactured for obese individuals, weight watchers, and diabetic patients. They are used quite successfully in bakery items such as cakes, biscuits, cookies, Indian sweetmeats, confectionery products, beverages, puddings, and chewing gum. Saccharin, aspartame, sodium cyclamate, and stugar are some of the commonly used substitutes for sugar. Their use is not recommended in soft drinks and other food consumed by children as these foods may be a substitute for essential nutrients.

Alcohol

Ethyl alcohol is produced by yeast fermentation of carbohydrates under anaerobic conditions. Different carbohydrates are used to manufacture alcoholic beverages.

Alcoholic beverages do not supply necessary nutrients but contribute significant amount of energy. Alcohol contributes 7 kcal/g or 5.6 kcal/ml and in people who consume alcoholic beverages, up to 10% of total energy needs may be derived from alcohol. Some chronic alcoholics may consume insufficient food and suffer from malnutrition while the reverse may be observed in the case of social drinkers who consume large amount of high-calorie foods such as starters, nuts, and wafers along with their drinks.

These high-calorie snacks are rich in carbohydrate, fat, and sodium. Alcohol is absorbed rapidly, directly into the blood stream. Drinking on an empty stomach increases the alcohol level in blood twice as fast as on a full stomach.

If alcohol is taken along with antidepressants or tranquilizers, it prolongs the sedative effect of these medicines.

Excessive consumption of alcohol accompanied by decreased intake of other nutrients can lead to malnutrition and serious liver disorders such as cirrhosis of the liver.

Summary

Carbohydrates are nutrients which form the bulk of our diet. They include sugars, starch and fibre and occur abundantly in the plant kingdom. They are made up of carbon, hydrogen, and oxygen.

Sugars and starches are available carbohydrates and provide 4 kcal/g of energy on oxidation. Sugars are classified as monosaccharides and disaccharides of which glucose is the sugar present in blood, and sucrose or table sugar is consumed in large quantities compared to other sugars. Polysaccharides include starch, the form in which carbohydrate is stored in plants, glycogen or animal starch stored in the muscles and liver and dextrins, which are formed on partial breakdown of starch. These polysaccharides are made up of glucose units and after digestion and absorption all available polysaccharides are converted to glucose and used as a source of energy by all body cells via the liver and blood. Unavailable polysaccharides play an important role in our diet by regular elimination of faecal matter and regulating the levels of bile acids and cholesterol.

Carbohydrates are an essential nutrient and a minimum quantity should be consumed daily. They perform many important functions in the body. The diet should not provide more than 70% energy from carbohydrates and at least 25-30 g fibre should be consumed daily. An excessive intake of sugar and starch may lead to obesity and dental caries, while excessive fibre may cause gastric irritability and malabsorption of minerals.

Glycogenolysis Breakdown of glycogen to glucose when energy is required.

Hollow calories or empty calories Term used to describe foods which only supply energy and have very few or no nutrients.

Insulin A hormone secreted by the pancreas, which regulates carbohydrate metabolism.

Invert sugar Mixture of glucose and fructose, sweeter than sucrose, produced by hydrolysis of sucrose and prevents crystallization in confectionery items. Lignin A substance which is not a carbohydrate but present along with carbohydrates in the cell wall of plants and forms part of dietary fibre.

Renal threshold Blood level of a substance at which it cannot be further reabsorbed by the kidneys and is excreted in the urine, e.g., renal threshold of glucose is 170 mg/100 ml.

Today, sugar is being replaced by artificial sweeteners, which are many hundred times sweeter than sugar and provide no calories. In people who consume alcoholic beverages, the intake of calories from alcohol need to be considered because alcohol does not provide any nutrients other than energy. Many beverages and fast foods contain large quantities of refined sugars and starches, which could be detrimental to health if they are not combined with nutrient-dense foods.

Proteins

Protein is the basic material of every living cell and is thè most important of all known substances in the organic kingdom. It is the only nutrient that can make new cells and rebuild tissues. Therefore, an adequate amount of protein in the diet is essential for normal growth and development and for the maintenance of health.

Definition

Proteins are large, complex, organic compounds made up of carbon, hydrogen, oxygen, and nitrogen. The presence of nitrogen distinguishes proteins from carbohydrates and fats. Apart from nitrogen, elements such as sulphur, phosphorus, copper, and iron are also found in some proteins.

The basic units from which proteins are built are the amino acids. Each amino acid contains a carboxyl group (COOH) or acid group and an amino group (NHS or basic group.

Proteins consist of chains of amino acids that are linked to each other by a pep. tide linkage (-CO-NH-).

Twenty-two different amino acids are widely distributed in nature. However, the proteins obtained from plants and animals are quite different both in amounts present and in quality. The proteins that make up the skin, bones, muscles, hair, and nails in the body are obviously very different from each other. Egg, milk, meat, and pulse proteins also differ both in quality and in quantity.

This is because the amino acids present in each of these proteins are in different permutations and combinations. Thousands of different proteins exist in nature and vary widely from one another in quality. No two proteins will have an identical amino acid content.

The protein content of any food can be estimated by measuring the nitrogen content of the food. Since proteins contain 16% nitrogen, each gram of nitrogen measured is equal to 6.25 g of protein.

Essential Amino Acids

Those amino acids which cannot be synthesized in sufficient amounts by the body and must be provided by the diet are called essential amino acids. The human adult requires eight essential amino acids, while growing children require ten essential amino acids. Essential amino acids are indispensable to life.

Non-essential Amino Acids

All amino acids are required by the body for tissue synthesis and repair. Non-essential amino acids does not mean that these amino acids are not required by the body. They are termed non-essential because they are not dietary essentials. If they are lacking in the diet, they can be synthesized by the body from other amino acids.

The twenty-two amino acids present in proteins could be compared with the letters of the Roman alphabet and the innumerable words present in our dictionary. Similarly, innumerable proteins can be formed by using the twenty-two amino acids in varying sequences and quantities.

Protein Quality

No two food proteins are identical in their quality, i.e., with the efficiency with which they can be used in the body. The quality of protein depends upon the kind and amount of amino acids present in them in relation to the body needs. Protein quality is an important criterion for tissue synthesis. Each body protein performs a specific function and cannot be replaced by another protein. When a new protein has to be synthesized, all the amino acids, which make up the protein, must be availableat the same time and in sufficient quantity. Even if one amino acid is missing or deficient, protein cannot be synthesized just like a word cannot be made if even one of the alphabets of which it is made up of is missing.

Biological Value

It is an index of protein quality. It is defined as the amount of absorbed nitrogen retained in the body. The digestibility factor is not taken into account. Biological value (BV) is a quantitative measure of the nutritive value of a protein food. A pro-tein of high BV will retain more nitrogen than a protein of low BV

Cereals and pulses consumed together will have a higher BV than the average value of the individual cereal or pulse. This is because of the complementary nature of proteins. Amino acids deficient in cereals will be compensated by the amino acids present in pulses.

Classification of Proteins

Proteins may be classified on (1) the basis of their structure or on (2) the basis of their quality, i.e., the amino acids present in them.

Classification by Structure

Simple proteins These proteins are made up of amino acids only, e.g., zein in corn, albumin in egg white, and gliadin in wheat consist of amino acids only.

Conjugated proteins These proteins have a nonprotein molecule attached to the protein, e.g., blood protein haemoglobin, which contains a haeme (iron) group attached to protein and milk protein casein, which has a phosphate group attached. Derived proteins These result from a partial breakdown of a native protein.

Proteoses, peptones, and polypeptides are formed when digestive enzymes begin their action on proteins.

From the nutritional point of view, classification of proteins on the basis of their quality is more relevant than classification by structure and is explained in the next section.

Classification by Quality

Proteins are classified into three groups on the basis of their quality.

Complete proteins These proteins contain all essential amino acids in sufficient proportions and amounts to meet the body's need for growth and repair of tissue cells. A complete protein food has a high BV Eggs, milk, meat, fish, and poultry are complete protein foods. They are found in animal foods.

Partially complete proteins These are proteins in which one or more essential amino acids are present in inadequate amounts. They cannot synthesize tissues without the help of other proteins. The value of each is increased when it is consumed in combination with another incomplete protein at the same meal. They can maintain life. They are found in plant foods. Cereals, pulses, nuts, and oilseeds are partially complete protein foods. Cereals contain inadequate amounts of essential amino acid lysine, and pulses are deficient in essential amino acid methionine.

Incomplete proteins These proteins are incapable of growth and repair of body cells. They cannot maintain life. One or more essential amino acids may be completely lacking in these proteins, e.g., gelatin and zein in corn. Gelatin lacks three essential amino acids and is the only animal protein which is incomplete.

Proteins perform three main functions - structural function, regulatory function, and energy.

Structural Function

Growth The primary function of food protein is the synthesis of body cells. All body tissues and fluids except urine and bile are made up of protein. Proteins are the major constituent of muscles, organs, endocrine glands, and collagen. Collagen is the main structural protein of bones, tendons, ligaments, skin, blood vessels, and connective tissue. All enzymes and some hormones, e.g., insulin are made up of proteins. Proteins are required for the formation and growth of all these substances. During periods of rapid growth, additional proteins are needed for synthesis of body components.

Energy

Maintenance or wear and tear Protein is required by all age groups for continuous maintenance of all the cells in the body. Cells have a varying lifespan and proteins are needed to replace the old or worn out cells.

Regulatory Functions

All amino acids from food protein are used for growth and maintenance. Certain amino acids and proteins have highly specialized functions in the regulation of body processes and protection against disease. Some of the regulatory functions are as follows.

1. Haemoglobin, an iron containing protein in the red blood cells, performs an important role by transporting oxygen to the tissue cells.
2. Plasma proteins maintain water balance and regulate the osmotic pressure in the body.
3. Antibodies that are protein in nature perform a protective function by increasing the body's resistance to disease.
4. All enzymes and some hormones, e.g., insulin are made up of protein. The hormone insulin regulates blood sugar levels. Enzymes act as specific catalysts to metabolic processes in the body.
5. Some amino acids have specific functions, e.g., tryptophan serves as a precursor for niacin, a B-complex vitamin. The amino acid tyrosine in combination with iodine forms the hormone thyroxine.

Like carbohydrates, proteins too provide 4 kcal/g when broken down in the body. The basic need of the body is energy and this takes priority over protein synthesis. If the diet does not supply adequate calories from carbohydrates and fats, the proteins from the diet will be oxidized to meet the energy needs of the body.

If the diet is deficient in calories, the body uses up its protein and fat stores. Using protein as a source of energy is not advisable as it puts an extra burden on the body and the pocket. Protein is used by the body as a source of energy only when no other source of energy is available.

Digestion, Absorption, and Metabolism

To enable proteins to perform their various functions, dietary protein needs to be broken down into its constituent amino acids.

The mechanical digestion of protein begins in the mouth, where the teeth grind the food into small pieces. The mouth does not produce any enzyme to digest proteins. Chemical digestion begins in the stomach. The hydrochloric acid (HC1) in the gastric juice activates the enzyme pepsin, which acts on proteins and reduces them to polypeptides. After the partially digested proteins reach the small intestine, three pancreatic enzymes - trypsin, chymotrypsin, and carboxypeptidase - continue the process of chemical digestion. The peptidases secreted by the intestine finally reduce the smaller peptides and dipeptides into amino acids, which are the end product of protein digestion.

After digestion, the amino acids in the small intestine are absorbed by the blood and carried to the liver and all body tissues where they are metabolized.

The body needs varying compositions of amino acids to build and repair the different tissues of the body. All essential amino acids must be present if body cells have to be built or repaired. Surplus amino acids are sent back to the liver where they are deaminated by splitting off the amino group. The remaining part of the protein is used for energy or stored as glycogen in the liver and muscles or as fat in the adipose tissue. The end products of the metabolism of amino acids are carbon dioxide, water, and nitrogen. Some of the nitrogen is excreted as urea by the kidneys. Some nitrogen may be retained and used again to synthesize non-essential amino acids as and when required by the body.

Methods of Improving Protein Quality

Animal proteins contain all essential amino acids in correct proportions and amounts and are good quality proteins. Four essential amino acids are in short supply in plant proteins. They are lysine, methionine, threonine, and tryptophan. Proteins in plant foods are generally deficient in one or two essential amino acids. Cereals are poor in lysine and pulses are poor in methionine. Egg protein has a BV of 100 and is the reference protein as its amino acid composition corresponds most closely to human requirements. Eggs sold in the market are unfertilized and could be included in a vegetarian diet, if acceptable.

We have already read that protein will be synthesized only when all amino acids, which form the protein, are present simultaneously. We have also read that vegetable proteins are partially complete proteins. These two points should be kept in mind while improving the protein quality of a meal.

The protein quality of a mainly vegetarian diet can be improved in the following ways.

1. By including a small quantity of complete protein food in every meal. Complete protein foods such as milk, curds, paneer, cheese, buttermilk, and eggs could be used in

small quantities in various preparations instead of including it in one meal only, e.g., cereal and milk, egg or cheese sandwiches, French toast, raita, curd rice, or butter-milk at all meals in place of a bowl of curd in one meal.

2. Correct mixtures of plant foods could provide all essential amino acids in suitable proportions and amounts. Cereal and pulse combinations will complement each other as cereals provide methionine, which is lacking in pulses, and pulses provide lysine, which is lacking in cereals, when cereal and pulses are consumed together in the same meal, e.g., Missi roti, thalipeeth, puran poli, idli, and rajmah chawal. This is possible because the same amino acids are not missing from all plant foods.
3. Synthetic amino acids may be added to processed foods to compensate for the amino acid deficient in them, e.g., lysine-enriched bread. Textured vegetable proteins are used successfully to improve the protein quality and reduce the cost of protein-rich foods.

Plant proteins are being used successfully to stretch the supply of expensive animal proteins. When plant proteins are consumed with a small quantity of animal protein, the quality of the mixture is likely to be as effective as if only animal protein has been consumed. A good rule while planning menus would be to include some animal protein at each meal instead of concentrating it all in one meal.

Factors Influencing Protein Requirements

Many factors affect the protein requirement of an individual such as:

1. Body weight:
2. Special physiological needs during:
   (a) Growth
   (b) Pregnancy and lactation
   (c) Convalescence
   (d) Infection and fever
   (e) Injury or surgery.
3. Adequacy of calorie intake
4. Quality of protein and efficiency of digestion
5. Previous state of nutrition.

Body weight The protein requirement is based on a persons ideal body weight. Adults require 1 g protein/kg body weight from a mixed diet. The Indian reference man weighs 60 kg and requires 60 g protein/day and the reference woman weighs 50 kg and requires 50 g protein/day from a mixed diet.

Special physiological needs Infants and growing children require additional protein for synthesis of new cells as compared to adults. They need 1.6-2 g pro-tein/kg body weight. Whenever new tissue or protein needs to be synthesized, additional protein greater than the amount needed for maintenance should be included in the diet. Protein requirement increases during illness or disease as pro-tein is needed for rebuilding new tissue. In traumatic injury, surgery, burns, and fever, there is breakdown of tissues, which need to be repaired. Extra physical activity does not require any additional intake of protein.

Adequacy of calorie intake The diet should contain adequate carbohydrates and fats to have a protein sparing effect.

Quality of protein and efficiency of digestion The quantity of protein required will be more if the protein quality is poor. Plant proteins have a lower digestibility. The method of cooking also affects the availability of protein. Overcooking and toughening of animal proteins affects digestibility.

Previous state of nutrition Malnourished and underweight individuals require more protein as compared to healthy individuals.

Dietary Sources

Proteins are present in both plant and animal foods. Animal food sources provide the highest quality or complete proteins such as eggs, milk and milk products - cheese, paneer, mawa, milk powder, curds, condensed milk - meat, fish, shell fish, poultry and organ meats.

Plant Food Sources

Pulses, especially soya bean (43% protein) and its products such as soya milk, tofu, textured vegetable proteins; nuts, and oilseeds - groundnut and gingelly seeds are important sources of protein in the Indian diet. Cereals contain 6-12% partially complete proteins and as they form the bulk of the diet, they contribute significantly to the protein content. Vegetables, with the exception of peas and beans, are poor sources of proteins. Green leafy vegetables contain a small percentage of good quality protein (approximately 1-3%). Fruits do not contribute towards the protein content of the diet.

Effect of Deficiency and Excess

A reduced protein intake over a prolonged period of time leads to loss of weight, fatigue, anaemia, nutritional oedema, lowered resistance to infection, and poor healing of wounds. Protein deficiency is more marked during periods when protein needs are more, e.g., during infancy, childhood, pregnancy, and lactation. The deficiency occurs when an individual does not eat enough proteins or obtains insufficient calories. Protein calorie malnutrition (PCM) is common in preschool children; in developing countries and manifests itself in the form of kwashiorkor, a deficiency of protein or marasmus, a deficiency of calories as well as proteins, which is equivalent to starvation in adults. Protein deficiency is also seen in people who follow a crash diet for weight loss. It can be prevented by including correct mixture of inexpensive protein-rich foods in the diet.

An excessive intake of protein is not beneficial to health. When the diet provides more protein than what is necessary for body building, repair, and regulatory functions, the excess protein is used as energy or converted to fat and stored in the adipose tissue in 'the body. A high protein intake has many disadvantages.

1. Once the body needs have been taken care of, the excess protein is deaminated by the liver and urea is synthesized. The kidneys have to work more to excrete the additional amount of urea. A high protein intake is an unnecessary burden on two vital organs, i.e., the liver and the kidneys. If these organs are diseased, toxic wastes tend to accumulate in the body.
2. When animal proteins such as meat, poultry, and whole milk products form a substantial part of the high-protein diet, there is a risk of high blood levels of cholesterol.
3. A high intake of protein increases the loss of calcium through the urine.
4. Protein-rich foods are much costlier, are in short supply, and are not an economical source of energy.

Summary

Proteins are important constituents of all living cells and are made up of units called amino acids. Proteins differ from one another because of the different kinds and amounts of amino acids of which they are composed. Amino acids are classified as essential and non-essential. Non-essential amino acids can be synthesized by the body in required amounts. Essential amino acids cannot be synthesized by the body and must be included in the diet. The quality of any protein depends upon the essential amino acids present. On the basis of quality, proteins are classified as complete, partially complete, and incomplete. Animal proteins except gelatin are complete proteins while plant proteins are partially complete proteins. The quality of plant proteins can be improved when several plant foods are combined together or small quantities of animal proteins are included in each meal. For tissue synthesis to take place all essential amino acids should be present at the same time.

Proteins perform three basic functions, namely the structural function of body building and repair, the regulatory and protective function, and as a source of energy when no other source is available.

The chemical digestion of protein begins in the stomach where protein is broken down to polypeptides. In the intestine, polypeptides are further broken down into dipeptides and amino acids, which are absorbed into the blood stream and sent to various tissue cells via the liver.

Proteins are present in abundance both in animal and plant foods such as eggs, milk, meat, pulses, especially soya beans, groundnuts, and textured vegetable proteins. Most vegetables and all fruits are poor sources of protein. How much protein an individual will require depends on many factors such as age, body weight, special physiological needs, adequacy of calorie intake, quality of protein, and previous state of nutrition.

Essential amino acid An amino acid that cannot be synthesized by our body and needs to be supplied by our diet.

Non-essential amino acid An amino acid that can be synthesized in the body and need not be present in the diet.

Peptidases Enzymes that breakdown short polypeptides and dipeptides into amino acids.

Peptide linkage The linkage between the amino group of one amino acid and the carboxyl group of another amino acid.

Proteolytic enzymes Protein-splitting enzymes that reduce proteins to shorter chain polypetides and dipeptides.

List and briefly explain the functions performed by proteins.

List the symptoms of protein deficiency in adults.

Why are proteins called an uneconomical source of energy?

Recollect and list the sources of animal and vegetable proteins, which you have consumed in your diet yesterday.

An excessive intake of protein is not beneficial as it increases the burden on two vital organs, namely the liver and kidneys to metabolize and excrete the wastes arising from amino acid breakdown. Protein-rich foods are costlier than carbohydrates, which provide the same number of calories per gram. When the protein intake is inadequate, protein cannot perform the required functions in the body and a deficiency results. Deficiency symptoms are common in the vulnerable age group in developing countries. Protein deficiency can be prevented by proper menu planning and including low-cost plant proteins such as textured vegetable proteins in the diet.

4

Vitamins and Minerals

Vitamins

he term vitamin was coined from the words 'vital amine' as early scientists felt these chemicals which are vital for life were amines. Vitamins were discovered one at a time from 1900 to 1950, some as a cure for classic diseases such as beri-beri, pellagra, and scurvy, while others were discovered after research on various body functions.

Vitamins like carbohydrates, proteins, and fats are organic compounds. Unlike these nutrients, vitamins are required in minute quantities and are also called micronutrients. They do not provide energy and are present in very small quanti-ties in food, but nonetheless are vital for life processes. All vitamins can be synthesized on a commercial scale, though fresh foods are always preferred.

Definition Vitamins is the term used for a group of potent organic compounds other than proteins, carbohydrates, and fats which occur in minute quantities in food and which are essential for some specific body functions such as regulation, maintenance, growth, and protection. Many of them cannot be synthesized, at least in adequate amounts, by the body and must be obtained from the diet.

Classification

Vitamins are grouped according to their solubility in either fat or water.

Fat-soluble vitamins The fat-soluble vitamins are vitamins A, D, E, and K. They require fat for their absorption and can be stored in the body. If their intake is poor, but body stores are ample, deficiency symptoms will not be seen immediately.

Water-soluble vitamins The water-soluble vitamins are B-complex vitamins and vitamin C. Being water soluble they are easily absorbed and the excess consumed is excreted in the urine. They are not stored in the body.

Fat Soluble Vitamins

Vitamin A

Vitamin A is the generic name given to a group of compounds having vitamin A activity. These compounds are retinol, retinal, and retinoic acid. They are found only in the fatty phases of foods of animal origin. Plant foods contain yellow, orange, and/or red coloured pigments called carotene which give colour to vegetables and fruits. Carotene pigments are converted to vitamin A in the body, i.e., carotene is a provitamin or precursor of vitamin A. Carotene is synthesized by plants and is the ultimate source of all vitamin A.

Pure vitamin A is a pale yellow crystalline compound occuring naturally in the animal kingdom. It is soluble in fat, insoluble in water, and relatively stable to heat, acids, and alkalis. It is easily oxidized and rapidly destroyed by UV rays.

Functions Vitamin A performs the following functions.

1. Vitamin A maintains normal vision in dim light. Rhodopsin or visual purple is present in the retina of the eye. It is required for vision in dim light. It is formed when vitamin A combines with protein opsin. In bright light rhodopsin absorbs light and breaks down into protein opsin and retinal, Every time rhodopsin breaks down, some retinal is lost. In dim light or darkness, retinal and opsin recombine rapidly to form rhodopsin provided there is an adequate supply of vitamin A. If there is a deficiency of vitamin A, the regeneration is slow and the person's eyes fail to adapt to changes in light.
2. It helps in synthesis and maintenance of healthy epithelium - outermost lining of skin and innermost lining of mucous membranes of respiratory, gastrointestinal, and genitourinary tract. Epithelial glands secrete mucous that lubricates the lining of the eyes, respiratory and gastrointestinal tract, etc.

3. Vitamin A is required for normal bone and tooth development, and proper growth.
4. It helps the body to fight against infections by keeping mucous membranes in a healthy condition which act as a barrier to infection.

Deficiency If the body has sufficient stores, deficiency does not develop at once.

Night blindness or nyctalopia It is one of the earliest signs of vitamin A deficiency. In this condition, an individual is unable to see well in dim light, especially after coming from a brightly lit area. This happens because there is insufficient vitamin A to bring about quick formation of rhodopsin.

Epithelial changes The epithelium becomes dry, scaly, and rough. Goose pimples are seen on upper forearms and thighs.

Changes in the eyes are:

(a) Secretion of tears decreases
(b) Eye ball becomes dry and lustreless
(c) Bitot spots (pigmented spots) are seen on conjunctiva
(d) Photophobia or sensitivity to bright light is observed
(e) Xeropthalmia - cornea becomes dry and inflammed. If not treated it leads to keratomalacia.
(f) Keratomalacia or softening of the cornea and permanent blindness results.

Bone development Growth failure and stunted bones are seen in children.

Hypervitaminosis A High doses of vitamin A is not recommended as excess is stored in the liver. This excessive accumulation of vitamin A in the body is toxic. Symptoms of toxicity are nausea, vomiting, abdominal pain, loss of hair, thickening of long bones, and joint pain.

Sources Animal foods such as whole milk and milk products, egg yolk, oily fish, fish-liver oils, organ meats, butter, cream, and clarified butter or pure ghee are rich sources.

Sources of carotene All yellow, orange, and red fruits and vegetables such as car-rots, pumpkin, mango, papaya, peaches, and apricots, and all green leafy vegetables such as fenugreek leaves, spinach, colocasia leaves, amaranth, curry leaves, and turnip greens are rich sources of provitamin A.

Requirement : An adult requires 600 tg of retinol or 2,400 gg of 13-carotene per day; 4 gg of (3-carotene is converted to 1 µg of retinol in the intestinal wall and liver.

Vitamin D

It is a fat-soluble vitamin. The two important forms are vitamin D_2 (activated ergos-terol or calciferol) and vitamin D_3 (activated 7-dehydrocholesterol or cholecalciferol), Vitamin D_3 is produced when 7-dehydrocholesterol in the skin is exposed to the UV rays in the sun. Vitamin D differs from other fat-soluble vitamins because it is synthesized in the body, and we do not depend on our diet for it. Being fat soluble it requires fat for its absorption.

Functions

1. Absorption of calcium and phosphorus from the small intestine requires the presence of vitamin D and the hormones of the parathyroid and thyroid gland.
2. Mineralization of bones and teeth - after calcium and phosphorus is absorbed, vitamin D is required to ensure that these minerals are deposited in bones and teeth to strengthen them.
3. Regulation of calcium and phosphorus levels in blood.

Sources Sunlight is the main source of vitamin D. The precursor in skin is converted to active vitamin D_3. Barriers such as clothing, soot, fog, window glass, and melanin (pigment in the skin) interfere with synthesis of vitamin D. Sunscreen lotions with high SPF also prevent vitamin D formation.

It is found in fish liver oils, fortified milk, vanaspati, and margarine. Natural foods such as butter, milk, and fish have it in small amounts.

Hypervitaminosis D Large doses of vitamin D can be toxic. Excessive use of forti-fied foods lead to loss of appetite, vomiting, diarrhoea, growth failure, and calcification of soft tissues and kidney stones.

Deficiency Vitamin D deficiency leads to lowered absorption of calcium, low serum levels of calcium, and reduced bone mineralization. Bones cannot withstand the weight and bend into deformities.

Rickets is seen in infants and children especially dark-skinned children. Bones are soft and yield to pressure. Joints are enlarged and there is delayed closing of the skull bones. Symptoms of rickets include enlarged skull, pigeon chest, poor muscle development, pot belly, and bowed legs or knocked knees.

Osteomalacia or adult rickets is more common in women who consume a diet deficient in calcium, phosphorus, and vitamin D, and have had several pregnancies. The softening of bones leads to a deformed spine, rheumatic pain in the legs and lower back, a waddling gait, and spontaneous fractures.

Vitamin E

Vitamin E or tocopherol is a fat-soluble vitamin. It is stable to heat and acids. It is rapidly oxidized in rancid fats.

Many claims are being made that supplements of this vitamin can prevent or cure a wide variety of diseases, from reproductive function to skin problems such as psoriasis and acne, but there is no proof.

Functions Vitamin E is the most potent natural antioxidant found in food. Polyunsaturated fatty acids form a structural part of all cell membranes. They are prone to oxidative breakdown by free radicals in the cell. The main function of vitamin E is to act as an antioxidant. Vitamin E itself gets oxidized and protects cell membranes from oxidative damage. It performs the following functions:

1. Prevents oxidation of vitamin A in the intestine
2. Protects normal cell membranes by preventing their breakdown 3. Prevents hemolysis of red blood cells
4. Prevents oxidation of PUFAs.

Sources Vitamin E is widely distributed in foods, particularly vegetable oils (corn, soya, sunflower, safflower), wheat germ, whole grains, legumes, nuts, and dark green leafy vegetables.

Deficiency In severe deficiency, although uncommon, increased haemolysis of red blood cells is seen in premature infants.

Vitamin K

Vitamin K is essential in the diet because it is needed for synthesis of prothrombin and other blood clotting factors. It exists as K_1 (found in plants), K_2 (synthesized by bacteria in the intestinal tract), and K_3 (synthetic form). Being fat soluble, it requires fat and bile salts for efficient absorption.

Functions Vitamin K is required for the formation of prothrombin and several other proteins involved in clotting of blood. The ability of blood to clot is dependent upon a high blood level of prothrombin.

Deficiency A deficiency of vitamin K is uncommon in adults. New born infants have a sterile intestinal tract, hence they are given a single dose of vitamin K to prevent haemorrhagic disease.

A deficiency interferes with formation of prothrombinogen and, thus, reduces clotting tendency of blood. It may occur during diseases of malabsorption, oral use of sulfa drugs and antibiotics, or certain drugs which are vitamin K antagonists and can cause haemorrhages.

Sources Bacterial synthesis in the intestinal tract supplies at least half of the daily needs. Green leafy vegetables, cabbage, cauliflower, and pork liver are excellent sources. Cheese, egg yolk, and tomato also supply vitamin K.

Water Soluble Vitamins

B-Complex Vitamins

Scientists discovered eleven water-soluble B-complex vitamins of which eight are considered essential for humans.

They differ from each other in their structure, distribution in foods, stability, and symptoms that result from their deficiency. They are:

1. Thiamine (vitamin B_1)
2. Riboflavin (vitamin B_2)
3. Niacin
4. Pyridoxine (vitamin B_6)
5. Pantothenic acid
6. Biotin
7. Folic acid
8. Cyanocobalamin (vitamin B_{12})

They are all water soluble.

These eight vitamins are grouped together because their functions are closely related. The remaining three B-complex vitamins, namely, para-aminobenzoic acid (PABA), choline, and inositol play an active role in cell metabolism but the diet and intestinal synthesis can make good this requirement. The B-complex vitamins which are essential in human nutrition are broadly grouped into the following categories:

1. Classic deficiency disease vitamins;
   (a) Thiamine
   (b) Riboflavin
   (c) Niacin.

Beri-beri Ariboflavinosis Pellagra

Thiamine (vitamin B_1) Thiamine performs the following functions:

1. Thiamine functions mainly as a co-enzyme, thiamine pyrophosphate (TPP), which is required in the breakdown of glucose to yield energy.
2. It helps to maintain a healthy nervous system.
3. It is required for normal appetite and digestion.

Daily requirement of thiamine is 0.5 mg/1,000 kcal. Thus, an adult who needs 3,000 calories would require 1.5 mg of vitamin B_1 per day.

Sources Foods rich in protein such as pork, liver, pulses, groundnut, and eggs are good sources. Whole grain and enriched cereals, parboiled rice, unpolished rice, and sprouted pulses contribute B_1. Soya bean is a rich source.

Effect of cooking and processing B_1 is easily destroyed by cooking food in neutral or alkaline medium. Losses are greater when food is cooked at high temperatures, overcooked, and cooking water discarded.

Deficiency The symptoms of deficiency occur because the tissue cells are unable to receive sufficient energy from glucose. Therefore, they cannot carry out their normal functions. The gastrointestinal, nervous, and cardiovascular systems are specially affected.

Early symptoms of deficiency include fatigue, irritability, depression, poor appetite, tingling, and numbness of the legs. A severe deficiency causes beri-beri. Beri-beri is of two types.

1. Dry beri-beri: Polyneuritis or inflammation of the nerves, numbness of extremities, muscle weakness, and cramps are the main symptoms.

2. Wet beri-beri: Severe oedema, enlargement of the heart, palpitation, and increase in rate of heart beat are seen in wet beri-beri.

A person may suffer from either type of beri-beri. Beri-beri is also known as 'rice-eaters' disease because it is seen in people whose chief diet consists of polished rice.

Prevention Parboiling rice to retain B_1.

Riboflavin (vitamin B_2) Riboflavin performs the following functions:

1. As a co-enzyme, just like B_1 is a vital factor in carbohydrate metabolism, B_2 is vital is protein metabolism.
2. As a co-enzyme in carbohydrate metabolism, B_2 is a constituent of co-enzymes flavin mono nucleotide (FMN) and flavin adenine dinucleotide (FAD).

Daily requirement is 0.55 mg/1,000 kcalories.

Sources Milk and cheese are rich in B_2. Organ meats, eggs, dark greer leafy vegetables, and enriched cereal foods.

Effect of cooking and processing B_2 is sensitive to light. If milk is kept in clear glass bottles, 3/4th of B_2 is lost in a short time. Cooking in open containers and in excess water is harmful.

Deficiency

1. Swelling of lips with cheilosis
2. Cracks in the skin at the corners of the lip, i.e., angular stomatitis
3. Redness and swelling of the tongue or glossitis
4. Eyes look bloodshot, eye fatigue, itching, burning, watering, and sensitivity to bright light, i.e., photophobia.

Niacin Niacin or nicotinic acid is a vitamin intimately connected with several metabolic reactions it takes part in as a component.

Functions Like B_1 and B_2, niacin is also required for enzymes that bring about breakdown of glucose, amino acids, and fatty acids to yield energy, i.e., for release of energy from food.

1. As a constituent of two co-enzymes, nicotinamide adenine dinucleotide (NAD) and nicotinamide adenine dinucleotide phosphate (NADP), to release energy from carbohydrates, proteins, and fats.

2. For a healthy skin, normal gastrointestinal tract, and maintenance of the nervous system.

Because this vitamin takes part in many reactions of energy metabolism in the breakdown of proteins, carbohydrates, and fats, its requirement is related to calorie intake (6.6 mg/1,000 kilocalories). Although milk is not a good source of niacin it con-tains essential amino acid tryptophan which is converted to niacin in the body.

Sources Protein rich foods such as poultry, fish, meat, groundnut, beans, and peas are good sources. Grains are fair sources except maize and rice, green leafy vegetables, potatoes, milk, eggs, and cheese are poor sources of preformed niacin but rich sources of tryptophan.

Effect of cooking and processing It is most stable of all B-complex vitamins. Fairly stable to heat, acid, alkali, light, oxidation, and autoclaving.

Deficiency It is seen in low-protein or maize-based diets. Pellagra, which means rough skin, is characterized by four D's - diarrhoea, dermatitis, dementia, and death. Deficiency begins with weakness, headache, loss of appetite and weight, and a sore and swollen tongue. Dermatitis is symmetrical and on exposed parts of the body - forearms, legs, and hands and is aggravated by sunlight.

Dementia or depression, confusion, poor memory, delirium, and hallucinations occur in severe deficiency. Without treatment it results in death.

Anaemia-preventing Vitamins

Folic acid, vitamin B_{12}, and vitamin B_6 help in the formation of either red blood corpuscles (RBCs) or haemoglobin and help in preventing anaemia. Folic acid or folacin Derives its name from Latin word 'folium' which means leaf.

Sources Liver, kidney, green leafy vegetables, whole pulses, and yeast, and in fermented food such as idli, dhokla, and dosa. Some bacteria present in the intestinal tract are capable of synthesizing the vitamin.

Functions In order to perform its functions, folic acid needs to be converted into its active form. Vitamin C is needed for this conversion.

Inactive Folic Acid Vit C 3 Active Folic Acid

It is a component of specific enzymes required for formation of DNA and haeme in the RBCs. B_{12} is required along with folic acid for maturation of RBCs.

Deficiency Deficiency results in megaloblastic anaemia which is common in underdeveloped countries, among the vulnerable age group. In folic acid deficiency, the bone marrow releases large nucleated cells into the circulation. The anaemia is a macrocytic, megaloblastic anaemia. Megaloblasts are large nucleated cells or immature RBCs. Other symptoms are weakness, loss of weight, pallor, and glossitis. Haemoglobin level may fall as low as 2-4 g/ 100 ml and blood transfusion may be needed. Normal Hb level is 11.5-14.5 g for women and 12.5-16.5 g % for adult men.

Cyanocobalamin (vitamin B_{12}) It is found only in foods of animal origin. Liver, kidney, milk, eggs, and cheese are good sources. Small amounts of animal protein in the diet take care of B_{12} requirement.

Functions

1. It helps folic acid in the synthesis and maturation of RBCs.
2. It is essential for formation of myelin sheath around nerve fibres.

Absorption Vitamin B_{12} is absorbed only if a glycoprotein known as 'intrinsic factor' is present in gastric juice.

Deficiency Vitamin B_{12} deficiency results either in megaloblastic anaemia or in per-nicious anaemia. The latter is more common and is serious. Megaloblastic anaemia is seen in strict vegetarians who do not consume milk. It is because of a dietary deficien. cy of B12-Pernicious anaemia occurs due to absence of intrinsic factor in the person's gastric juice. So, even if diet provides enough B_{12} it will not be absorbed.

Symptoms The person appears well nourished with respect to body weight. Skin and eyes are pale, tongue is raw and red, and mouth ulcers are present. There is numbness, tingling sensation, and a feeling of pins and needles in the fingers, as nervous system is affected. Haemoglobin level is low and megaloblasts appear in blood. Treatment of pernicious anaemia involves injections of B_{12} throughout life as oral doses cannot be absorbed due to lack of intrinsic factor.

Pyridoxine (vitamin B_6) Liver, kidney, meat, whole grain cereals, soya beans, and groundnuts are sources of pyridoxine.

Functions

1. Essential for synthesis and breakdown of amino acids
2. Helps in conversion of tryptophan to niacin
3. Conversion of linoleic acid to arachidonic acid
4. Needed for synthesis of haeme
5. Production of antibodies.

The requirement increases with an increase in protein content of diet.

Deficiency Anaemia is hypochromic anaemia because Hb is not synthesized for the red colour of RBCs. Red blood cells are pale in colour. Soreness of tongue, depression, and sleepiness are other symptoms. Deficiency occurs along with other nutrient deficiencies, e.g., PCM and B-complex deficiency.

Pantothenic acid and biotin They are both co-enzymes required for release of energy from carbohydrates, fats, and proteins. Biotin is synthesized in the intestinal tract. Both vitamins are widely present in foods and deficiency is rare in normal circumstances.

Egg white contains a protein avidin that interferes with absorption of biotin from the intestinal tract. Only raw egg whites can cause a deficiency as avidin is inactivated when eggs are cooked. Having a few raw egg whites in a week is not harmful and do not cause a deficiency.

Vitamin C

Vitamin C, also known as the fresh fruit and vegetable vitamin, was discovered as an acid in lime juice which prevented scurvy among British sailors on long voyages at sea. It was named ascorbic acid because of its antiscorbutic or antiscurvy properties.

It is highly soluble in water and most easily destroyed as compared to all other vitamins. It is readily oxidized and destroyed by heat and presence of alkali. It is lost when food is dehydrated.

Functions

1. Synthesis of collagen which is the intercellular cementing substance that keeps cells in bone and muscle tissue together

2. Making haemoglobin by helping in absorption of iron from food
3. Healing of wounds and fractures
4. Increasing resistance to infections and fevers
5. Proper growth during periods of increased need or during rapid growth
6. As an antioxidant, like vitamin E, it prevents the oxidation of vitamin A and unsaturated fatty acids.

Deficiency Deprivation of vitamin C results in defective formation of the intercellular cementing substance.

Symptoms

1. Poor wound healing because collagen is not synthesized
2. Increased susceptibility to infections
3. Painful joints and bleeding gums
4. Skin bruises by slightest injury
5. Severe deficiency causes scurvy. The symptoms are swelling, infection and bleeding of gums, and anaemia.

Excessive intake The benefits of consuming megadoses of vitamin C to prevent the common cold and cancer is still controversial. An increased intake beyond the RDA is advised in certain cases such as surgical cases, infections, and drug therapies, but benefits of megadoses of 1-5 g daily is still under study.

Sources Fresh citrus fruits such as orange, sweet lime, grape fruit, lemon; other fruits and vegetables such as guava, amla, cabbage, capsicum, green chillies, green leafy vegetables, and tomatoes are excellent sources of vitamin C. Cereals and pulses are poor in vitamin C, but when dry pulses are sprouted ascorbic acid is

formed in them. 85% of the vitamin is formed in the grain and 15% in the sprout. Green gram contains thrice as much vitamin C as compared to bengal gram. Sprouted pulses are a good alternative to fresh fruits and vegetables during periods of scarcity. Sprouts can be lightly steamed or consumed raw.

Berries such as zizyphus, strawberries, gooseberries, and cashewfruit are seasonal rich sources. Amla is the richest source providing 600 mg/100 g as compared to oranges which provide 30 mg/100 g, i.e., amla contains 20 times as much vitamin C as compared to orange. Heating and dehydration reduces the vitamin C content of all fresh fruits except amla which retains some vitamin C in the preserve.

Effect of Cooking on Vitamins

Water-soluble vitamins are more easily lost during cooking and storing food. Losses occur due to oxidation or exposure to air which is catalysed by enzymes. Blanching fruits and vegetables, which need to be refrigerated or frozen, destroys the enzymes and preserves vitamin C. High temperature, prolonged heating, and alkaline medium favour destruction of vitamins. To retain maximum vitamins in our food, observe the following rules:

1. Select good quality, fresh fruits and vegetables. Stale, wilted, and poor quality produce may be cheaper, but has lower vitamin content.
2. Always wash fruits and vegetable before peeling or cutting and not afterwards, as water-soluble vitamins get leached into water and are lost.
3. Cut fruits and vegetables for salads just before they are to be served and store in a cool place. Keep food covered. This prevents oxidative losses.
4. Avoid cutting into small pieces as more surface area is exposed.
5. Avoid soaking in water as water-soluble vitamins leach out.
6. Cook in minimum quantity water so that extra cooking is not required to dry up the excess liquid. Use shortest cooking time.
7. Cook in a covered pan, except while cooking greens - cook uncovered for a few minutes to allow volatile acids to escape which helps in preserving green colour.
8. Do not overcook. Refresh greens and use pot liquor or cooking liquid in soups, gravies, or for kneading dough.
9. Do not add alkali (soda bicarbonate) to enhance green colour or hasten the cooking of pulses such as kabuli channa as B-complex and vitamin C are readily destroyed in an alkaline medium.
10. Store food in a refrigerator, covered with a lid, aluminium foil, or cling film to retain nutrients.

11. Reheat only what is required.
12. Pressure cooking helps in retaining vitamins as food is cooked in a covered container for a shorter time.
13. Fat-soluble vitamins are lost during deep fat frying, if the food to be fried is not coated prior to frying.
14. Vitamin A and carotene are lost due to oxidation and dehydration.

Vitamins are vital organic compounds required by the body to perform specific functions such as the release of energy from food and other growth related, protective and regulatory functions. They are required in minute amounts and hence are categorized as micronutrients. They are broadly classified as fat soluble (vitamin A, D, E, and K) and water soluble (B-complex and vitamin C) vitamins. Each vitamin has a specific role to perform and cannot be replaced by another vitamin. Fat-soluble vitamins require fat for their absorption and can be stored in the body. Water-soluble vitamins are readily absorbed but are not stored in the body. Excessive intake of fat-soluble vitamins leads to toxicity or hypervitaminosis.

Vitamin A is present in animal foods only. Carotene, a precursor of vitamin A, is present in yellow, orange, and red fruits and vegetables, and in green leafy vegetables. We get our requirement of vitamin D from sunlight. The precursor in the skin 7-dehydrocholesterol is activated by UV rays from sunlight. A deficiency of vitamins E and K is rarely seen in adults as both vitamins are wide-spread in nature.

The B-complex vitamins are water soluble and include eight vitamins, namely, thiamine or B_1, riboflavin or B_2, niacin, pyridoxine or B_6, folic acid, cyanocobalamine *or* B_{12}, *pantothenic acid, and biotin. They mainly function as co-enzymes in the* release of energy from carbohydrates, fats, and proteins. Three B-complex vitamins are designated 'anaemia preventing vitamins' as they are needed for synthesis of haeme and for the maturation of red blood cells. Apart from the food sources, the bacterial flora in the intestine are capable of synthesizing vitamins, namely, vitamin K and B-complex vitamins.

Vitamin C is the most susceptible of all vitamins. It is present in fresh fruits and vegetables and in sprouted grain. It is destroyed by oxidation, heat, and an alkaline medium. Proper cooking practices need to be followed if vitamin content of food has to be retained.

Minerals

Mineral elements are inorganic substances found in body tissues and fluid They occur in foods as salts, e.g., sodium chloride, calcium phosphate, and ferrous sulfate. They constitute 4% of our body weight. Unlike carbohydrates, fats, and proteins they do not furnish energy. They have many functions in our body such as tissue building, regulation of body fluids, and other functions. Like vitamins, they are required in small quantities and are vital to the body. They should be supplied daily as they are excreted through the kidney, the bowel, and the skin.

Minerals are present in the body as:

(a) components of organic compounds, e.g., haemoglobin contains iron and thyroxine contains iodine

(b) as inorganic compounds, e.g., calcium phosphate in the bones (c) as free ions in every cell in the body and (d) in all body fluids.

Sodium is the main electrolyte in the extracellular fluid, and potassium is the main electrolyte in the intracellular fluid.

The mineral elements are not destroyed by heat, oxidation, acid, or alkali. Since they are soluble in water some loss occurs due to leaching when cooking water is discarded.

Definition

Minerals are inorganic elements required by the body in varying amounts to carry out various body functions. They remain largely as ash when plant and animal tissues are ignited.

Classification

Minerals may be classified into three groups.

Major minerals or macrominerals Seven minerals are required in large amounts of over 100 mg/day, e.g., calcium, phosphorus, sodium, chlorine, potassium, magnesium, and sulphur.

Minor minerals These are required in small quantities, less than 100 mg/day, e.g., iron and manganese. Trace elements A few micrograms to a few milligrams are required per day, e.g., iodine, fluorine, zinc, and molybdenum.

General Functions of Minerals

1. Minerals form the structural components of bones, teeth, soft tissues, blood, and muscles, e.g., calcium, phosphorus, and magnesium in bones.
2. They regulate activity of nerves with regard to stimuli and contraction of muscles, e.g., calcium.
3. Maintain acid-base balance of body fluids, e.g., sodium and chlorine.
4. They control water balance by means of osmotic pressure and permeability of cell membranes, e.g., sodium and potassium.
5. They are constituents of vitamins, e.g., thiamine contains sulphur and cyanocobalamin contains cobalt.
6. They form part of molecules of hormones and enzymes, e.g., iodine in thyroxine and zinc in insulin.
7. They activate enzymes, e.g., calcium activates enzyme lipase.
8. They regulate cellular oxidation, e.g., iron and manganese.
9. Necessary for clotting of blood, e.g., calcium.

Calciurn

The adult body contains 1.2 kg of calcium of which 99% is present in bones and teeth. The bones provide:

1. A rigid framework for the body and
2. Reserves of calcium

The remaining 1% is distributed in extracellular and intracellular fluids and has the following functions:

1. Calcium acts as a cataiyst in clotting of blood.

It increases permeability of cell membranes thus helping in absorption.

It regulates contraction and relaxation of muscles including the heart beat. It activates a number of enzymes such as pancreatic lipase and acts as a cofactor, Factors affecting calcium absorption The amount of calcium absorbed by humans depends on the body's need. Approximately 40% of calcium ingested is absorbed.

1. Phosphate and phytic acid is present in cereals and form insoluble calcium salts if present in excess.

2. An alkaline intestinal pH (above 7) reduces absorption by forming insoluble salts.
3. Excess fibre decreases absorption of calcium.
4. Oxalic acid in green leafy vegetable forms insoluble calcium oxalate, which is excreted.
5. Faulty absorption of fats and fatty acids form insoluble calcium salts, which are excreted.
6. Lactose increases calcium absorption.
7. High protein intake increases absorption.

The parathyroids regulate the calcium level in blood and calcium metabolism in bone. The calcium to phosphorus ratio should always be 1:1.

Sources Various sources of calcium are:

1. Milk and milk products excluding butter, ghee, and cream
2. Ragi, green leafy vegetables especially drumstick leaves, cabbage, curry leaves, carrot, and cauliflower tops, and amaranth
3. Small dried fish, nuts, and oilseeds such as gingelly seeds
4. Betel leaf with slaked lime is a rich source of calcium.

Deficiency A severe deficiency of calcium leads to rickets in children and osteomalacia and osteoporosis in adults.

1. Osteoporosis In osteoporosis, the bones become porous because of bone mineral loss. This causes compression of the vertebrae that results in loss of height, back and hip pain, and increased susceptibility to fractures. It is seen in post-menopausal women and can be controlled by weight bearing exercises such as walking, calcium supplements, and hormone therapy.
2. Tetany A decrease in serum calcium levels gives rise to a condition called tetany. The symptoms of tetany are severe intermittent spasms of the muscles of hands and feet accompanied by muscular pain. Twitching of facial muscles occurs.

Phosphorus

Phosphorus comprises 1% of total body weight. It occurs along with calcium in human nutrition and also has many other functions in the body.

1. Building bones and teeth along with calcium and magnesium.
2. DNA and RNA, the nucleic acids needed for genetic coding contain phosphorus.
3. As phospholipids, they regulate the absorption and transport of fats.
4. Adenosine triphosphate (ATP) and adenosine diphosphate (ADP)are necessary for storing and releasing energy according to body needs.
5. As part of enzymes needed for the metabolism of carbohydrates, fats, and proteins.

Sources Phosphorus is widely distributed in foods. Milk and meat are rich in phosphorus. Whole grain cereals, legumes, nuts, carrots, and fish are also rich sources of phosphorus.

Deficiency Phosphorus deficiency is rare since a diet that contains adequate pro-tein and calcium will be rich in phosphorus. Deficiency symptoms are similar to calcium deficiency.

The human body contains 3-5 g of iron of which 70% is in the circulating haemoglobin. Functions:

1. Essential for carrying 0_2 to the lungs where 0_2 is released and CO_2 is picked up to be exhaled by haemoglobin in the red blood cells.
2. It is an essential part of several oxidative enzymes.
3. It helps in specific brain functions such as a good attention span and capacity to learn and memorize.
4. It facilitates the complete oxidation of carbohydrates, proteins, and fats with in the cell and release of energy for performing physical work.

Diet provides iron in two forms:

1. Haeme iron, i.e., iron associated to the protein, globin, to form haemoglobin. Haeme iron is found in flesh food only.
2. Non-haeme iron is the form present in all plant sources and in 60% of animal sources.

Haeme iron is present in small quantities in food. About 40% iron in flesh food is haeme iron while 60% is non-haeme iron. It is rapidly absorbed and transported. About 23% is absorbed.

Non-haeme iron is the larger portion of iron in food. It is tightly bound to organic molecules in the form of ferric iron (Fe +++) In the acidic medium of the stomach, it is dissociated and reduced to its more soluble ferrous form (Fe^{++}). The absorption rate of non-haeme iron is slow and approximately 8% is absorbed.

Vitamin C from the diet and hydrochloric acid in gastric juice help in converting ferric iron to ferrous iron.

Factors affecting iron absorption The following factors enhance absorption:

Body need In periods of extra demand or in a deficiency, more iron is absorbed.

Acidic medium Gastric acidity and ascorbic acid in the meal favour absorption. Form of iron Haeme iron and ferrous form are better absorbed. Complete proteins Complete proteins such as meat favour absorption.

The following factors decrease absorption:

1. Ferric iron or non-haeme iron in the absence of protein and ascorbic acid are poorly absorbed.
2. Achlorhydria or lack of hydrochloric acid in gastric juice and use of antacids with meals interfere with absorption.
3. Tea and coffee with meals.
4. Excessive intake of phytates and oxalates interferes with absorption. 5. Malabsorption due to intestinal disorders.

Iron is required for replacement of daily losses through excretion in urine, sweat, hair, and worn-out cells. It is also needed for replacement of blood losses and an expanding blood volume in all stages of growth.

Iodine

Sources Various sources of iron are:

1. Liver, organ meats, shellfish, lean meat, egg yolk are all good sources
2. Green leafy vegetables, whole grain, and enriched cereals, legumes, and jaggery
3. Garden cress seeds and niger seeds are excellent sources
4. Peaches, apricots, manukas, and figs
5. Use of iron cooking utensils contributes significantly to the iron content of the diet.

Non-haeme iron is present in plant foods such as green vegetables, and cereals. 40% iron in meat, poultry, and fish is haeme iron and 60% is non-haeme iron. Deficiency Iron deficiency or anaemia is very common in the vulnerable age groups in all developing countries. Haemoglobin level may be as low as 5-9 g. Normal haemoglobin levels for females are 11.5-14.5 g% and for males 12.5-16.5 g%.

Symptoms General fatigue, breathlessness on exertion, giddiness and pallor of skin (paleness), oedema of ankles and spoon shaped nails are the common symptoms of iron deficiency.

Iron deficiency causes microcytic and hypochromic anaemia. Red blood cell's appear pale and smaller in size. Iron deficiency may also be seen if excessive blood loss occurs or because of faulty absorption, intestinal disease, or parasites especially hookworm and roundworm infestations.

Most of the iodine in an adult body is found in the thyroid gland. The only known function of iodine is as a constituent of thyroxine. The thyroid hormone regulates the rate of oxidation within the cells. The iodine absorbed is incorporated into the amino acid tyrosine to form the hormone thyroxine.

Iodine + Tyrosine = Thyroxine.

If intake of iodine is inadequate, the stores of thyroxine are gradually depleted and the thyroid gland enlarges in an attempt to produce the necessary thyroxine.

Sources Seafood contains maximum iodine and fruits contain the least. Wide variations are seen because food content of iodine depends upon the soil where they are grown. To provide sufficient iodine, salt is being iodized. Salt is a universally used dietary item. It is cheap and addition of iodine does not affect its flavour. It is added in the form of sodium or potassium iodide in the proportion of 1 mg for every 10 g of salt.

Deficiency Deficiency occurs when iodine content of the soil is so low that insufficient iodine is obtained through food, e.g., the soil in the Kangra valley in the Himalayan belt is deficient in iodine. Deficiency of iodine results in goitre.

5

Dietary Supplement

Overview

Increased intakes of fruits, vegetables, whole grains, and fat-free or low-fat milk and milk products are likely to have important health benefits for most Americans. While protein is an important macronutrient in the diet, most Americans are already currently consuming enough (AMDR = 10 to 35 percent of calories) and do not need to increase their intake. As such, protein consumption, while important for nutrient adequacy, is not a focus of this document. Although associations have been identified between specific food groups (e.g., fruits and vegetables) and reduced risk for chronic diseases, the effects are interrelated and the health benefits should be considered in the context of an overall healthy diet that does not exceed calorie needs (such as the USDA Food Guide or the DASH Eating Plan). The strength of the evidence for the association between increased intake of fruits and vegetables and reduced risk of chronic diseases is variable and depends on the specific disease, but an array of evidence points to beneficial health effects.

Compared with the many people who consume a dietary pattern with only small amounts of fruits and vegetables, those who eat more generous amounts as part of a healthful diet are likely to have reduced risk of chronic diseases, including stroke and perhaps other cardiovascular diseases, type 2 diabetes, and cancers in certain sites (oral cavity and pharynx, larynx, lung, esophagus, stomach, and colon-rectum). Diets rich in foods containing fiber, such as fruits, vegetables, and whole grains, may reduce the risk of coronary heart disease. Diets rich in milk and milk products can reduce the risk of low bone mass throughout the life cycle. The consumption of milk products is especially important for children and adolescents who are building their peak bone mass and developing lifelong habits. Although each of these food groups may have a different relationship with disease outcomes, the adequate consumption of all food groups contributes to overall health.

Key Recommendations

- Consume a sufficient amount of fruits and vegetables while staying within energy needs. Two cups of fruit and 2½ cups of vegetables per day are recommended for a reference 2,000-calorie intake, with higher or lower amounts depending on the calorie level.
- Choose a variety of fruits and vegetables each day. In particular, select from all five vegetable subgroups (dark green, orange, legumes, starchy vegetables, and other vegetables) several times a week.
- Consume 3 or more ounce-equivalents of whole-grain products per day, with the rest of the recommended grains coming from enriched or whole-grain products. In general, at least half the grains should come from whole grains.
- Consume 3 cups per day of fat-free or low-fat milk or equivalent milk products.

Key Recommendations for Specific Population Groups;

- *Children and adolescents.* Consume whole-grain products often; at least half the grains should be whole grains. Children 2 to 8 years should consume 2 cups per day of fat-free or low-fat milk or equivalent milk products. Children 9 years of age and older should consume 3 cups per day of fat-free or low-fat milk or equivalent milk products.

Discussion

Fruits, vegetables, whole grains, and milk products are all important to a healthful diet and can be good sources of the nutrients of concern. When increasing intake of fruits, vegetables, whole grains, and fat-free or low-fat milk and milk products, it is important to decrease one's intake of less-nutrient-dense foods to control calorie intake. The 2,000-calorie level used in the discussion is a reference level only; it is not a recommended calorie intake because many Americans should be consuming fewer calories to maintain a healthy weight.

Fruits and Vegetables

Four and one-half cups (nine servings) of fruits and vegetables are recommended daily for the reference 2,000-calorie level, with higher or lower amounts depending on the caloric level. This results in a range of 2½ to 6½ cups (5 to 13 servings) of fruits and vegetables each day for the 1,200- to 3,200-calorie levels. Fruits and vegetables provide a variety of micronutrients and fiber. In the fruit group, consumption of whole fruits (fresh, frozen, canned, dried) rather than fruit juice for the majority of the total daily amount is suggested to ensure adequate fiber intake. Different vegetables are rich in different nutrients. In the vegetable group, weekly intake of specific amounts from each of five vegetable subgroups (dark green, orange, legumes [dry beans], starchy, and other vegetables)[12] is recommended for adequate nutrient intake. Each subgroup provides a somewhat different array of nutrients. In the USDA Food Guide at the reference 2,000-calorie level, the following weekly amounts are recommended:

Dark green vegetables	3 cups/week
Orange vegetables	2 cups/week
Legumes (dry beans)	3 cups/week
Starchy vegetables	3 cups/week
Other vegetables	6 ½ cups/week

Most current consumption patterns do not achieve the recommended intakes of many of these vegetables. The DASH Eating Plan and the USDA Food Guide suggest increasing intakes of dark green vegetables, orange vegetables, and legumes (dry beans) as part of the overall recommendation to have an adequate intake of fruits and vegetables.

Whole Grains

In addition to fruits and vegetables, whole grains are an important source of fiber and other nutrients. Whole grains, as well as foods made from them, consist of the entire grain seed, usually called the kernel. The kernel is made of three components—the bran, the germ, and the endosperm. If the kernel has been cracked, crushed, or flaked, then it must retain nearly the same relative proportions of bran, germ, and endosperm as the original grain to be called whole grain. In the grain-refining process, most of the bran and some of the germ is removed, resulting in the loss of dietary fiber (also known as cereal fiber), vitamins, minerals, lignans, phytoestrogens, phenolic compounds, and phytic acid. Some manufacturers add bran to grain products to increase the dietary fiber content. Refined grains are the resulting product of the grain-refining processing. Most refined grains are enriched before being further processed into foods. Enriched refined grain products that conform to standards of identity are required by law to be fortified with folic acid, as well as thiamin, riboflavin, niacin, and iron. Food manufacturers may fortify whole-grain foods where regulations permit the addition of folic acid. Currently, a number of whole-grain, ready-to-eat breakfast cereals are fortified with folic acid. Many nutrients occur at higher or similar levels in whole grains when compared to enriched grains, but whole grains have less folate unless they have been fortified with folic acid.

Consuming at least 3 or more ounce-equivalents of whole grains per day can reduce the risk of several chronic diseases and may help with weight maintenance. Thus, daily intake of at least 3 ounce-equivalents of whole grains per day is recommended by substituting whole grains for refined grains. However, because three servings may be difficult for younger children to achieve, it is recommended that they increase whole grains into their diets as they grow. At all calorie levels, all age groups should consume at least half the grains as whole grains to achieve the fiber recommendation. All grain servings can be whole-grain; however, it is advisable to include some folate-fortified products, such as folate-fortified whole-grain cereals, in these whole-grain choices.

Whole grains cannot be identified by the colour of the food; label-reading skills are needed. For information about the ingredients in whole-grain and enriched-grain products, read the ingredient list on the food label. For many whole-grain products, the words "whole" or "whole grain" will appear before the grain ingredient's name. The whole grain should be the first ingredient listed. Wheat flour, enriched flour, and degerminated cornmeal are not whole grains. The Food and Drug Administration requires foods that bear the whole-grain health claim to (1) contain 51 percent or more whole-grain ingredients by weight per reference amount and (2) be low in fat.

Milk and Milk Products

Another source of nutrients is milk and milk products. Milk product consumption has been associated with overall diet quality and adequacy of intake of many nutrients. The intake of milk products is especially important to bone health during childhood and adolescence. Studies specifically on milk and other milk products, such as yogurt and cheese, showed a positive relationship between the intake of milk and milk products and bone mineral content or bone mineral density in one or more skeletal sites.

Adults and children should not avoid milk and milk products because of concerns that these foods lead to weight gain. There are many fat-free and low-fat choices without added sugars that are available and consistent with an overall healthy dietary plan. If a person wants to consider milk alternatives because of lactose intolerance, the most reliable and easiest ways to derive the health benefits associated with milk and milk product consumption is to choose alternatives within the milk food group, such as yogurt or lactose-free milk, or to consume the enzyme lactase prior to the consumption of milk products.

For individuals who choose to or must avoid all milk products (e.g., individuals with lactose intolerance, vegans), non-dairy calcium-containing alternatives may be selected to help meet calcium needs.

Fruits, Vegetables, and Legumes (Dry Beans) That Contain Vitamin A (Carotenoids), Vitamin C, Folate, and Potassium

Many of the fruits, vegetables, and legumes (beans) are considered to be important sources of vitamin A (as carotenoids), vitamin C, and potassium in the adult population. Intakes of these nutrients, based on dietary intake data or evidence of public health problems, may be of concern. Also listed are sources of naturally occurring folate, a nutrient considered to be of concern for women of childbearing age and those in the first trimester of pregnancy. Folic acid-fortified grain products, not listed in this table, are also good sources.

Sources of Vitamin A (Carotenoids)

- Bright orange vegetables like carrots, sweetpotatoes, and pumpkin
- Tomatoes and tomato products, red sweet pepper

- Leafy greens such as spinach, collards, turnip greens, kale, beet and mustard greens, green leaf lettuce, and romaine
- Orange fruits like mango, cantaloupe, apricots, and red or pink grapefruit.

Sources of Vitamin C

- Citrus fruits and juices, kiwi fruit, strawberries, guava, papaya, and cantaloupe
- Broccoli, peppers, tomatoes, cabbage (especially Chinese cabbage), brussels sprouts, and potatoes
- Leafy greens such as romaine, turnip greens, and spinach.

Sources of Folate

- Cooked dry beans and peas
- Oranges and orange juice
- Deep green leaves like spinach and mustard greens.

Sources of Potassium

- Baked white or sweetpotatoes, cooked greens (such as spinach), winter (orange) squash
- Bananas, plantains, many dried fruits, oranges and orange juice, cantaloupe, and honeydew melons
- Cooked dry beans
- Soybeans (green and mature)
- Tomato products (sauce, paste, puree)
- Beet greens.

Fats

Overview

Fats and oils are part of a healthful diet, but the type of fat makes a difference to heart health, and the total amount of fat consumed is also important. High intake of saturated fats, *trans* fats, and cholesterol increases the risk of unhealthy blood lipid levels, which, in turn, may increase the risk of coronary heart disease. A high intake of fat (greater than 35 percent of calories) generally increases saturated fat intake and makes it more difficult to avoid consuming excess calories. A low intake of fats and oils (less than 20 percent of calories) increases the risk of inadequate intakes of vitamin E and of essential fatty acids and may contribute to unfavorable changes in high-density lipoprotein (HDL) blood cholesterol and triglycerides.

Key Recommendations

- Consume less than 10 percent of calories from saturated fatty acids and less than 300 mg/day of cholesterol, and keep *trans* fatty acid consumption as low as possible.
- Keep total fat intake between 20 to 35 percent of calories, with most fats coming from sources of polyunsaturated and monounsaturated fatty acids, such as fish, nuts, and vegetable oils.
- When selecting and preparing meat, poultry, dry beans, and milk or milk products, make choices that are lean, low-fat, or fat-free.
- Limit intake of fats and oils high in saturated and/or *trans* fatty acids, and choose products low in such fats and oils.

Key Recommendations for Specific Population Groups;

- *Children and adolescents.* Keep total fat intake between 30 to 35 percent of calories for children 2 to 3 years of age and between 25 to 35 percent of calories for children and adolescents 4 to 18 years of age, with most fats coming from sources of polyunsaturated and monounsaturated fatty acids, such as fish, nuts, and vegetable oils.

Discussion

Fats supply energy and essential fatty acids and serve as a carrier for the absorption of the fat-soluble vitamins A, D, E, and K and carotenoids. Fats serve as building blocks of membranes and play a key regulatory role in numerous biological functions. Dietary fat is found in foods derived from both plants and animals. The recommended total fat intake is between 20 and 35 percent of calories for adults. A fat intake of 30 to 35 percent of calories is recommended for children 2 to 3 years of age and 25 to 35 percent of calories for children and adolescents 4 to 18 years of age. Few Americans consume less than 20 percent of calories from fat. Fat intakes that exceed 35 percent of calories are associated with both total increased saturated fat and calorie intakes.

To decrease their risk of elevated low-density lipoprotein (LDL) cholesterol in the blood, most Americans need to decrease their intakes of saturated fat and *trans* fats, and many need to decrease their dietary intake of cholesterol. Because men tend to have higher intakes of dietary cholesterol, it is especially important for them to meet this recommendation. Population-based studies of American diets show that intake of saturated fat is more excessive than intake of *trans* fats and cholesterol. Therefore, it is most important for Americans to decrease their intake of saturated fat. However, intake of all three should be decreased to meet recommendations.

Based on 1994-1996 data, the estimated average daily intake of *trans* fats in the United States was about 2.6 percent of total energy intake. Processed foods and oils provide approximately 80 percent of *trans* fats in the diet, compared to 20 percent that occur naturally in food from animal sources. *Trans* fat content of certain processed foods has changed and is likely to continue to change as the industry reformulates products.

Because the *trans* fatty acids produced in the partial hydrogenation of vegetable oils account for more than 80 percent of total intake, the food industry has an important role in decreasing *trans* fatty acid content of the food supply. Limited consumption of foods made with processed sources of *trans* fats provides the most effective means of reducing intake of *trans* fats. By looking at the food label, consumers can select products that are lowest in saturated fat, *trans* fats, and cholesterol.

To meet the total fat recommendation of 20 to 35 percent of calories, most dietary fats should come from sources of polyunsaturated and monounsaturated fatty acids. Sources of omega-6 polyunsaturated fatty acids are liquid vegetable oils, including soybean oil, corn oil, and safflower oil.

Plant sources of omega-3 polyunsaturated fatty acids include soybean oil, canola oil, walnuts, and flaxseed. Eicosapentaenoic acid (EPA) and docosahexaenoic acid (DHA) are omega-3 fatty acids that are contained in fish and shellfish. Fish that naturally contain more oil (e.g., salmon, trout, herring) are higher in EPA and DHA than are lean fish (e.g., cod, haddock, catfish). Limited evidence suggests an association between consumption of fatty acids in fish and reduced risks of mortality from cardiovascular disease for the general population. Other sources of EPA and DHA may provide similar benefits; however, more research is needed. Plant sources that are rich in monounsaturated fatty acids include vegetable oils (e.g., canola, olive, high oleic safflower, and sunflower oils) that are liquid at room temperature and nuts.

Considerations for Specific Population Groups

Evidence suggests that consuming approximately two servings of fish per week may reduce the risk of mortality from coronary heart disease and that consuming EPA and DHA may reduce the risk of mortality from cardiovascular disease in people who have already experienced a cardiac event.

Federal and State advisories provide current information about lowering exposure to environmental contaminants in fish. For example, methylmercury is a heavy metal toxin found in varying levels in nearly all fish and shellfish. For most people, the risk from mercury by eating fish and shellfish is not a health concern. However, some fish contain higher levels of mercury that may harm an unborn baby or young child's developing nervous system. The risks from mercury in fish and shellfish depend on the amount of fish eaten and the levels of mercury in the fish. Therefore, the Food and Drug Administration (FDA) and the Environmental Protection Agency are advising women of childbearing age who may become pregnant, pregnant women, nursing mothers, and young children to avoid some types of fish and shellfish and eat fish and shellfish that are lower in mercury.

Lower intakes (less than 7 percent of calories from saturated fat and less than 200 mg/day of cholesterol) are recommended as part of a therapeutic diet for adults with elevated LDL blood cholesterol (i.e., above their LDL blood cholesterol goal. People with an elevated LDL blood cholesterol level should be under the care of a healthcare provider.

Carbohydrates

Overview

Carbohydrates are part of a healthful diet. The AMDR for carbohydrates is 45 to 65 percent of total calories. Dietary fiber is composed of nondigestible carbohydrates and lignin intrinsic and intact in plants. Diets rich in dietary fiber have been shown to have a number of beneficial effects, including decreased risk of coronary heart disease and improvement in laxation. There is also interest in the potential relationship between diets containing fiber-rich foods and lower risk of type 2 diabetes. Sugars and starches supply energy to the body in the form of glucose, which is the only energy source for red blood cells and is the preferred energy source for the brain, central nervous system, placenta, and fetus. Sugars can be naturally present in foods (such as the fructose in fruit or the lactose in milk) or added to the food. Added sugars, also known as caloric sweeteners, are sugars and syrups that are added to foods at the table or during processing or preparation (such as high fructose corn syrup in sweetened beverages and baked products). Although the body's response to sugars does not depend on whether they are naturally present in a food or added to the food, added sugars supply calories but few or no nutrients.

Consequently, it is important to choose carbohydrates wisely. Foods in the basic food groups that provide carbohydrates—fruits, vegetables, grains, and milk—are important sources of many nutrients. Choosing plenty of these foods, within the context of a calorie-controlled diet, can promote health and reduce chronic disease risk. However, the greater the consumption of foods containing large amounts of added sugars, the more difficult it is to consume enough nutrients without gaining weight. Consumption of added sugars provides calories while providing little, if any, of the essential nutrients.

Key Recommendations

- Choose fiber-rich fruits, vegetables, and whole grains often.
- Choose and prepare foods and beverages with little added sugars or caloric sweeteners, such as amounts suggested by the USDA Food Guide and the DASH Eating Plan.
- Reduce the incidence of dental caries by practicing good oral hygiene and consuming sugar- and starch-containing foods and beverages less frequently.

Discussion

The recommended dietary fiber intake is 14 grams per 1,000 calories consumed. Initially, some Americans will find it challenging to achieve this level of intake. However, making fiber-rich food choices more often will move people toward this goal and is likely to confer significant health benefits.

The majority of servings from the fruit group should come from whole fruit (fresh, frozen, canned, dried) rather than juice. Increasing the proportion of fruit that is eaten in the form of whole fruit rather than juice is desirable to increase fiber intake. However, inclusion of some juice, such as orange juice, can help meet recommended levels of potassium intake. Appendixes B-1 and B-8 list some of the best sources of potassium and dietary fiber, respectively.

Legumes—such as dry beans and peas—are especially rich in fiber and should be consumed several times per week. They are considered part of both the vegetable group and the meat and beans group as they contain nutrients found in each of these food groups.

Consuming at least half the recommended grain servings as whole grains is important, for all ages, at each calorie level, to meet the fiber recommendation. Consuming at least 3 ounce-equivalents of whole grains per day can reduce the risk of coronary heart disease, may help with weight maintenance, and may lower risk for other chronic diseases. Thus, at lower calorie levels, adults should consume more than half (specifically, at least 3 ounce-equivalents) of whole grains per day, by substituting whole grains for refined grains.

Individuals who consume food or beverages high in added sugars tend to consume more calories than those who consume food or beverages low in added sugars; they also tend to consume lower amounts of micronutrients. Although more research is needed, available prospective studies show a positive association between the consumption of calorically sweetened beverages and weight gain. For this reason, decreased intake of such foods, especially beverages with caloric sweeteners, is recommended to reduce calorie intake and help achieve recommended nutrient intakes and weight control.

Total discretionary calories should not exceed the allowance for any given calorie level, as shown in the USDA Food Guide. The discretionary calorie allowance covers all calories from added sugars, alcohol, and the additional fat found in even moderate fat choices from the milk and meat group. For example, the 2,000-calorie pattern includes only about 267 discretionary calories. At 29 percent of calories from total fat (including 18 g of solid fat), if no alcohol is consumed, then only 8 teaspoons (32 g) of added sugars can be afforded. This is less than the amount in a typical 12-ounce calorically sweetened soft drink. If fat is decreased to 22 percent of calories, then 18 teaspoons (72 g) of added sugars is allowed. If fat is increased to 35 percent of calories, then no allowance remains for added sugars, even if alcohol is not consumed. In some cases, small amounts of sugars added to nutrient-dense foods, such as breakfast cereals and reduced-fat milk products, may increase a person's intake of such foods by enhancing the palatability of these products, thus improving nutrient intake without contributing excessive calories.

The Nutrition Facts Panel on the food label provides the amount of total sugars but does not list added sugars separately. People should examine the ingredient list to find out whether a food contains added sugars. The ingredient list is usually located under the Nutrition Facts Panel or on the side of a food label. Ingredients are listed in order of predominance, by weight; that is, the ingredient with the greatest contribution to the product weight is listed first and the ingredient contributing the least amount is listed last.

Sugars and starches contribute to dental caries by providing substrate for bacterial fermentation in the mouth. Thus, the frequency and duration of consumption of starches and sugars can be important factors because they increase exposure to cariogenic substrates. Drinking fluoridated water and/or using fluoride-containing dental hygiene products help reduce the risk of dental caries. Most bottled water is not fluoridated. With the increase in consumption of bottled water, there is concern that Americans may not be getting enough fluoride for maintenance of oral health. A combined approach of reducing the frequency and duration of exposure to fermentable carbohydrate intake and optimizing oral hygiene practices, such as drinking fluoridated water and brushing and flossing teeth, is the most effective way to reduce incidence of dental caries.

Considerations for Specific Population Groups

Older Adults

Dietary fiber is important for laxation. Since constipation may affect up to 20 percent of people over 65 years of age, older adults should choose to consume foods rich in dietary fiber. Other causes of constipation among this age group may include drug interactions with laxation and lack of appropriate hydration.

Children

Carbohydrate intakes of children need special considerations with regard to obtaining sufficient amounts of fiber, avoiding excessive amounts of calories from added sugars, and preventing dental caries. Several cross-sectional surveys on U.S. children and adolescents have found inadequate dietary fiber intakes, which could be improved by increasing consumption of whole fruits, vegetables, and whole-grain products. Sugars can improve the palatability of foods and beverages that otherwise might not be consumed.

This may explain why the consumption of sweetened dairy foods and beverages and presweetened cereals is positively associated with childrens' and adolescents' nutrient intake. However, beverages with caloric sweeteners, sugars and sweets, and other sweetened foods that provide little or no nutrients are negatively associated with diet quality and can contribute to excessive energy intakes, affirming the importance of reducing added sugar intake substantially from current levels. Most of the studies of preschool children suggest a positive association between sucrose consumption and dental caries, though other factors (particularly infrequent brushing or not using fluoridated toothpaste) are more predictive of caries outcome than is sugar consumption.

Sodium and Potassium

Overview

On average, the higher an individual's salt (sodium chloride) intake, the higher an individual's blood pressure. Nearly all Americans consume substantially more salt than they need. Decreasing salt intake is advisable to reduce the risk of elevated blood pressure. Keeping blood pressure in the normal range reduces an individual's risk of coronary heart disease, stroke, congestive heart failure, and kidney disease. Many American adults will develop hypertension (high blood pressure) during their lifetime. Lifestyle changes can prevent or delay the onset of high blood pressure and can lower elevated blood pressure. These changes include reducing salt intake, increasing potassium intake, losing excess body weight, increasing physical activity, and eating an overall healthful diet.

Key Recommendations

- Consume less than 2,300 mg (approximately 1 tsp of salt) of sodium per day.
- Choose and prepare foods with little salt. At the same time, consume potassium-rich foods, such as fruits and vegetables.

Key Recommendations for Specific Population Groups;

- *Individuals with hypertension, blacks, and middle-aged and older adults.* Aim to consume no more than 1,500 mg of sodium per day, and meet the potassium recommendation (4,700 mg/day) with food.

Discussion

Salt is sodium chloride. Food labels list sodium rather than salt content. When reading a Nutrition Facts Panel on a food product, look for the sodium content. Foods that are low in sodium (less than 140 mg or 5 percent of the Daily Value [DV]) are low in salt.

On average, the natural salt content of food accounts for only about 10 percent of total intake, while discretionary salt use (i.e., salt added at the table or while cooking) provides another 5 to 10 percent of total intake. Approximately 75 percent is derived from salt added by manufacturers. In addition, foods served by food establishments may be high in sodium. It is important to read the food label and determine the sodium content of food, which can vary by several hundreds of milligrams in similar foods. For example, the sodium content in regular tomato soup may be 700 mg per cup in one brand and 1,100 mg per cup in another brand. Reading labels, comparing sodium contents of foods, and purchasing the lower sodium brand may be one strategy to lower total sodium intake.

An individual's preference for salt is not fixed. After consuming foods lower in salt for a period of time, taste for salt tends to decrease. Use of other flavorings may satisfy an individual's taste. While salt substitutes containing potassium chloride may be useful for some individuals, they can be harmful to people with certain medical conditions. These individuals should consult a healthcare provider before trying salt substitutes. Discretionary salt use is fairly stable, even when foods offered are lower in sodium than typical foods consumed. When consumers are offered a lower sodium product, they typically do not add table salt to compensate for the lower sodium content, even when available. Therefore, any program for reducing the salt consumption of a population should concentrate primarily on reducing the salt used during food processing and on changes in food selection (e.g., more fresh, less-processed items, less sodium-dense foods) and preparation.

Reducing salt intake is one of several ways that people may lower their blood pressure. The relationship between salt intake and blood pressure is direct and progressive without an apparent threshold. On average, the higher a person's salt intake, the higher the blood pressure. Reducing blood pressure, ideally to the normal range, reduces the risk of stroke, heart disease, heart failure, and kidney disease.

Another dietary measure to lower blood pressure is to consume a diet rich in potassium. A potassium-rich diet also blunts the effects of salt on blood pressure, may reduce the risk of developing kidney stones, and possibly decrease bone loss with age. The recommended intake of potassium for adolescents and adults is 4,700 mg/day. Recommended intakes for potassium for children 1 to 3 years of age is 3,000 mg/day, 4 to 8 years of age is 3,800 mg/day, and 9 to 13 years of age is 4,500 mg/day. Potassium should come from food sources. Fruits and vegetables, which are rich in potassium with its bicarbonate precursors, favourably affect acid-base metabolism, which may reduce risk of kidney stones and bone loss. Potassium-rich fruits and vegetables include leafy green vegetables, fruit from vines, and root vegetables. Meat, milk, and cereal products also contain potassium, but may not have the same effect on acid-base metabolism.

Considerations for Specific Population Groups

Individuals With Hypertension, Blacks, and Middle-Aged and Older Adults. Some individuals tend to be more salt sensitive than others, including people with hypertension, blacks, and middle-aged and older adults. Because blacks commonly have a relatively low intake of potassium and a high prevalence of elevated blood pressure and salt sensitivity, this population subgroup may especially benefit from an increased dietary intake of potassium. Dietary potassium can lower blood pressure and blunt the effects of salt on blood pressure in some individuals. While salt substitutes containing potassium chloride may be useful for some individuals, they can be harmful to people with certain medical conditions. These individuals should consult a healthcare provider before using salt substitutes.

Food Safety

Overview

Avoiding foods that are contaminated with harmful bacteria, viruses, parasites, toxins, and chemical and physical contaminants are vital for healthful eating. The signs and symptoms of foodborne illness range from gastrointestinal symptoms, such as upset stomach, diarrhea, fever, vomiting, abdominal cramps, and dehydration, to more severe systemic illness, such as paralysis and meningitis. It is estimated that every year about 76 million people in the United States become ill from pathogens in food; of these, about 5,000 die. Consumers can take simple measures to reduce their risk of foodborne illness, especially in the home.

Key Recommendations

- To avoid microbial foodborne illness:
  - o Clean hands, food contact surfaces, and fruits and vegetables. Meat and poultry should *not* be washed or rinsed.
  - o Separate raw, cooked, and ready-to-eat foods while shopping, preparing, or storing foods.
  - o Cook foods to a safe temperature to kill microorganisms.
  - o Chill (refrigerate) perishable food promptly and defrost foods properly.
  - o Avoid raw (unpasteurized) milk or any products made from unpasteurized milk, raw or partially cooked eggs or foods containing raw eggs, raw or undercooked meat and poultry, unpasteurized juices, and raw sprouts.

Key Recommendations for Specific Population Groups

- *Infants and young children, pregnant women, older adults, and those who are immunocompromised.* Do not eat or drink raw (unpasteurized) milk or any products made from unpasteurized milk, raw or partially cooked eggs or foods containing raw eggs, raw or undercooked meat and poultry, raw or undercooked fish or shellfish, unpasteurized juices, and raw sprouts.

- *Pregnant women, older adults, and those who are immunocompromised:* Only eat certain deli meats and frankfurters that have been reheated to steaming hot.

Discussion

The most important food safety problem is microbial foodborne illness. All those who handle food, including farmers, food producers, individuals who work in markets and food service establishments, and other food preparers, have a responsibility to keep food as safe as possible. To keep food safe, people who prepare food should clean hands, food contact surfaces, and fruits and vegetables; separate raw, cooked, and ready-to-eat foods; cook foods to a safe internal temperature; chill perishable food promptly; and defrost food properly. For more important information on cooking, cleaning, separating, and chilling.

When preparing and consuming food, it is essential to wash hands often, particularly before and after preparing food, especially after handling raw meat, poultry, eggs, or seafood. A good hand washing protocol includes wetting hands; applying soap; rubbing hands vigorously together for 20 seconds; rinsing hands thoroughly under clean, running warm water; and drying hands completely using a clean disposable or cloth towel.

Washing may be the only method that consumers have to reduce pathogen load on fresh produce that will not be either peeled or subsequently cooked. A good protocol for washing fresh fruits and vegetables includes removing and discarding outer leaves, washing produce just before cooking or eating, washing under running potable water, scrubbing with a clean brush or with hands, and drying the fruits or vegetables using a clean disposable or cloth towel. Free moisture on produce may promote survival and growth of microbial populations. Therefore, drying the food is critical if the item will not be eaten or cooked right away.

People should read the labels of bagged produce to determine if it is ready-to-eat. Ready-to-eat, prewashed bagged produce can be used without further washing if kept refrigerated and used by the "use-by" date. If desired, prewashed, ready-to-eat produce can be washed again. Raw meat and poultry should not be washed because this creates the danger of cross-contamination and is not necessary. Washing these foods can allow most bacteria that are present on the surface of the meat or poultry to spread to ready-to-eat foods, kitchen utensils, and counter surfaces.

It is important to separate raw, cooked, and ready-to-eat foods while shopping, preparing, or storing. This prevents cross-contamination from one food to another. In addition, refrigerator surfaces can become contaminated from high-risk foods such as raw meats, poultry, fish, uncooked hot dogs, certain deli meats, or raw vegetables. If not cleaned, contaminated refrigerator surfaces can, in turn, serve as a vehicle for contaminating other foods.

Uncooked and undercooked meat, poultry and eggs and egg products are potentially unsafe. Raw meat, poultry and eggs should always be cooked to a safe internal temperature. The best way to tell if meat, poultry and egg dishes are cooked safely is to use a food thermometer. Leftover refrigerator foods should also be reheated to the proper internal temperature. Bacteria grow most rapidly in the range of 40°F and 140°F. To keep food out of this danger zone, keep cold food cold (below 40°F) and hot food hot (above 140°F).

The refrigerator should be set at no higher than 40°F and the freezer at 0°F, and these temperatures should be checked with an appliance thermometer. Refrigerated leftovers may become unsafe within 3 to 4 days. Despite the appearance of a food, it may not be safe to eat. Not all bacterial growth causes a food's surface to discolor or smell bad. It may be unsafe to taste fresh or leftover food items when there is any doubt about their safety. Safe disposal of the food is indicated if there is a question about whether or not a food is safe to eat. "If in doubt—throw it out."

Considerations for Specific Population Groups

Some people may be at high risk for developing foodborne illness. These include pregnant women and their fetuses, young children, older adults, people with weakened immune systems, and individuals with certain chronic illnesses. These people should pay extra attention to food safety advice.

For example, pregnant women, older adults, and those who are immunocompromised are at risk of developing listeriosis, a potentially life-threatening illness caused by the bacterium *Listeria monocytogenes*. Some deli meats and frankfurters that have not been reheated to steaming hot and some ready-to-eat foods are associated with listeriosis and pose a high-risk to certain individuals. All these foods should be heated to a safe internal temperature. In addition, these individuals should take special care not to eat or drink raw (unpasteurized) milk or any products made from unpasteurized milk (such as some soft cheeses), raw or partially cooked eggs or foods containing raw eggs, raw or undercooked meat and poultry, unpasteurized juices, and raw sprouts. They should also avoid raw or undercooked fish or shellfish.

New information on food safety is constantly emerging. Recommendations and precautions for people at high risk are updated as scientists learn more about preventing foodborne illness. Individuals in high-risk categories should seek guidance from a healthcare provider.

Vitamin

A vitamin is an organic compound required as a nutrient in tiny amounts by an organism. A compound is called a vitamin when it cannot be synthesized in sufficient quantities by an organism, and must be obtained from the diet. Thus, the term is conditional both on the circumstances and the particular organism. For example, ascorbic acid functions as vitamin C for some animals but not others, and vitamins D and K are required in the human diet only in certain circumstances.

Vitamins are classified by their biological and chemical activity, not their structure. Thus, each "vitamin" may refer to several *vitamer* compounds that all show the biological activity associated with a particular vitamin. Such a set of chemicals are grouped under an alphabetized vitamin "generic descriptor" title, such as "vitamin A," which includes the compounds retinal, retinol, and many carotenoids. Vitamers are often inter-converted in the body. The term *vitamin* does not include other essential nutrients such as dietary minerals, essential fatty acids, or essential amino acids, nor does it encompass the large number of other nutrients that promote health but are otherwise required less often.

Vitamins have diverse biochemical functions, including function as hormones (e.g. vitamin D), antioxidants (e.g. vitamin E), and mediators of cell signaling and regulators of cell and tissue growth and differentiation (e.g. vitamin A). The largest number of vitamins (e.g. B complex vitamins) function as precursors for enzyme cofactor bio-molecules (coenzymes), that help act as catalysts and substrates in metabolism. When acting as part of a catalyst, vitamins are bound to enzymes and are called prosthetic groups. For example, biotin is part of enzymes involved in making fatty acids. Vitamins also act as coenzymes to carry chemical groups between enzymes. For example, folic acid carries various forms of carbon group – methyl, formyl and methylene - in the cell. Although these roles in assisting enzyme reactions are vitamins' best-known function, the other vitamin functions are equally important.

Until the 1900s, vitamins were obtained solely through food intake, and changes in diet (which, for example, could occur during a particular growing season) can alter the types and amounts of vitamins ingested. Vitamins have been produced as commodity chemicals and made widely available as inexpensive pills for several decades, allowing supplementation of the dietary intake.

History

The value of eating a certain food to maintain health was recognized long before vitamins were identified. The ancient Egyptians knew that feeding a patient liver would help cure night blindness, an illness now known to be caused by a vitamin A deficiency. The advancement of ocean voyage during the Renaissance resulted in prolonged periods without access to fresh fruits and vegetables, and made illnesses from vitamin deficiency common among ship's crew.

In 1749, the Scottish surgeon James Lind discovered that citrus foods helped prevent scurvy, a particularly deadly disease in which collagen is not properly formed, causing poor wound healing, bleeding of the gums, severe pain, and death. In 1753, Lind published his *Treatise on the Scurvy*, which recommended using lemons and limes to avoid scurvy, which was adopted by the British Royal Navy. This led to the nickname Limey for sailors of that organization. Lind's discovery, however, was not widely accepted by individuals in the Royal Navy's Arctic expeditions in the 19th century, where it was widely believed that scurvy could be prevented by practicing good hygiene, regular exercise, and by maintaining the morale of the crew while on board, rather than by a diet of fresh food. As a result, Arctic expeditions continued to be plagued by scurvy and other deficiency diseases. In the early

20th century, when Robert Fálcon Scott made his two expeditions to the Antarctic, the prevailing medical theory was that scurvy was caused by "tainted" canned food.

In 1881, Russian surgeon Nikolai Lunin studied the effects of scurvy while at the University of Tartu in present-day Estonia. He fed mice an artificial mixture of all the separate constituents of milk known at that time, namely the proteins, fats, carbohydrates, and salts. The mice that received only the individual constituents died, while the mice fed by milk itself developed normally. He made a conclusion that "a natural food such as milk must therefore contain, besides these known principal ingredients, small quantities of unknown substances essential to life." However, his conclusions were rejected by other researchers when they were unable to reproduce his results. One difference was that he had used table sugar (sucrose), while other researchers had used milk sugar (lactose) that still contained small amounts of vitamin B.

The Discovery of Vitamins and their Sources

Year of discovery	*Vitamin*	*Source*
1909	Vitamin A (Retinol)	Cod liver oil
1912	Vitamin B_1 (Thiamin)	Rice bran
1912	Vitamin C (Ascorbic acid)	Lemons
1918	Vitamin D (Calciferol)	Cod liver oil
1920	Vitamin B_2 (Riboflavin)	Eggs
1922	Vitamin E (Tocopherol)	Wheat germ oil, Cosmetic and Liver
1926	Vitamin B_{12} (Cyanocobalamin)	Liver
1929	Vitamin K (Phylloquinone)	Alfalfa
1931	Vitamin B_5 (Pantothenic acid)	Liver
1931	Vitamin B_7 (Biotin)	Liver
1934	Vitamin B_6 (Pyridoxine)	Rice bran
1936	Vitamin B_3 (Niacin)	Liver
1941	Vitamin B_9 (Folic acid)	Liver

In east Asia, where polished white rice was the common staple food of the middle class, beriberi resulting from lack of vitamin B was endemic. In 1884, Takaki Kanehiro, a British trained medical doctor of the Japanese Navy observed that beriberi was endemic among low ranking crew who often ate nothing but rice but not among crews of Western navies and officers who consumed a Western-style diet. Kanehiro initially believed that lack of protein was the chief cause of beriberi. With the support of Japanese navy, he experimented using crews of two battleships, one crew was fed only white rice, while the other was fed a diet of meat, fish, barley, rice, and beans. The group that ate only white rice documented 161 crew members with beriberi and 25 deaths, while the latter group had only 14 cases of beriberi and no deaths. This convinced Kanehiro and the Japanese Navy that diet was the cause of beriberi. This was confirmed in 1897, when Christiaan Eijkman discovered that feeding unpolished rice instead of the polished variety to chickens helped to prevent beriberi in the chickens. The following year, Frederick Hopkins postulated that some foods contained "accessory factors"—in addition to proteins, carbohydrates, fats, et cetera—that were necessary for the functions of the human body. Hopkins was awarded the 1929 Nobel Prize for Physiology or Medicine with Christiaan Eijkman for their discovery of several vitamins.

In 1910, Japanese scientist Umetaro Suzuki succeeded in extracting a water-soluble complex of micronutrients from rice bran and named it aberic acid. He published this discovery in a Japanese scientific journal. When the article was translated into German, the translation failed to state that it was a newly discovered nutrient, a claim made in the original Japanese article, and hence his discovery failed to gain publicity. Polish biochemist Kazimierz Funk isolated the same complex of micronutrients and proposed the complex be named "Vitamine" (a portmanteau of "vital amine") in 1912. The name soon became synonymous with Hopkins' "accessory factors", and by the time it was shown that not all vitamins were amines, the word was already ubiquitous. In 1920, Jack Cecil Drummond proposed that the final "e" be dropped to deemphasize the "amine" reference after the discovery that vitamin C had no amine component.

Throughout the early 1900s, the use of deprivation studies allowed scientists to isolate and identify a number of vitamins. Initially, lipid from fish oil was used to cure rickets in rats, and the fat-soluble nutrient was called "antirachitic A". Thus, the first "vitamin" bioactivity ever isolated, which cured rickets, was initially called "vitamin A", although confusingly the bioactivity of this compound is now called vitamin D. What we now call "vitamin A" was identified in fish oil as a separate factor that was inactivated by ultraviolet light. In 1931, Albert Szent-Györgyi and a fellow researcher Joseph Svirbely determined that "hexuronic acid" was actually vitamin C and noted its anti-scorbutic activity. In 1937, Szent-Györgyi was awarded the Nobel Prize for his discovery. In 1943 Edward Adelbert Doisy and Henrik Dam were awarded the Nobel Prize for their discovery of vitamin K and its chemical structure.

In humans

Vitamins are classified as either water-soluble, meaning that they dissolve easily in water, or fat-soluble vitamins, which are absorbed through the intestinal tract with the help of lipids (fats). In general, water-soluble vitamins are readily excreted from the body. Each vitamin is typically used in multiple reactions and, therefore, most have multiple functions.

In Nutrition and Diseases

Vitamins are essential for the normal growth and development of a multicellular organism. Using the genetic blueprint inherited from its parents, a fetus begins to develop, at the moment of conception, from the nutrients it absorbs. It requires certain vitamins and minerals to be present at certain times. These nutrients facilitate the chemical reactions that produce among other things, skin, bone, and muscle. If there is serious deficiency in one or more of these nutrients, a child may develop a deficiency disease. Even minor deficiencies may cause permanent damage.

For the most part, vitamins are obtained with food, but a few are obtained by other means. For example, microorganisms in the intestine—commonly known as "gut flora"—produce vitamin K and biotin, while one form of vitamin D is synthesized in the skin with the help of the natural ultraviolet wavelength of sunlight. Humans can produce some vitamins from precursors they consume. Examples include vitamin A, produced from beta carotene, and niacin, from the amino acid tryptophan.

Once growth and development are completed, vitamins remain essential nutrients for the healthy maintenance of the cells, tissues, and organs that make up a multicellular organism; they also enable a multicellular life form to efficiently use chemical energy provided by food it eats, and to help process the proteins, carbohydrates, and fats required for respiration.

Deficiencies

Deficiencies of vitamins are classified as either primary or secondary. A primary deficiency occurs when an organism does not get enough of the vitamin in its food. A secondary deficiency may be due to an underlying disorder that prevents or limits the absorption or use of the vitamin, due to a "lifestyle factor", such as smoking, excessive alcohol consumption, or the use of medications that interfere with the absorption or use of the vitamin. People who eat a varied diet are unlikely to develop a severe primary vitamin deficiency. In contrast, restrictive diets have the potential to cause prolonged vitamin deficits, which may result in often painful and potentially deadly diseases.

Because human bodies do not store most vitamins, humans must consume them regularly to avoid deficiency. Human bodily stores for different vitamins vary widely; vitamins A, D, and B_{12} are stored in significant amounts in the human body, mainly in the liver, and an adult human's diet may be deficient in vitamins A and B_{12} for many months before developing a deficiency condition. Vitamin B_3 is not stored in the human body in significant amounts, so stores may only last a couple of weeks.

Well-known human vitamin deficiencies involve thiamine (beriberi), niacin (pellagra), vitamin C (scurvy) and vitamin D (rickets). In much of the developed world, such deficiencies are rare; this is due to (1) an adequate supply of food; and (2) the addition of vitamins and minerals to common foods, often called fortification.

Some evidence also suggests that there is a link between vitamin deficiency and mental disorders.

Side Effects and Overdose

In large doses, some vitamins have documented side effects that tend to be more severe with a larger dosage. The likelihood of consuming too much of any vitamin from food is remote, but overdosing from vitamin supplementation does occur. At high enough dosages some vitamins cause side effects such as nausea, diarrhea, and vomiting.

When side effects emerge, recovery is often accomplished by reducing the dosage. The concentrations of vitamins an individual can tolerate vary widely, and appear to be related to age and state of health. In the United States, overdose exposure to all formulations of vitamins was reported by 62,562 individuals in 2004 (nearly 80% of these exposures were in children under the age of 6), leading to 53 "major" life-threatening outcomes and 3 deaths &m dash;a small number in comparison to the 19,250 people who died of unintentional poisoning of all kinds in the U.S. in the same year (2004).

Supplements

Dietary supplements, often containing vitamins, are used to ensure that adequate amounts of nutrients are obtained on a daily basis, if optimal amounts of the nutrients cannot be obtained through a varied diet. Scientific evidence supporting the benefits of some dietary supplements is well established for certain health conditions, but others need further study. A meta-analysis in 2006 suggested that Vitamin A and E supplements not only provide no tangible health benefits for generally healthy individuals, but may actually increase mortality, although two large studies included in the analysis involved smokers, for which it was already known that beta-carotene supplements can be harmful.

In the United States, advertising for dietary supplements is required to include a disclaimer that the product is not intended to treat, diagnose, mitigate, prevent, or cure disease, and that any health claims have not been evaluated by the Food and Drug Administration. In some cases, dietary supplements may have unwanted effects, especially if taken before surgery, with other dietary supplements or medicines, or if the person taking them has certain health conditions. Vitamin supplements may also contain levels of vitamins many times higher, and in different forms, than one may ingest through food.

Intake of excessive quantities can cause vitamin poisoning, often due to overdose of Vitamin A and Vitamin D (The most common poisoning with multinutrient supplement pills does not involve a vitamin, but is rather due to the mineral iron). Due to toxicity, most common vitamins have recommended upper daily intake amounts.

Since 2005, suppliers have distinguished their products as either Medical Grade or Pharmeceutical Grade products. Both of these classifications indicate products that are manufactured to be easily absorbed by the body. Normal vitamin manufacturing is not regulated in the United States to the same standards as are medicinal pharmaceuticals, although U.S. vitamins which are manufactured for food consumption by humans or animals must be manufactured to Food Chemicals Codex (FCC), grade, commonly called "food grade".

Governmental Regulation of Vitamin Supplements

Most countries place dietary supplements in a special category under the general umbrella of *foods,* not drugs. This necessitates that the manufacturer, and not the government, be responsible for ensuring that its dietary supplement products are safe before they are marketed. Unlike drug products, which must explicitly be proven safe and effective for their intended use before marketing, there are often no provisions to "approve" dietary supplements for safety or effectiveness before they reach the consumer. Also unlike drug products, manufacturers and distributors of dietary supplements are not generally required to report any claims of injuries or illnesses that may be related to the use of their products.

Names in Current and Previous Nomenclatures

The reason the set of vitamins seems to skip directly from E to K is that the vitamins corresponding to "letters" F-J were either reclassified over time, discarded as false leads, or renamed because of their relationship to "vitamin B", which became a "complex" of vitamins. The German-speaking scientists who isolated and described vitamin K (in addition to naming it as such) did so because the vitamin is intimately involved in the *Koagulation* of blood following wounding. At the time, most (but not all) of the letters from F through to J were already designated, so the use of the letter K was considered quite reasonable.

The following table lists chemicals that had previously been classified as vitamins, as well as the earlier names of vitamins that later became part of the B-complex:

Previous name	*Chemical name*	*Reason for name change*
Vitamin B_4	Adenine	DNA metabolite
Vitamin B_8	Adenylic acid	DNA metabolite
Vitamin F	Essential fatty acids	Needed in large quantities (doesnot fit the definition of a vitamin).
Vitamin G	Riboflavin	Reclassified as Vitamin B_2
Vitamin H	Biotin	Reclassified as Vitamin B_7

Vitamin J	Catechol, Flavin	Protein metabolite
Vitamin L_1	Anthranilic acid	Protein metabolite
Vitamin L_2	Adenylthiomethylpentose	RNA metabolite
Vitamin M	Folic acid	Reclassified as Vitamin B_9
Vitamin O	Carnitine	Protein metabolite
Vitamin P	Flavonoids	No longer classified as a vitamin
Vitamin PP	Niacin	Reclassified as Vitamin B_3
Vitamin U	S-Methylmethionine	Protein metabolite

Vitamin A

Vitamin A, a bi-polar molecule formed with bi-polar bonds between carbon and hydrogen, is linked to a family of similarly shaped molecules, the retinoids, which complete the remainder of the vitamin sequence.

Its important part is the retinyl group, which can be found in several forms. In foods of animal origin, the major form of vitamin A is an ester, primarily retinyl palmitate, which is converted to an alcohol (retinol) in the small intestine.

Vitamin A can also exist as an aldehyde (retinal), or as an acid (retinoic acid). Precursors to the vitamin (provitamins) are present in foods of plant origin as some of the members of the carotenoid family of compounds.

All forms of vitamin A have a Beta-ionone ring to which an isoprenoid chain is attached. This structure is essential for vitamin activity. The orange pigment of carrot - Beta-carotene - can be represented as two connected retinyl groups. The retinyl group, when attached to a specific protein, is the only primary light absorber in visual perception, and the compound name is related to the retina of the eye.

Vitamin A can be found in various forms:

- retinol, the form of vitamin A absorbed when eating animal food sources, is a yellow, fat-soluble, vitamin with importance in vision and bone growth. Since the alcohol form is unstable, the vitamin is usually produced and administered in a form of retinyl acetate or palmitate.
- other retinoids, a class of chemical compounds that are related chemically to vitamin A, are used in medicine.

Discovery of Vitamin A

The discovery of vitamin A stemmed from research dating back to 1906, indicating that factors other than carbohydrates, proteins, and fats were necessary to keep cattle healthy. By 1917 one of these substances was independently discovered by Elmer McCollum at the University of Wisconsin-Madison, and Lafayette Mendel and Thomas Osborne at Yale University. Since "water-soluble factor B" (Vitamin B) had recently been discovered, the researchers chose the name "fat-soluble factor A" (vitamin A). Vitamin A was first synthesized in 1947 by two Dutch chemists, David Adriaan van Dorp and Jozef Ferdinand Arens.

Equivalencies of Vetinoids and Carotenoids (IU)

Since some carotenoids can be converted into vitamin A, attempts have been made to determine how much of them in the diet is equivalent to a particular amount of retinol, so that comparisons can be made of the benefit of different foods. Unfortunately the situation is confusing because the accepted equivalences have changed. For many years, a system of equivalencies was used in which an international unit (IU) was equal to 0.3 micrograms of retinol, 0.6 ìg of â-carotene, or 1.2 ìg of other provitamin-A carotenoids. Later, a unit called retinol equivalent (RE) was introduced. 1 RE corresponded to 1 ìg retinol, 2 ìg â-carotene dissolved in oil (as in supplement pills), 6 ìg â-carotene in normal food (because it is not absorbed as well as from supplements), and 12 ìg of either a-carotene or â-cryptoxanthin in food.

The conclusion that can be drawn from the newer research is that fruits and vegetables are not as useful for obtaining vitamin A as was thought—in other words, the IU's that they were reported to contain were worth much less than the same number of IU's of fat-dissolved supplements. This is important for vegetarians. (Night blindness is prevalent in countries where little meat or vitamin A-fortified foods are available.) A sample vegan diet for one day that provides sufficient vitamin A has been published by the Food and Nutrition Board (page 120). On the other hand, reference values for retinol or its equivalents, provided by the National Academy of Sciences, have decreased. The RDA (for men) of 1968 was 5000 IU (1500 ìg retinol). In 1974 the RDA was set to 1000 RE (1000 ìg retinol), whereas now the Dietary Reference

Intake is 900 RAE (900 ìg or 3000 IU retinol). This is equivalent to 1800 ìg of â-carotene supplement (3000 IU) or 10800 ìg of â-carotene in food (18000 IU).

According to the Institute of Medicine of the National Academies, "RDAs are set to meet the needs of almost all (97 to 98 percent) individuals in a group. For healthy breastfed infants, the AI is the mean intake. The AI for other life stage and gender groups is believed to cover the needs of all individuals in the group, but lack of data prevent being able to specify with confidence the percentage of individuals covered by this intake."

Sources of Vitamin A

Vitamin A is found naturally in many foods:

- liver (beef, pork, chicken, turkey, fish) (6500 ìg 722%)
- carrots (835 ìg 93%)
- Broccoli leaves (800 ìg 89%) - Acc. to USDA database. Broccoli florets supposedly have much less -
- sweet potatoes (709 ìg 79%)
- kale (681 ìg 76%)
- butter (684 ìg 76%)
- spinach (469 ìg 52%)
- leafy vegetables
- pumpkin (369 ìg 41%)
- collard greens (333 ìg 37%)
- cantaloupe melon (169 ìg 19%)
- eggs (140 ìg 16%)
- apricots (96 ìg 11%)
- papaya (55 ìg 6%)
- mango (38 ìg 4%)
- peas (38 ìg 4%)
- broccoli (31 ìg 3%)
- winter squash.

Note: bracketed values are retinol equivalences and percentage of the adult male RDA per 100g.

Conversion of carotene to retinol varies from person to person and bioavailability of carotene in food varies.

Metabolic Functions of Vitamin A

Vitamin A plays a role in a variety of functions throughout the body, such as:

- Vision
- Gene transcription
- Immune function
- Embryonic development and reproduction
- Bone metabolism
- Haematopoiesis
- Skin health
- Reducing risk of heart disease
- Antioxidant Activity.

Vision

The role of vitamin A in the vision cycle is specifically related to the retinal form. Within the eye, 11-*cis*-retinal is bound to rhodopsin (rods) and iodopsin (cones) at conserved lysine residues. As light enters the eye the 11-*cis*-retinal is isomerized to the all-"trans" form. The all-"trans" retinal dissociates from the opsin in a series of steps called bleaching. This isomerization induces a nervous signal along the optic nerve to the visual centre of the brain. Upon completion of this cycle, the all-"trans"-retinal can be recycled and converted back to the 11-"cis"-retinal form via a series of enzymatic reactions. Additionally, some of the all-"trans" retinal may be converted to all-"trans" retinol form and then transported with an interphotoreceptor retinol-binding protein (IRBP) to the pigment epithelial cells. Further esterification into all-"trans" retinyl esters allow this final form to be stored within the pigment epithelial cells to be reused when needed. The final conversion of 11-*cis*-retinal will rebind to opsin to reform rhodopsin in the retina. Rhodopsin is needed to see black and white as well as see at night. It is for this reason that a deficiency in vitamin A will inhibit the reformation of rhodopsin and lead to night blindness.

Gene Transcription

Vitamin A, in the retinoic acid form, plays an important role in gene transcription. Once retinol has been taken up by a cell, it can be oxidized to retinal (by retinol dehydrogenases) and then retinal can be oxidized to retinoic acid (by retinal oxidase). The conversion of retinal to retinoic acid is an irreversible step, meaning that the production of retinoic acid is tightly regulated, due to its activity as a ligand for nuclear receptors. Retinoic acid can bind to two different nuclear receptors to initiate (or inhibit) gene transcription: the retinoic acid receptors (RARs) or the retinoid "X" receptors (RXRs). RAR and RXR must dimerize before they can bind to the DNA. RAR will form a heterodimer with RXR (RAR-RXR), but it does not readily form a homodimer (RAR-RAR). RXR, on the other hand, readily forms a homodimer (RXR-RXR) and will form heterodimers with many other nuclear receptors as well, including the thyroid hormone receptor (RXR-TR), the Vitamin D_3 receptor (RXR-VDR), the peroxisome proliferator-activated receptor (RXR-PPAR) and the liver "X" receptor (RXR-LXR). The RAR-RXR heterodimer recognizes retinoid acid response elements (RAREs) on the DNA whereas the RXR-RXR homodimer recognizes retinoid "X" response elements (RXREs) on the DNA. The other RXR heterodimers will bind to various other response elements on the DNA. Once the retinoic acid binds to the receptors and dimerization has occurred, the receptors undergo a conformational change that causes co-repressors to dissociate from the receptors. Coactivators can then bind to the receptor complex, which may help to loosen the chromatin structure from the histones or may interact with the transcriptional machinery. The receptors can then bind to the response elements on the DNA and upregulate (or downregulate) the expression of target genes, such as cellular retinol-binding protein (CRBP) as well as the genes that encode for the receptors themselves.

Dermatology

Vitamin A appears to function in maintaining normal skin health. The mechanisms behind retinoid's therapeutic agents in the treatment of dermatological diseases are being researched. For the treatment of acne, the most effective drug is 13-cis retinoic acid (isotretinoin). Although its mechanism of action remains unknown, it is the only retinoid that dramatically reduces the size and secretion of the sebaceous glands. Isotretinoin reduces bacterial numbers in both the ducts and skin surface. This is thought to be a result of the reduction in sebum, a nutrient source for the bacteria. Isotretinoin reduces inflammation via inhibition of chemotatic responses of monocytes and neutrophils. Isotretinoin also has been shown to initiate remodeling of the sebaceous glands; triggering changes in gene expression that selectively induces apoptosis. Isotretinoin is a teratogen and its use is confined to medical supervision.

Deficiency

Vitamin A deficiency is estimated to affect millions of children around the world. Approximately 250,000-500,000 children in developing countries become blind each year owing to vitamin A deficiency, with the highest prevalence in Southeast Asia and Africa. According to the World Health Organization (WHO), vitamin A deficiency is under control in the United States, but in developing countries vitamin A deficiency is a significant concern. With the high prevalence of vitamin A deficiency, the WHO has implemented several initiatives for supplementation of vitamin A in developing countries. Some of these strategies include intake of vitamin A through a combination of breast feeding, dietary intake, food fortification, and supplementation. Through the efforts of WHO and its partners, an estimated 1.25 million deaths since 1998 in 40 countries due to vitamin A deficiency have been averted.

Vitamin A deficiency can occur as either a primary or secondary deficiency. A primary vitamin A deficiency occurs among children and adults who do not consume an adequate intake of yellow and green vegetables, fruits and liver. Early weaning can also increase the risk of vitamin A deficiency. Secondary vitamin A deficiency is associated with chronic malabsorption of lipids, impaired bile production and release, low fat diets, and chronic exposure to oxidants, such as cigarette smoke. Vitamin A is a fat soluble vitamin and depends on micellar solubilization for dispersion into the small intestine, which results in poor utilization of vitamin A from low-fat diets. Zinc deficiency can also impair absorption, transport, and metabolism of vitamin A because it is essential for the synthesis of the vitamin A transport proteins and the oxidation of retinol to retinal. In malnourished populations, common low intakes of vitamin A and zinc increase the risk of vitamin A deficiency and lead to several physiological events. A study in Burkina Faso showed major reduction of malaria morbidity with combined vitamin A and zinc supplementation in young children. Since the unique function of retinyl group is the light absorption in

Retinylidene protein, one of the earliest and specific manifestations of vitamin A deficiency is impaired vision, particularly in reduced light - Night blindness. Persistent deficiency gives rise to a series of changes, the most devastating of which occur in the eyes. Some oiher ocular changes are referred to as xerophthalmia. First there is dryness of the conjunctiva (xerosis) as the normal lacrimal and mucus secreting epithelium is replaced by a keratinized epithelium. This is followed by the build-up of keratin debris in small opaque plaques (Bitot's spots) and, eventually, erosion of the roughened corneal surface with softening and destruction of the cornea (keratomalacia) and total blindness. Other changes include impaired immunity, hypokeratosis (white lumps at hair follicles), keratosis pilaris and squamous metaplasia of the epithelium lining the upper respiratory passages and urinary bladder to a keratinized epithelium. With relations to dentistry, a deficiency in Vitamin A leads to enamel hypoplasia.

Adequate supply of Vitamin A is especially important for pregnant and breastfeeding women, since deficiencies cannot be compensated by postnatal supplementation.

Toxicity

As vitamin A is fat-soluble, disposing of any excesses taken in through diet is much harder than with water-soluble vitamins B and C. As such, vitamin A toxicity can result. This can lead to nausea, jaundice, irritability, anorexia (not to be confused with anorexia nervosa, the eating disorder), vomiting, blurry vision, headaches, muscle and abdominal pain and weakness, drowsiness and altered mental status.

Acute toxicity generally occurs at doses of 25,000 IU/kg of body weight, with chronic toxicity occurring at 4,000 IU/kg of body weight daily for 6-15 months. However, liver toxicities can occur at levels as low as 15,000 IU per day to 1.4 million IU per day, with an average daily toxic dose of 120,000 IU per day. In people with renal failure 4000 IU can cause substantial damage. Additionally excessive alcohol intake can increase toxicity. Children can reach toxic levels at 1500IU/kg of body weight.

In chronic cases, hair loss, drying of the mucous membranes, fever, insomnia, fatigue, weight loss, bone fractures, anemia, and diarrhea can all be evident on top of the symptoms associated with less serious toxicity.

It has been estimated that 75% of people may be ingesting more than the RDA for vitamin A on a regular basis in developed nations. Intake of twice the RDA of preformed vitamin A chronically may be associated with osteoporosis and hip fractures. High vitamin A intake has been associated with spontaneous bone fractures in animals. Cell culture studies have linked increased bone resorption and decreased bone formation with high vitamin A intakes. This interaction may occur because vitamins A and D may compete for the same receptor and then interact with parathyoid hormone which regulates calcium.

Toxic effects of vitamin A have been shown to significantly affect developing fetuses. Therapeutic doses used for acne treatment have been shown to disrupt cephalic neural cell activity. The fetus is particularly sensitive to vitamin A toxicity during the period of organogenesis.

These toxicities only occur with preformed (retinoid) vitamin A (such as from liver). The carotenoid forms (such as beta-carotene as fcund in carrots), give no such symptoms, but excessive dietary intake of beta-carotene can lead to carotenodermia, which causes orange-yellow discoloration of the skin.

A study by Siri Forsmo *et al.* shows a correlation between low bone mineral density and too high intake of vitamin A.

Researchers have succeeded in creating water-soluble forms of vitamin A, which they believed could reduce the potential for toxicity. However, a 2003 study found that water-soluble vitamin A was approximately 10 times as toxic as fat-soluble vitamin. A 2006 study found that children given water-soluble vitamin A and D, which are typically fat-soluble, suffer from asthma twice as much as a control group supplemented with the fat-soluble vitamins.

Chronically high doses of Vitamin A can produce the syndrome of "pseudotumor cerebri". This syndrome includes headache, blurring of vision and confusion. It is associated with increased intracerebral pressure.

Vitamins Hang out in Water and Fat

There are two types of vitamins: fat soluble and water soluble.

When you eat foods that contain fat-soluble vitamins, the vitamins are stored in the fat tissues in your body and in your liver.

They wait around in your body fat until your body needs them. Fat-soluble vitamins are happy to stay stored in your body for awhile — some stay for a few days, some for up to 6 months! Then, when it's time for them to be used, special carriers in your body take them to where they're needed. Vitamins A, D, E, and K are all fat-soluble vitamins.

Water-soluble vitamins are different. When you eat foods that have water-soluble vitamins, the vitamins don't get stored as much in your body. Instead, they travel through your bloodstream. Whatever your body doesn't use comes out when you urinate (pee).

So these kinds of vitamins need to be replaced often because they don't stick around! This crowd of vitamins includes vitamin C and the big group of B vitamins — B1 (thiamin), B2 (riboflavin), niacin, B6 (pyridoxine), folic acid, B12 (cobalamine), biotin, and pantothenic acid.

Vitamins Feed Your Needs

Your body is one powerful machine, capable of doing all sorts of things by itself. But one thing it can't do is make vitamins. That's where food comes in. Your body is able to get the vitamins it needs from the foods you eat because different foods contain different vitamins. The key is to eat different foods to get an assortment of vitamins. Though some kids take a daily vitamin, most kids don't need one if they're eating a variety of healthy foods.

Now, let's look more closely at vitamins — from A to K:

Vitamin A

This vitamin plays a really big part in eyesight. It's great for night vision, like when you're trick-or-treating on Halloween. Vitamin A helps you see in colour, too, from the brightest yellow to the darkest purple. In addition, it helps you grow properly and aids in healthy skin.

Which foods are rich in vitamin A?

- milk fortified with vitamin A
- liver
- orange fruits and vegetables (like cantaloupe, carrots, sweet potatoes)
- dark green leafy vegetables (like kale, collards, spinach).

B Vitamins

There's more than one B vitamin. Here's the list: B1, B2, B6, B12, niacin, folic acid, biotin, and pantothenic acid. Whew — that's quite a group!

The B vitamins are important in metabolic (say: meh-tuh-bah-lik) activity — this means that they help make energy and set it free when your body needs it. So the next time you're running to third base, thank those B vitamins.

This group of vitamins is also involved in making red blood cells, which carry oxygen throughout your body. Every part of your body needs oxygen to work properly, so these B vitamins have a really important job.

Which foods are rich in vitamin B?

- whole grains, such as wheat and oats
- fish and seafood
- poultry and meats
- eggs
- dairy products, like milk and yogurt
- leafy green vegetables
- beans and peas.

Vitamin C

This vitamin is important for keeping body tissues, such as gums and muscles in good shape. C is also key if you get a cut or wound because it helps you heal. This vitamin also helps your body resist infection. This means that even though you can't always avoid getting sick, vitamin C makes it a little harder for your body to become infected with an illness.

Which foods are rich in vitamin C?

- citrus fruits, like oranges
- cantaloupe
- strawberries
- tomatoes
- broccoli
- cabbage
- kiwi fruit
- sweet red peppers.

Vitamin D

No bones about it... vitamin D is the vitamin you need for strong bones! It's also great for forming strong teeth. Vitamin D even lends a hand to an important mineral — it helps your body absorb the amount of calcium it needs.

Which foods are rich in vitamin D?

- milk fortified with vitamin D
- fish
- egg yolks
- liver
- fortified cereal.

Vitamin E

Everybody needs E. This hard-working vitamin maintains a lot of your body's tissues, like the ones in your eyes, skin, and liver. It protects your lungs from becoming damaged by polluted air. And it is important for the formation of red blood cells.

Which foods are rich in vitamin E?

- whole grains, such as wheat and oats
- wheat germ
- leafy green vegetables
- sardines
- egg yolks
- nuts and seeds.

Vitamin K

Vitamin K is the clotmaster! Remember the last time you got a cut? Your blood did something special called clotting. This is when certain cells in your blood act like glue and stick together at the surface of the cut to help stop the bleeding.

Which foods are rich in vitamin K?

- leafy green vegetables
- dairy products, like milk and yogurt
- broccoli
- soybean oil.

When your body gets this vitamin and the other ones it needs, you'll be feeling A-OK!

Dietary Supplement Fact Sheet: Vitamin A and Carotenoids

Vitamin A: What is it?

Vitamin A is a group of compounds that play an important role in vision, bone growth, reproduction, cell division, and cell differentiation (in which a cell becomes part of the brain, muscle, lungs, blood, or other specialized tissue.). Vitamin A helps regulate the immune system, which helps prevent or fight off infections by making white blood cells that destroy harmful bacteria and viruses. Vitamin A also may help lymphocytes (a type of white blood cell) fight infections more effectively.

Vitamin A promotes healthy surface linings of the eyes and the respiratory, urinary, and intestinal tracts. When those linings break down, it becomes easier for bacteria to enter the body and cause infection. Vitamin A also helps the skin and mucous membranes function as a barrier to bacteria and viruses.

In general, there are two categories of vitamin A, depending on whether the food source is an animal or a plant.

Vitamin A found in foods that come from animals is called preformed vitamin A. It is absorbed in the form of retinol, one of the most usable (active) forms of vitamin A. Sources include liver, whole milk, and some fortified food products. Retinol can be made into retinal and retinoic acid (other active forms of vitamin A) in the body.

Vitamin A that is found in colorful fruits and vegetables is called provitamin A carotenoid. They can be made into retinol in the body. In the United States, approximately 26% of vitamin A consumed by men and 34% of vitamin A consumed by women is in the form of provitamin A carotenoids. Common provitamin A carotenoids found in foods that come from plants are beta-carotene, alpha-carotene, and beta-cryptoxanthin. Among these, beta-carotene is most efficiently made into retinol. Alpha-carotene and beta-cryptoxanthin are also converted to vitamin A, but only half as efficiently as beta-carotene.

Of the 563 identified carotenoids, fewer than 10% can be made into vitamin A in the body. Lycopene, lutein, and zeaxanthin are carotenoids that do not have vitamin A activity but have other health promoting properties. The Institute of Medicine (IOM) encourages consumption of all carotenoid-rich fruits and vegetables for their health-promoting benefits.

Some provitamin A carotenoids have been shown to function as antioxidants in laboratory studies; however, this role has not been consistently demonstrated in humans. Antioxidants protect cells from free radicals, which are potentially damaging by-products of oxygen metabolism that may contribute to the development of some chronic diseases.

What Foods Provide Vitamin A?

Retinol is found in foods that come from animals such as whole eggs, milk, and liver. Most fat-free milk and dried nonfat milk solids sold in the United States are fortified with vitamin A to replace the amount lost when the fat is removed. Fortified foods such as fortified breakfast cereals also provide vitamin A. Provitamin A carotenoids are abundant in darkly colored fruits and vegetables. The 2000 National Health and Nutrition Examination Survey (NHANES) indicated that major dietary contributors of retinol are milk, margarine, eggs, beef liver and fortified breakfast cereals, whereas major contributors of provitamin A carotenoids are carrots, cantaloupes, sweet potatoes, and spinach.

Vitamin A in foods that come from animals is well absorbed and used efficiently by the body. Vitamin A in foods that come from plants is not as well absorbed as animal sources of vitamin A.

What are Vecommended Intakes of Vitamin A?

Recommendations for vitamin A are provided in the Dietary Reference Intakes (DRIs) developed by the Institute of Medicine (IOM). DRI is the general term for a set of reference values used for planning and assessing nutrient intake in healthy people. Three important types of reference values included in the DRIs are *Recommended Dietary Allowances* (RDA), *Adequate Intakes* (AI), and *Tolerable Upper Intake Levels* (UL).

The RDA recommends the average daily dietary intake level that is sufficient to meet the nutrient requirements of nearly all (97% to 98%) healthy individuals in each age and gender group. An AI is set when there are insufficient scientific data to establish an RDA. AIs meet or exceed the amount needed to maintain nutritional adequacy in nearly all people. The UL, on the other hand, is the maximum daily intake unlikely to result in adverse health effects.

When can Vitamin A Deficiency Occur?

Vitamin A deficiency is common in developing countries but rarely seen in the United States. Approximately 250,000 to 500,000 malnourished children in the developing world become blind each year from a deficiency of vitamin A. In the United States, vitamin A deficiency is most often associated with strict dietary restrictions and excess alcohol intake. Severe zinc deficiency, which is also associated with strict dietary limitations, often accompanies vitamin A deficiency. Zinc is required to make retinol binding protein (RBP) which transports vitamin A. Therefore, a deficiency in zinc limits the body's ability to move vitamin A stores from the liver to body tissues.

Night blindness is one of the first signs of vitamin A deficiency. In ancient Egypt, it was known that night blindness could be cured by eating liver, which was later found to be a rich source of the vitamin. Vitamin A deficiency contributes to blindness by making the cornea very dry and damaging the retina and cornea.

Vitamin A deficiency diminishes the ability to fight infections. In countries where such deficiency is common and immunization programs are limited, millions of children die each year from complications of infectious diseases such as measles. In vitamin A-deficient individuals, cells lining the lungs lose their ability to remove disease-causing microorganisms. This may contribute to the pneumonia associated with vitamin A deficiency.

There is increased interest in early forms of vitamin A deficiency, described as low storage levels of vitamin A that do not cause obvious deficiency symptoms. This mild degree of vitamin A deficiency may increase children's risk of developing respiratory and diarrheal infections, decrease growth rate, slow bone development, and decrease likelihood of survival from serious illness. Children in the United States who are considered to be at increased risk for subclinical vitamin A deficiency include:

- toddlers and preschool age children;
- children living at or below the poverty level;
- children with inadequate health care or immunizations;
- children living in areas with known nutritional deficiencies;
- recent immigrants or refugees from developing countries with high incidence of vitamin A deficiency or measles; and

- children with diseases of the pancreas, liver, or intestines, or with inadequate fat digestion or absorption.

A deficiency can occur when vitamin A is lost through chronic diarrhea and through an overall inadequate intake, as is often seen with protein-energy malnutrition. Low blood retinol concentrations indicate depleted levels of vitamin A. This occurs with vitamin A deficiency but also can result from an inadequate intake of protein, calories, and zinc, since these nutrients are needed to make RBP. Iron deficiency can also affect vitamin A metabolism, and iron supplements provided to iron-deficient individuals may improve body stores of vitamin A and iron.

Excess alcohol intake depletes vitamin A stores. Also, diets high in alcohol often do not provide recommended amounts of vitamin A. It is very important for people who consume excessive amounts of alcohol to include good sources of vitamin A in their diets. Vitamin A supplements may not be recommended for individuals who abuse alcohol, however, because their livers may be more susceptible to potential toxicity from high doses of vitamin A. A medical doctor will need to evaluate this situation and determine the need for vitamin A supplements.

Who may need Extra Vitamin A to Prevent a Deficiency?

Vitamin A deficiency rarely occurs in the United States, but the World Health Organization (WHO) and the United Nations Children's Fund (UNICEF) recommend vitamin A administration for all children diagnosed with measles in communities where vitamin A deficiency is a serious problem and where death from measles is greater than 1%. In 1994, the American Academy of Pediatrics recommended vitamin A supplements for two subgroups of children likely to be at high risk for subclinical vitamin A deficiency: children aged 6 months to 24 months who are hospitalized with measles, and hospitalized children older than 6 months.

Fat malabsorption can result in diarrhea and prevent normal absorption of vitamin A. Over time this may result in vitamin A deficiency. Those conditions include:

Celiac disease: Often referred to as sprue, celiac disease is a genetic disorder. People with celiac disease become sick when they eat a protein called gluten found in wheat and some other grains. In celiac disease, gluten can trigger damage to the small intestine, where most nutrient absorption occurs. Approximately 30% to 60% of people with celiac disease have gastrointestinal-motility disorders such as diarrhea. They must follow a gluten-free diet to avoid malabsorption and other symptoms.

Crohn's disease: This inflammatory bowel disease affects the small intestine. People with Crohn's disease often experience diarrhea, fat malabsorption, and malnutrition.

Pancreatic disorders: Because the pancreas secretes enzymes that are important for fat absorption, pancreatic disorders often result in fat malabsorption. Without these enzymes, it is difficult to absorb fat. Many people with pancreatic disease take pancreatic enzymes in pill form to prevent fat malabsorption and diarrhea.

Healthy adults usually have a reserve of vitamin A stored in their livers and should not be at risk of deficiency during periods of temporary or short-term fat malabsorption. Long-term problems absorbing fat, however, may result in deficiency. In these instances physicians may recommend additional vitamin A.

Vegetarians who do not consume eggs and dairy foods need provitamin A carotenoids to meet their need for vitamin A. They should include a minimum of five servings of fruits and vegetables in their daily diet and regularly choose dark green leafy vegetables and orange and yellow fruits to consume recommended amounts of vitamin A.

What are some Current Issues and Controversies about Vitamin A?

Vitamin A, Beta Carotene, and Cancer

Dietary intake studies suggest an association between diets rich in beta-carotene and vitamin A and a lower risk of many types of cancer. A higher intake of green and yellow vegetables or other food sources of beta carotene and/or vitamin A may decrease the risk of lung cancer. However, a number of studies that tested the role of beta-carotene supplements in cancer prevention did not find them to protect against the disease. In the Alpha-Tocopherol Beta-Carotene (ATBC) Cancer Prevention Study, more than 29,000 men who regularly smoked cigarettes were randomized to receive 20 mg beta-carotene alone, 50 mg alpha-tocopherol alone, supplements of both, or a placebo for 5 to 8 years. Incidence of lung cancer was 18% higher among men who took the beta-carotene supplement. Eight percent more men in this group died, as compared to those receiving other treatments or placebo. Similar results were seen in the Carotene and Retinol Efficacy Trial (CARET), a lung cancer chemoprevention study that provided subjects with supplements of 30 mg beta-carotene and 25,000 IU retinyl palmitate (a form of vitamin A) or a placebo. This study was stopped after researchers discovered that subjects receiving beta-carotene had a 46% higher risk of dying from lung cancer.

The IOM states that "beta-carotene supplements are not advisable for the general population," although they also state that this advice "does not pertain to the possible use of supplemental beta-carotene as a provitamin A source for the prevention of vitamin A deficiency in populations with inadequate vitamin A".

Vitamin A and Osteoporosis

Osteoporosis, a disorder characterized by porous and weak bones, is a serious health problem for more than 10 million Americans, 80% of whom are women. Another 18 million Americans have decreased bone density which precedes the development of osteoporosis. Many factors increase the risk for developing osteoporosis, including being female, thin, inactive, at advanced age, and having a family history of osteoporosis. An inadequate dietary intake of calcium, cigarette smoking, and excessive intake of alcohol also increase the risk.

Researchers are now examining a potential new risk factor for osteoporosis: an excess intake of vitamin A. Animal, human, and laboratory research suggests an association between greater vitamin A intake and weaker bones. Worldwide, the highest incidence of osteoporosis occurs in northern Europe, a population with a high intake of vitamin A. However, decreased biosynthesis of vitamin D associated with lower levels of sun exposure in this population may also contribute to this finding.

One small study of nine healthy individuals in Sweden found that the amount of vitamin A in one serving of liver may impair the ability of vitamin D to promote calcium absorption. To further test the association between excess dietary intakes of vitamin A and increased risk for hip fractures, researchers in Sweden compared bone mineral density and retinol intake in approximately 250 women with a first hip fracture to 875 age-matched controls.

They found that a dietary retinol intake greater than 1,500 mcg/day (more than twice the recommended intake for women) was associated with reduced bone mineral density and increased risk of hip fracture as compared to women who consumed less than 500 mcg/day.

This issue was also examined by researchers with the Nurses Health Study, who looked at the association between vitamin A intake and hip fractures in over 72,000 postmenopausal women. Women who consumed the most vitamin A in foods and supplements (3,000 mcg or more per day as retinol equivalents, which is over three times the recommended intake) had a significantly increased risk of experiencing a hip fracture as compared to those consuming the least amount (less than 1,250 mcg/day). The effect was lessened by use of estrogens. These observations raise questions about the effect of retinol because retinol intakes greater than 2,000 mcg/day were associated with an increased risk of hip fracture as compared to intakes less than 500 mcg.

A longitudinal study in more than 2,000 Swedish men compared blood levels of retinol to the incidence of fractures in men. The investigators found that the risk of fractures was greatest in men with the highest blood levels of retinol (more than 75 mcg per deciliter [dL]). Men with blood retinol levels in the 99th percentile (greater than 103 mcg per dL) had an overall risk of fracture that exceeded the risk among men with lower levels of retinol by a factor of seven. High vitamin A intake, however, does not necessarily equate to high blood levels of retinol. Age, gender, hormones, and genetics also influence these levels. Researchers did not find any association between blood levels of beta-carotene and risk of hip fracture. Researchers' findings, which are consistent with the results of animal, in vitro (laboratory), and epidemiologic studies, suggest that intakes above the UL, or approximately two times that of the RDA for vitamin A, may pose subtle risks to bone health that require further study.

The Centers for Disease Control and Prevention (CDC) reviewed data from NHANES III (1988-94) to determine whether there was any association between bone mineral density and blood levels of retinyl esters, a form of vitamin A. No significant associations between blood levels of retinyl esters and bone mineral density in 5,800 subjects were found.

There is no evidence of an association between beta-carotene intake, especially from fruits and vegetables, and increased risk of osteoporosis. Current evidence points to a possible association with vitamin A as retinol only. If you have specific questions regarding your intake of vitamin A and risk of osteoporosis, discuss this information with your physician or other qualified healthcare provider to determine what's best for your personal health.

What are the Health risks of Too much Vitamin A?

Hypervitaminosis A refers to high storage levels of vitamin A in the body that can lead to toxic symptoms. There are four major adverse effects of hypervitaminosis A: birth defects, liver abnormalities, reduced bone mineral density that may result in osteoporosis, and central nervous system disorders.

Toxic symptoms can also arise after consuming very large amounts of preformed vitamin A over a short period of time. Signs of acute toxicity include nausea and vomiting, headache, dizziness, blurred vision, and muscular uncoordination. Although hypervitaminosis A can occur when large amounts of liver are regularly consumed, most cases result from taking excess amounts of the nutrient in supplements.

The IOM has established Tolerable Upper Intake Levels (ULs) for vitamin A that apply to healthy populations. The UL was established to help prevent the risk of vitamin A toxicity. The risk of adverse health effects increases at intakes greater than the UL. The UL does not apply to malnourished individuals receiving vitamin A either periodically or through fortification programs as a means of preventing vitamin A deficiency. It also does not apply to individuals being treated with vitamin A by medical doctors for diseases such as retinitis pigmentosa.

What are the Health Risks of Too Many Carotenoids?

Provitamin A carotenoids such as beta-carotene are generally considered safe because they are not associated with specific adverse health effects. Their conversion to vitamin A decreases when body stores are full. A high intake of provitamin A carotenoids can turn the skin yellow, but this is not considered dangerous to health.

Clinical trials that associated beta-carotene supplements with a greater incidence of lung cancer and death in current smokers raise concerns about the effects of beta-carotene supplements on long-term health; however, conflicting studies make it difficult to interpret the health risk. For example, the Physicians Health Study compared the effects of taking 50 mg beta-carotene every other day to a placebo in over 22,000 male physicians and found no adverse health effects. Also, a trial that tested the ability of four different nutrient combinations to help prevent the development of esophageal and gastric cancers in 30,000 men and women in China suggested that after five years those participants who took a combination of beta-carotene, selenium, and vitamin E had a 13% reduction in cancer deaths. In one lung cancer trial, men who consumed more than 11 grams/day of alcohol (approximately one drink per day) were more likely to show an adverse response to beta-carotene supplements, which may suggest a potential relationship between alcohol and beta-carotene.

The IOM did not set ULs for carotene or other carotenoids. Instead, it concluded that beta-carotene supplements are not advisable for the general population. As stated earlier, however, they may be appropriate as a provitamin A source for the prevention of vitamin A deficiency in specific populations.

Vitamin A Intakes and Healthful Diets

According to the 2005 *Dietary Guidelines for Americans*, "Nutrient needs should be met primarily through consuming foods. Foods provide an array of nutrients and other compounds that may have beneficial effects on health. In certain cases, fortified foods and dietary supplements may be useful sources of one or more nutrients that otherwise might be consumed in less than recommended amounts. However, dietary supplements, while recommended in some cases, cannot replace a healthful diet."

Dietary Supplement Fact Sheet: Vitamin B6

Vitamin B_6: What is it?

Vitamin B_6 is a water-soluble vitamin that exists in three major chemical forms: pyridoxine, pyridoxal, and pyridoxamine. It performs a wide variety of functions in your body and is essential for your good health. For example, vitamin B_6 is needed for more than 100 enzymes involved in protein metabolism. It is also essential for red blood cell metabolism. The nervous and immune systems need vitamin B_6 to function efficiently, and it is also needed for the conversion of tryptophan (an amino acid) to niacin (a vitamin). Hemoglobin within red blood cells carries oxygen to tissues. Your body needs vitamin B_6 to make hemoglobin. Vitamin B_6 also helps increase the amount of oxygen carried by hemoglobin. A vitamin B_6 deficiency can result in a form of anemia that is similar to iron deficiency anemia.

An immune response is a broad term that describes a variety of biochemical changes that occur in an effort to fight off infections. Calories, protein, vitamins, and minerals are important to your immune defenses because they promote the growth of white blood cells that directly fight infections. Vitamin B_6, through its involvement in protein metabolism and cellular growth, is important to the immune system. It helps maintain the health of lymphoid organs (thymus, spleen, and lymph nodes) that make your white blood cells. Animal studies show that a vitamin B_6 deficiency can decrease your antibody production and suppress your immune response.

Vitamin B_6 also helps maintain your blood glucose (sugar) within a normal range. When caloric intake is low your body needs vitamin B_6 to help convert stored carbohydrate or other nutrients to glucose to maintain normal blood sugar levels. While a shortage of vitamin B_6 will limit these functions, supplements of this vitamin do not enhance them in well-nourished individuals.

What Foods Provide Vitamin B_6?

Vitamin B_6 is found in a wide variety of foods including fortified cereals, beans, meat, poultry, fish, and some fruits and vegetables. The table of selected food sources of vitamin B_6 suggests many dietary sources of B_6.

What is the Recommended Dietary Allowance for vitamin B_6 for Adults?

The Recommended Dietary Allowance (RDA) is the average daily dietary intake level that is sufficient to meet the nutrient requirements of nearly all (97 to 98 percent) healthy individuals in each life-stage and gender group.

When can a Vitamin B_6 Deficiency Occur?

Clinical signs of vitamin B_6 deficiency are rarely seen in the United States. Many older Americans, however, have low blood levels of vitamin B_6, which may suggest a marginal or sub-optimal vitamin B_6 nutritional status. Vitamin B_6 deficiency can occur in individuals with poor quality diets that are deficient in many nutrients. Symptoms occur during later stages of deficiency, when intake has been very low for an extended time. Signs of vitamin B_6 deficiency include dermatitis (skin inflammation), glossitis (a sore tongue), depression, confusion, and convulsions. Vitamin B_6 deficiency also can cause anemia. Some of these symptoms can also result from a variety of medical conditions other than vitamin B_6 deficiency. It is important to have a physician evaluate these symptoms so that appropriate medical care can be given.

Who may need Extra Vitamin B_6 to Prevent a Deficiency?

Individuals with a poor quality diet or an inadequate B_6 intake for an extended period may benefit from taking a vitamin B_6 supplement if they are unable to increase their dietary intake of vitamin B_6. Alcoholics and older adults are more likely to have inadequate vitamin B_6 intakes than other segments of the population because they may have limited variety in their diet. Alcohol also promotes the destruction and loss of vitamin B_6 from the body.

Asthmatic children treated with the medicine theophylline may need to take a vitamin B_6 supplement. Theophylline decreases body stores of vitamin B_6, and theophylline-induced seizures have been linked to low body stores of the vitamin. A physician should be consulted about the need for a vitamin B_6 supplement when theophylline is prescribed.

What are some Current Issues and Controversies about Vitamin B_6?

Vitamin B_6 and the Nervous System

Vitamin B_6 is needed for the synthesis of neurotransmitters such as serotonin and dopamine. These neurotransmitters are required for normal nerve cell communication. Researchers have been investigating the relationship between vitamin B_6 status and a wide variety of neurologic conditions such as seizures, chronic pain, depression, headache, and Parkinson's disease.

Lower levels of serotonin have been found in individuals suffering from depression and migraine headaches. So far, however, vitamin B_6 supplements have not proved effective for relieving these symptoms. One study found that a sugar pill was just as likely as vitamin B_6 to relieve headaches and depression associated with low dose oral contraceptives. Alcohol abuse can result in neuropathy, abnormal nerve sensations in the arms and legs. A poor dietary intake contributes to this neuropathy and dietary supplements that include vitamin B_6 may prevent or decrease its incidence.

Vitamin B_6 and Carpal Tunnel Syndrome

Vitamin B_6 was first recommended for carpal tunnel syndrome almost 30 years ago. Several popular books still recommend taking 100 to 200 milligrams (mg) of vitamin B_6 daily to treat carpal tunnel syndrome, even though scientific studies do not indicate it is effective. Anyone taking large doses of vitamin B_6 supplements for carpal tunnel syndrome needs to be aware that the Institute of Medicine recently established an upper tolerable limit of 100 mg per day for adults. There are documented cases in the literature of neuropathy caused by excessive vitamin B_6 taken for treatment of carpal tunnel syndrome.

Vitamin B_6 and Premenstrual Syndrome

Vitamin B_6 has become a popular remedy for treating the discomforts associated with premenstrual syndrome (PMS). Unfortunately, clinical trials have failed to support any significant benefit. One recent study indicated that a sugar pill was as likely to relieve symptoms of PMS as vitamin B_6. In addition, vitamin B_6 toxicity has been seen in increasing numbers of women taking vitamin B_6 supplements for PMS. One review indicated that neuropathy was present in 23 of 58 women taking daily vitamin B_6 supplements for PMS whose blood levels of B_6 were above normal. There is no convincing scientific evidence to support recommending vitamin B_6 supplements for PMS.

Vitamin B_6 and Interactions with Medications

There are many drugs that interfere with the metabolism of vitamin B_6. Isoniazid, which is used to treat tuberculosis, and L-DOPA, which is used to treat a variety of neurologic problems such as Parkinson's disease, alter the activity of vitamin B_6. There is disagreement about the need for routine vitamin B_6 supplementation when taking isoniazid. Acute isoniazid toxicity can result in coma and seizures that are reversed by vitamin B_6, but in a group of children receiving isoniazid, no cases of neurological or neuropsychiatric problems were observed regardless of whether or not they took a vitamin B_6 supplement.

Some doctors recommend taking a supplement that provides 100% of the RDA for B_6 when isoniazid is prescribed, which is usually enough to prevent symptoms of vitamin B_6 deficiency. It is important to consult with a physician about the need for a vitamin B_6 supplement when taking isoniazid.

What is the Velationship between Vitamin B_6, Homocysteine, and Heart Disease?

A deficiency of vitamin B_6, folic acid, or vitamin B12 may increase your level of homocysteine, an amino acid normally found in your blood. There is evidence that an elevated homocysteine level is an independent risk factor for heart disease and stroke. The evidence suggests that high levels of homocysteine may damage coronary arteries or make it easier for blood clotting cells called platelets to clump together and form a clot. However, there is currently no evidence available to suggest that lowering homocysteine level with vitamins will reduce your risk of heart disease. Clinical intervention trials are needed to determine whether supplementation with vitamin B_6, folic acid, or vitamin B12 can help protect you against developing coronary heart disease.

What is the Health Risk of Too much Vitamin B_6?

Too much vitamin B_6 can result in nerve damage to the arms and legs. This neuropathy is usually related to high intake of vitamin B_6 from supplements, and is reversible when supplementation is stopped. According to the Institute of Medicine, "Several reports show sensory neuropathy at doses lower than 500 mg per day". As previously mentioned, the Food and Nutrition Board of the Institute of Medicine has established an upper tolerable intake level (UL) for vitamin B_6 of 100 mg per day for all adults. "As intake increases above the UL, the risk of adverse effects increases."

Vitamin B_6 Intakes and Healthful Diets

Vitamin B_6 is found in a wide variety of foods. Foods such as fortified breakfast cereals, fish including salmon and tuna fish, meats such as pork and chicken, bananas, beans and peanut butter, and many vegetables will contribute to your vitamin B_6 intake. According to the 2005 *Dietary Guidelines for Americans*, "Nutrient needs should be met primarily through consuming foods. Foods provide an array of nutrients and other compounds that may have beneficial effects on health. In certain cases, fortified foods and dietary supplements may be useful sources of one or more nutrients that otherwise might be consumed in less than recommended amounts. However, dietary supplements, while recommended in some cases, cannot replace a healthful diet."

The Dietary Guidelines for Americans describes a healthy diet as one that:

- emphasizes a variety of fruits, vegetables, whole grains, and fat-free or low-fat milk and milk products;
- includes lean meats, poultry, fish, beans, eggs, and nuts;
- is low in saturated fats, trans fats, cholesterol, salt (sodium), and added sugars; and
- stays within your daily calorie needs.

For more information about building a healthful diet, refer to the Dietary Guidelines for Americans and the U.S. Department of Agriculture's food guidance system, MyPyramid.

Mineral Resources

India has a large number of economically useful minerals and they constitute one-quarter of the world's known mineral resources. About two-thirds of its iron deposits lies in a belt along Orissa and Bihar border. Other haemaite deposits are found in Madhya Pradesh, Karnataka, Maharastra and Goa. Magnetite iron-ore is found in Tamilnadu, Bihar and Himachal.

India has the world's largest deposits of coal. Bituminous coal is found in Jharia and Bokaro in Bihar and Ranigunj in West Bengal. Lignite coals are found in Neyveli in Tamilnadu.

Next to Russia, India has the largest supply of Manganese. The manganese mining areas are Madhya Pradesh, Maharastra and Bihar-Orissa area. Chromite deposits are found in Bihar, Cuttack district in Orissa, Krishna district in Andhra and Mysore and Hassan in Karnataka. Bauxite deposits are found in western Bihar, southwest Kashmir, Central Tamilnadu, and parts of Kerala, U.P, Maharastra and Karnataka.

India also produces third quarters of the world's mica. Belts of high quality mica are, Bihar, Andhra and Rajasthan. Gypsum reserves are in Tamilnadu and Rajasthan. Nickel ore is found in Cuttack in Bihar and Mayurbanj in Orissa. Ileminite reserves are in Kerala and along the east and the west coastal beaches.

Silimanite reserves are in Sonapahar of Meghalaya and in Pipra in M.P. Copper ore bearing areas are Agnigundala in Andhra, Singhbum in Bihar, Khetri and Dartiba in Rajasthan and parts of Sikkhim and Karnataka. The Ramagiri field in Andhra, Kolar and Hutti in Karnataka are the important gold mines. The Panna diamond belt is the only diamond producing area in the country, which covers the districts of Panna, Chatarpur and Satna in Madya Pradesh, as well as some parts of Banda in Uttar Pradesh.

Petroleum deposits are found in Assam and Gujarat. Fresh reserves were located off Bombay. The potential oil bearing areas are, Assam, Tripura, Manipur, west Bengal, Punjab, Himachal, Kutch and the Andamans. India also possesses the all-too valuable nuclear uranium as well as some varieties of rare earths.

Soils

Soil-types in India can be classified into three groups. The first group comprises of the alluvial, black and red soils, which are basically fertile and are arable and cultivatable.

The second group consists of the peaty and marshy, the saline and alkaline soils which are potentially arable.

The third group is the laterite and forest and hill soils, which are not at all suitable for cultivation.

The main alluvial area is found in the Indo-Gangetic plain and the Peninsular regions. The main crops are rice, sugarcane and wheat. Black soil is found in the northwestern regions and in the Deccan lava areas and Tamilnadu.

Black soil is especially suited for cotton. Red soil is particularly rich in potash and is found in northern and central India. The peaty and marshy soils are found in the Bengal deltas, Saline and alkaline soils in the semi-arid regions of Bihar, U.P, Gujarat, Punjab and Rajasthan. Desert soils are found in the minimum rain receiving areas of Gujarat, Punjab and Rajasthan. Laterite soil is common in the low hills of Andhra, Karnataka, Kerala, Madhya Pradesh, Orissa and Assam.

There are two crop seasons: Kharif, Rabi. The major Kharif crops are rice, jowar, maize, cotton, sugarcane, sesame and groundnut. The Rabi crops are wheat, jowar, barley, gram, rapeseed and mustard and the summer crops are rice, maize, groundnut and some cash crops.

6

Vitamin A and Food: The Current Situation

Overview: What this Book is About

The purpose of this book is to contribute to understanding the sociocultural and environmental factors that affect vitamin A intake and responses to vitamin A deficiency. The enterprise described here is based on the assumption that knowledge about the sociocultural and environmental contexts of vitamin A is essential for instituting and sustaining food-based prevention of vitamin A deficiency. It describes how a group of nutritionists and anthropologists worked together to create a protocol to evaluate the natural food sources of vitamin A in areas at risk for vitamin A deficiency. A manual describing the creation of a locally contextual protocol is a companion to this volume, and is titled *Community Assessment of Natural Food Sources of Vitamin A: Guidelines for an Ethnographic Protocol*. The protocol combines nutrition and anthropological tools, and is called focused ethnographic study (FES). FES is within the realm of rapid assessment procedures (RAP) of anthropologically-based methods for relatively rapid evaluation of health problems and prevention programs. In this case, FES is applied to understand how culture, environment, and food can prevent vitamin A deficiency.

We wrote this book for development planners in health, agriculture, education, or other: areas. It is also suitable for scholars and students of nutrition, public health, agriculture, anthropology and human cultural ecology to describe and discuss the issues surrounding the use of natural food sources for the prevention of vitamin A deficiency. Ethnographic research tools and their testing in a broad range of cultures and environments in five developing countries are outlined, as are the findings from this work. Chapters contributed by the investigators in these countries describe the suitability and generalizability of the research tools, the data generated, practical applications, and directions for policy.

The Vitamin A Situation

Vitamin A deficiency is a major global problem, affecting populations in developing areas of more than seventy-five countries where clinical and subclinical conditions have been observed (McLaren, 1986; WHO, 1994). Worldwide, this public health problem involves 2.8 to 3 million children with clinical deficiency and 251 million with subclinical deficiency. Vitamin A affects many physiological systems; it plays an essential role in vision and eye health, and it affects growth and susceptibility to infection (particularly diarrhea and measles) and anemia in children. The consequences of vitamin A deficiency include blindness, poor growth, severe infection, and death; its control and prevention are central in child health and survival programs (Wasantwisut and Attig, 1995). The International Conference on Nutrition (WHO/FAO, 1993) pledged the elimination of vitamin A deficiency by the year 2000.

The prevention of vitamin A deficiency at the community and household levels depends on the availability and consumption of vitamin A-rich food from either plant or animal sources, and on the presence of other dietary factors needed for bioavailability, absorption, and metabolism of vitamin A, such as sufficient fat, protein, zinc, and other essential nutrients (Booth et al., 1992). Inadequate intake of the appropriate quantity and quality of food to meet vitamin A requirements affects all members of populations with deficiency, but is most common in infants, young children, and pregnant/lactating women. Extensive reviews of the variety of foods containing vitamin A and the effects of vitamin A deficiency are presented elsewhere, and will not be covered here.

Proposed Solutions to the Problem

Actions aimed at preventing vitamin A deficiency may draw on several potential types of solutions. Solutions at the community level can be diverse and may involve a variety of multisectoral community and development programs. Public health programs in breastfeeding, immunizations, family planning, health education, and maternal and child care are relevant, as are agricultural extension, agricultural education, horticultural promotion, etc. Education sector involvement might include food education, school gardens, and hygiene promotion for the prevention of infection (WHO/UNICEF, 1994). The training of professionals delivering services and programs is key to appropriate activities that will effect positive change.

In general, providing more vitamin A to vulnerable populations has been undertaken in three major intervention activity categories: distribution of large doses of vitamin A supplements, fortification of selected food items, and dietary modification to include more vitamin A-rich food. These have been accomplished in context with public health, agriculture, and/or education sector programs as noted above. A combination of these activities together with various public health measures and economic improvements is considered appropriate and effective (Subcommittee on Nutrition, 1994).

It is recognized that distribution of supplements provides a quick-acting intervention, best accomplished with sufficient health infrastructure to targeted populations, in particular to children at risk for protein-energy malnutrition and various infections. Improving vitamin A status in this way resulted in reduced mortality and morbidity (Beaton et al., 1993).

Fortification of food with vitamin A and its distribution is most feasible where the processed food industry is well-developed and supported, which may not be the case in resource-poor areas where vitamin A is lacking in the diet, deficiency is most extreme, and various barriers exist for the most vulnerable to access fortified food (Trowbridge et al., 1993). Examples of vitamin A fortification programs have been reported (McKigney, 1983), and include cod liver oil in margarine, and vitamin A in milk, sugar, and monosodium glutamate.

Lack of vitamin A in the diet is the root cause of vitamin A deficiency and dietary modification is generally regarded as the ultimate goal for the prevention of vitamin A deficiency in all members of households and communities. This is a long-term approach and requires improvements in food availability and education of those most vulnerable to take advantage of improved food supplies. One important dietary modification is the sustained breastfeeding of infants when mothers have sufficient dietary vitamin A. It is thought that the most effective dietary modification programs target improvement of dietary intake of vitamin A for women in the child-bearing years, during pregnancy and lactation, and for young children at weaning and during rapid growth and development.

Considerations for Sustainability

To solve the root cause of vitamin A deficiency, more vitamin A must be present in the diets of vulnerable people. Program planners and development leaders in health, agriculture, education, and other sectors must understand the culture and ecology of food availability and consumption at the local level. This understanding will lead to improvements in the dietary quality and quantity of vitamin A, through dietary modification and food fortification programs. With respect to food supplies, it requires understanding the species of vitamin A-rich foods that are culturally acceptable and available, their seasonality, methods of preservation and preparation, and barriers to their use due to cost, health beliefs, or other reasons of accessibility are also important. Only when these factors are known will agricultural, food processing, social marketing, and public health education programs have a sustained impact on behavior change and in improving dietary modification for vitamin A (Wasantwisut and Attig, 1995).

The elements of understanding the culture and ecology of food availability and consumption at the local level are addressed in several avenues of scientific communications including agriculture, food science, nutrition and social science journals, and other publications. The use of food sources to solve the vitamin A problem has recently been reported by Gopalan et al., 1992; IVACG, 1992; Smitasiri et al., 1993; Wasantwisut et al., 1994; and Wasantwisut and Attig, 1995. These publications give examples of successful programs to improve dietary vitamin A.

Focused Ethnography to Understand Local Culture and Environment for Vitamin A Programs

The methodology that was used in the studies reported in this book can be described as focused ethnography. We drew on research techniques from anthropology and nutrition to create a manual that facilitates the collection and interpretation of data on cultural and environmental aspects of food use and vitamin A deficiency.

Focused ethnography evolved as an approach based on principles of contemporary method and theory in cultural anthropology, modified by the requirements and constraints of program development in public health, agriculture/horticulture, and other public service sectors (Gove and Pelto, 1994). These methods are akin to the pioneering developments widely known as rapid assessment procedures (RAPs) (Scrimshaw and Hurtado, 1987; Scrimshaw and Gleason, 1992). FES shares many fundamental characteristics with general ethnography:

- Data-gathering is carried out in a specific locality (community or regional cluster of communities).
- In-depth key-informant interviewing is a primary data-gathering.
- The research design produces a qualitative description of cultural and behavioural patterns, that is, the models or systems of relationships among elements in a sociocultural domain.
- Data-gathering places an emphasis on describing the perspective of the client (their own language, concepts, and cultural beliefs) the *emic* perspective.
- The theoretical approach of cultural ecology directs data-gathering, that is, attention is given to the description of culture, behavior/practices, and to the physical and social environment.

In contrast to general ethnography, program requirements determine several special features of the FES approach:

- Data-collection is focused on a specific set of predetermined questions. In our work the questions relate to: (i) identifying key foods, particularly those important for vitamin A; (ii) cultural beliefs regarding these foods; (iii) food acquisition, preparation and storage; (iv) patterns of food use and the vitamin A content of diets; and (v) community perceptions about the signs and symptoms of vitamin A deficiency.
- To be feasible with respect to cost, time, and organizational/political logistics, the Protocol is designed to be completed in a short period of time - six to eight weeks.

- Standardized methods are applied in which data-collection is very clearly specified, and forms for data-recording and analysis are provided. As a result, the investigator and field assistants have a dear picture of the expected products of the dare. It is therefore possible to have interviewers without university training.
- A manual of the procedures in the protocol provides a framework for training the field team. A pre-study training workshop, with step-by-step instruction in data-collection, insures that interviewers fully understand the purposes and procedures, and that they record data accurately and completely.

The FES approach is intended to demystify the processes of qualitative data-collection, in this case to understand how culture, environment, and food can prevent vitamin A deficiency. FES approaches have been developed for acute respiratory illness, malaria, and diarrhea (Herman and Bentley, 1993; WHO, 1993a, 1993b, 1994). This approach has also been applied to situation analysis of high risk behaviors in relation to HIV/AIDS (Pelto, 1993; NACO, 1994). Similar manuals, some of which include methods for assessing child labour situations in countries such as Bangladesh, are in various stages of preparation (personal communication, P. J. Pelto, 1994).

The Complexities of Understanding Vitamin A in Food and Diets: The Problem

We began our work with the premise that to prevent vitamin A deficiency, more vitamin A needs to be present in diets of those vulnerable to deficiency. Where deficiency exists the solution rests in getting more vitamin A into diets on a regular basis. The problem, therefore, is to find out how to do this - and this requires knowing the following:

- How much vitamin A is already in the diet: What and how much food is eaten, what is the vitamin A content of that food?
- Why people eat what they do: what are the food beliefs and behaviors that are practiced?
- What would bring about positive dietary change to prevent vitamin A deficiency: What vitamin A-rich food is available in the local environment that can be used to better

advantage, perhaps by better processing? What other dietary and health factors would make dietary vitamin A more physiologically active? How and why would those who are vulnerable to deficiency change their behavior to improve their diet?

In this chapter we review current knowledge of food sources of vitamin A present in nature (natural food sources), and discuss the current status of food composition data. This is followed by a discussion of factors that influence dietary intake of foods rich in vitamin A activity (that is, both retinol and carotene), and the impact these have on assessment of diets for this nutrient. We also include brief reviews of methods that have been used to assess diets for vitamin A in populations vulnerable to deficiency, and of food programs that have improved dietary vitamin A.

Overview of Natural Food Sources of Vitamin A

Vitamin A in food is found as retinol or as carotenes. Retinol is found exclusively in animal foods including eggs, milk, and milk products (Heinonen, 1991; Booth et al., 1992). Storage of retinol in animal species is not evenly distributed among tissues, with the highest levels of preformed vitamin A found in animal and fish livers and fish oils (Leth and Jacobsen, 1993; Morrison and Kuhnlein, 1993). Retinol is also stored in the intestinal walls of fish, in the body fat of eels, and in the eyes of certain species of shrimp. With the exception of fowl, meat products, including beef and pork, do not contain significant quantities of preformed vitamin A.

Carotenoids are found primarily in plant foods (Simpson and Tsou, 1986), whereas meats, fats, and dairy products are reportedly low in carotenoid content (Heinonen, 1991). The richest known sources of provitamin A are the palm oils. Red palm oil, a common cooking product in West Africa, is usually cited as having the highest concentration of provitamin A activity (Cottrell, 1991).

However, recent studies indicate that the oil of the buriti palm tree has a tenfold greater concentration of vitamin A activity when compared with red palm oil (Rains-Mariath et al., 1989). Other food categories rich in provitamin A activity include dark green, leafy vegetables; algae; red/yellow vegetables and tubers; and red/orange fruits, flowers, and juices (Booth et al., 1992). White roots and tubers and whole grains are considered very low in provitamin

A content. Colour intensity, however, is not necessarily a reliable indicator of biologically active carotenoids. For example, the chlorophyll of green leafy vegetables masks the carotenoid pigmentation, yet as a group these vegetables are excellent sources of provitamin A (Simpson and Tsou, 1986).

Vitamin A Food Composition Data

Nomenclature

Vitamin A can be obtained in two forms from the diet: preformed vitamin A, also referred to as retinol, and provitamin A, also known as the carotenoid precursors that are biologically active as retinol. The term vitamin A is used in two contexts; a generic term for all b-ionone derivatives, excluding the carotenoids; and as a generic term for all those compounds, including carotenoids, that are precursors to retinol and can reverse symptoms of deficiency associated with this fat-soluble vitamin (Davison et al., 1993).

The parent compound of vitamin A is all-trans retir.ol, which is an isoprenoid compound found in animal tissue. The major storage form, retinyl palmitate, is an ester of a fatty acid chain, 90% of which is stored in the liver. Carotenoids are a class of more than 600 known naturally occurring pigments found in certain fruits, vegetables, and oils, and animal foods, such as egg yolk and shrimp (Daun, 1988; Erdman, 1988). The nutritional functions of the carotenoids have recently been reviewed in response to the interest in the role of carotenoids as chemoprotective agents. Only fifty of these carotenoids, of which b-carotene comprises 10% to 15% of total serum carotenoids in humans, are known to be converted to retinol by oxidative cleavage (Thurnham, 1994).

Units of Expression

Nutrient values of preformed vitamin A and provitamin A can be combined into a single numerical value of vitamin A activity (Thompson, 1986). Originally, the internationally accepted values were international units (IU). One IU was defined as 0.30 mg of all-trans retinol, or 0.60 mg of all-trans b-carotene. These units are still found in many food composition tables.

In theory, one mmol of all-trans b-carotene should cleave to form 2 mmols of all-trans retinol (Olson, 1989). However, the absorption rate for carotene is 20% to 50% compared with that of retinol, which is estimated at 70% to 90%, and the absorption of the former becomes less efficient with increasing levels of intake (Olson, 1990). Discrepancies in the conversion of carotenoids to retinol have been attributed to factors influencing bioavailability and absorption, including the amount of carotenoid in the diet, interactions with other carotenoids, dietary fat and fibre, nutritional deficiencies of zinc and/or protein, and the substrate requirements for absorption (Olson, 1986; Erdman, 1988).

Analysis of Vitamin A

With recent interest in the possible link between cancer and the intake of carotenoids , an extensive literature has emerged describing the available methods for analyzing carotenoids, particularly those by high-pressure liquid chromatography (HPLC). Several thorough reviews exist, with descriptions of the theoretical and practical applications of each method.

Carotenoid analysis is accomplished by extraction, followed by partial purification, separation according to hydroxyl groups, isolation by chromatography, and then measurement by spectral absorption (Lee et al., 1989). The Association of Official Analytical Chemists (AOAC) method for carotene analysis is an open-column chromatography method using a magnesium oxide column, which separates carotenoids from xanthophylls on the basis of polarity, followed by visible absorption spectrophotometry (AOAC, 1984). The first fraction eluted is assumed to be, b-carotene.

Recent studies in carotenoid analyses revealed that assumptions inherent in the AOAC method are incorrect, so much of the published provitamin A nutrient data are overestimates of the true carotenoid value of certain foods (Simpson and Tsou, 1986). This is most critical for food items with mixed carotenoid activity, particularly those carotenoids that do not have vitamin A activity but elute out with the b-carotene fraction.

Reversed-phase HPLC is rapidly becoming the preferred method for carotenoid analysis, given its flexibility in the identification and quantification of the numerous carotenoids (Rizzolo and Polesello, 1992). The use of HPLC is also becoming the preferred method of retinol analysis. However, the complexity of carotenoids, their isomers, and other chemical substances in foods prevented the development of a single HPLC method for carotenoid analysis (Lee et al., 1989) until recently. Also, while the methodologies using HPLC for carotenoid and retinol analyses are evolving, standardization among and within different laboratories is difficult to attain. In a recent study on the intercomparison of methods used for vitamin A determination of foods, the results for retinol analyses in milk agreed very well (Hollman et al., 1993). However, comparison of b-carotene contents in green beans analyzed by different laboratories showed poor agreement. Another limiting factor for all analytical methods, particularly HPLC, is the cost of equipment and solvents, which is prohibitive in most developing regions (Rodriguez-Amaya, 1989).

Effect of Food Processing on Vitamin A

Carotenoids and retinol are affected by pH, enzymatic activity, light, and oxidation associated with the conjugated double bond system (Elkins and Dudek, 1985). The chemical changes occurring in carotenoids during processing has been reviewed by Simpson (1986). Fresh plant tissue may contain enzymes that are only activated during and following processing. Therefore, the preformed and provitamin A content of the raw form of a food item may be reduced as a consequence of food preparation. The most dramatic example of this is found in red palm oil, which in its raw form is considered one of the richest sources of provitamin A (Cottrell, 1991). After heating to 200°C for thirty minutes, the b-carotene content becomes negligible.

Numerous reports document changes in carotenoid content attributed to various cooking methods. As a general rule, foods boiled in an open container show the greatest losses. Regardless of the method used, most report that dehydration significantly reduces the carotene content in vegetables, which has implications for storage of seasonally available foods (Renquist et al., 1978; Park, 1987). However, in a study that controlled for complete extraction of carotenoids in raw samples, Khachik et al., (1992) reported no significant changes in the b-carotene content in several green vegetables, after microwaving, steaming, or boiling. Likewise, the carotenoid content of tomatoes did not change when they were dehydrated. It should be noted though that dehydration was performed in a laboratory environment and by sundrying.

Sweeney and Marsh (1971) reported that processing of fruits and vegetables induced isomerization of carotenoids, resulting in an estimated 15% to 20% reduction in vitamin A potency in green leafy vegetables, and 30% to 35% in yellow vegetables. Traditional processing methods, including preservation, induce formation of the cis-isomer of carotenoids from the all-trans form (O'Neil and Schwartz, 1992). With increased temperature, the presence of light, and catalysts such as acid, isomerization from the bans form to the cis form of carotenoids increases (Chandler and Schwartz, 1988).

The documentation of processing effects on retinol is less abundant. Losses of up to 40% in fish sources rich in vitamin A have been reported following boiling (Burt, 1988). In a study on the traditional food system of the Sahtu Dene/Metis, there were no consistent trends in retinol levels between raw and cooked forms of various food samples probably due to biological variation (Morrison and Kuhnlein, 1993). Smoking fish and mammal meat did not appear to reduce retinol levels.

Food Composition Tables for Vitamin A

Reasonably accurate food composition data is needed to calculate the vitamin A intake of a population from dietary surveys, or to select food items rich in this nutrient, for education programs. However, food tables contain nutrient values from chemical analyses of foods, with no allowance for the biological utilization of the item (Ferrando, 1987), so these values are estimates, at best, of active vitamin A. The limitations of vitamin A nutrient values in food composition tables have been reviewed (Simpson and Tsou, 1986; Booth et al., 1992); in their current state, most contain inconsistencies in preformed and provitamin A values. Differential use of units and conversion rates and reliance on outdated analytical techniques limit their use in the identification of vitamin A-rich foods and the calculation of dietary intake of vitamin A, particularly from carotenoid sources.

With the strong evidence that an increased intake of fruits and vegetables is associated with a reduced risk of certain types of cancers, the current food composition database of carotenoid values for foods consumed the United States was recently re-evaluated (Mangers et al., 1993). An artificial intelligence system was developed to evaluate existing carotenoid data, including indicators of data quality, and to prioritize future laboratory analyses. Only HPLC-generated data were incorporated into the database to eliminate the problem of overestimation associated with analytical methods that quantify total carotenoids instead of individual carotenoids. A modified version of this artificial intelligence system was subsequently used by West and Poortvliet (1993) to evaluate existing carotenoid data for developing countries. Most carotenoid values reported are for vegetables and fruits, although there were limited data for meat, fish, fats, eggs, cereals, and dairy products. Given the paucity of carotenoid data in many geographical regions, particularly African, these authors used less stringent criteria for including food composition data into their data base. In particular, carotenoid data generated from methods other than HPLC were included. This decision was made by West and Poortvliet (1993) in recognition of the limited number of resources available to laboratories in many developing countries.

A common criticism of food composition data is the inadequate amount of information available on sampling methods. Regardless of the analytical method selected for carotenoid and retinol determination, error introduced during the collection and preparation of samples can create large discrepancies in the final nutrient values. Sources of sampling and preparation error have been reviewed (Elkins and Dudek, 1985; Kuhnlein, 1986), and show that much of the variation is attributable to the nature of the item being analyzed (Thompson, 1986). West and Poortvliet (1993) reported multiple problems in compiling carotenoid data: use of different languages and nomenclature for identification of food items; inadequate data on the sample size and handling; limited data on the time between sampling and analyses, and sample treatment in the interim; exposure to light and air; details on the analytical methods used; and absence of information on the use of quality control procedures. In the absence of information on sampling, it is not known whether discrepancies in the published literature on vitamin A content reflect natural and/or analytical variation.

Heterogeneity in nutrient content is a consequence of numerous factors, including soil pH, amount of rainfall, seasonality, genetic diversity, and the stage of maturation. Vitamin A is not uniformly distributed within the animal or plant tissue, so the accuracy of the nutrient value is determined in part by the portion size and the number of individual units selected for a representative sample. Retinol concentrations in liver oils among fish and mammalian species can differ by more than a thousandfold, and mammalian liver retinol concentrations within species can vary in a range of more than 200-fold. Bureau and Bushway (1986) found a very large range in provitamin A values for a sample of twenty-two fruits and vegetables, but this was not consistent across seasons or location. Nutrient data of green leaves analyzed in two different seasons also showed inconsistent variation among seasons (Tagaki, 1985).

When compiling carotenoid data from multiple sources, Forman et al. (1993) grouped similar foods into a single general food description. Variability was indicated by the range of individual carotenoid values. Unfortunately, there were insufficient data to desegregate carotenoid values for a single food item based on factors such as season, that may influence carotenoid levels. In contrast, West and Poortvliet (1993) limited the amount of aggregation of carotenoid data due to the wide variation in globally generated values.

Factors Influencing the Dietary Intake of Vitamin A

Differential intake of provitamin A and preformed vitamin A can be explained in part by the natural variation in the nutrient content of individual foods. It is also determined by dietary beliefs and practices. In the first part of this paper, the seven general food categories presented in the preceding paper are explored in terms of factors influencing their intake. The discussion of each category is divided into four sections: inclusion in the diet, exclusion from the diet, seasonal factors, and economic factors.

The sections entitled "Inclusion in the diet" provide summaries of documented use of food items rich in vitamin A activity. In some societies, certain foods are prescribed as preventive measures or as treatment for illness. Traditional beliefs and practices in many societies are being modified by the influence of the media and government programmes. So that both historical and contemporary factors contribute to actual dietary intake. This extends to methods of food preparation which modify the vitamin A activity estimated in the raw form.

Exclusion of a food item rich in vitamin A activity from the diet can relate to dietary beliefs, although this effect is usually limited to certain sectors of the population. Certain foods are often proscribed from the diet in response to alterations in physiological status, e.g. menstruation, pregnancy and lactation, and illness.

Ecological factors such as climate, soil and water, and general environmental integrity all affect the availability of a food item' particularly in regions where transport and storage facilities are not well developed. The availability of time is a determinant of food consumption, particularly time to gather and prepare food. Cross-cultural differences in parental control and dietary beliefs influence the timing of the introduction of foods rich in vitamin A activity during the weaning period' and the quantity ingested. This has important implications for the vitamin A status of infants and children, whose liver stores of vitamin A are more rapidly depleted than those of adults and who can eat relatively small quantities of food.

The availability of foods rich in vitamin A activity is often seasonal. For example, in some regions the rainy season is marked by an abundance of wild leafy greens. When liver retinol stores are low or vitamin A status is compromised by disease, seasonal fluctuations can lead to periods of greater risk of hypovitaminosis A.

Dietary intake of foods rich in vitamin A activity is also determined by economic factors. Vitamin A intake is positively correlated with household income level. This correlation is most evident when provitamin A and preformed vitamin A food sources are not readily available. Market value is also linked to issues of social status associated with a given food item.

The literature about food beliefs and practices related to vitamin A intake is multidisciplinary. The sources consulted for this review include the following kinds of materials:

- nutrition surveys in regions where xerophthalmia is endemic,
- evaluations of programmes designed to improve vitamin A status in target populations. »clinical and case studies of xerophthalmia,
- anthropological studies of dietary practices in various societies,
- general reviews of dietary beliefs and practices,
- studies of traditional medicine that include dietary prescriptions and proscriptions.

(In addition, some of the information from Guatemala and East Africa is based on the personal observations of the authors.)

The available literature has at least four significant limitations for our purposes:

1. Nutritional data are often lacking, so that we have had to make assumptions about the potential vitamin A activity of the foods being discussed. This is problematic in light of the wide range of natural variation in vitamin A activity within species of animal and plant foods.
2. Wild foods, particularly local green leafy vegetables and fruits, are often overlooked in dietary surveys. It is hard to evaluate the dietary intake of provitamin A of children who eat fruit outside the home. As a consequence, the intake of foods rich in vitamin A activity is often underestimated. The same dilemma occurs when other foods are eaten outside the home (e.g., at the kill site for game, or at the market).
3. Some authors do not include scientific names, or even the common names of foods, in their discussion of dietary practices. It is impossible to differentiate poor from excellent sources of vitamin A within the commonly used categories of "vegetables" and "meat." Likewise, differential dietary practices are observed in different ethnic groups within the same region, or within the same ethnic group in different communities. When authors do not give details on the specific ethnic group and the location of the study, generalizations are often erroneously made.
4. Anthropological studies cover both reported behaviour and statements of beliefs and attitudes but rarely include reports of direct observations. There are important differences between reported practice, which tends to fit the ideal or norm, and real practice. Furthermore, although the statements of belief may be true, there is not always a direct relation between belief and practice. This is why it is so important not to assume that beliefs and attitudes dictate the way people act, especially in regard to food.

Given the diffuse distribution of literature pertaining to food choice and intake, the references cited should of course not be interpreted as an exhaustive evaluation of all dietary beliefs and practices associated with foods rich in vitamin A activity. The discussion highlights factors that have a documented influence on vitamin A intake, and the differential nature of their influence. Most of the examples cited are very specific and cannot be extrapolated to other populations. This emphasizes the necessity of evaluating the dietary practices of a group targeted for vitamin A intervention programmes before promoting natural food sources rich in vitamin A activity.

Green Vegetables, Algae, and Flowers

Inclusion in the Diet

The literature makes ample reference to the dietary use of green leafy vegetables, particularly of gathered wild species.

Leaves of tuber-producing plants are used for sauces, and wild greens make up 80% of the total vegetable intake among certain groups in Tanzania. The Bemba and Lamba tribes in the Zambezian woodlands identify 241 edible wild species, and boiling the leaves is the most common method of preparation.

Among the Twi-speaking people in Ghana,. the leaves of cocoyam are eaten regularly. The consumption of cassava leaves, however, is low; more often they are fed to poultry and other livestock. Gathering is not an organized activity but is practiced by both men and women during the course of farm work.

Among the Tswana of Botswana, gathering is a female activity, and the plants within the village are rejected to avoid possible contamination by human or animal faeces. The young plants are eaten fresh or are sun-dried after cooking and then shaped into cakes that can be stored up to three years. The children of this tribe also eat the flowers of certain species of wild plants.

Among the Oto and Twa of Zaire, members of both sexes participate in gathering, which includes the collection of honey, tubers, and caterpillars in addition to green leafy vegetables. In some societies in Zimbabwe, both women and children gather greens that are then eaten in cooked form or are dried for storage in anticipation of drought. Among the Luo of Kenya, leaves are boiled until dry, or the water is discarded, and Magadi soda is sometimes added to soften the leaves.

In rural Malaysia, 72 species of edible wild greens have been identified in the diet, which contradicts earlier literature claiming that green leafy vegetables are only used for 'taste". Consumption of the flower of the banana by children has also been documented in this region. Among the Gujarat in India, flowers are eaten to satiety. In northern India, the green leaves of root crops are eaten; in the southern part they are not.

In certain regions of Mexico, green leafy vegetables are considered the main source of vitamin A. It has been suggested that variation in preference for different species of wild greens among populations in Oaxaca, Mexico, may reflect differences in availability according to ecological conditions and agricultural practices, whereas in Tlaxcala, Mexico, selective weeding encourages growth of preferred species of wild greens.

Several indigenous groups in western Canada use the fronds of certain species of algae to gather herring spawn, which are then eaten together. Other species of algae are consumed in various forms, including fermented and dried. The young leaves of species of the celery family are preserved in seal oil by the Inupiaq Eskimos of Alaska and eaten year-round.

Dettwyler and Fishman noted that the infusion of papaya leaf was used in at least one village in Mali to treat night blindness in pregnant women. In Java, it has been reported that the majority of women increase their consumption of leafy green vegetables during lactation to increase vitamin intake, a reflection of beliefs introduced by the media and government programmes. Among Greek immigrants in the United States, certain species of greens are believed to be health-promoting during pregnancy and post-partum.

The only case we have found mentioned of a society in which a green leafy vegetable has high status is that of the Wamiri of Papua New Guinea, who value taro leaves as a feast food.

Exclusion from the Diet

As a general rule, consumption of green leafy vegetables is not limited by dietary beliefs, but they are underutilized relative to their availability and potential nutrient contribution. As pointed out by Pereira and Begum, those dietary restrictions that do exist may be limited to individual species of plants, so other species of greens could be substituted in promoting this category of foods rich in provitamin A.

Among the Yoruba in Nigeria, 57% of pregnant women were reported to avoid a green called "bitter leaf" because it tastes bitter. Three reasons are given why pregnant women in certain regions of the Gambia do not eat enough greens: the greens dilute sauces; they dislike the taste; there is not enough time available for gathering greens. A time constraint was also mentioned in reference to a generally low intake of greens among the Hopi of Arizona.

Several programmes under the auspices of Helen Keller International that are promoting the use of provitamin A-rich foods have been hampered by a consistent belief that infants are unable to digest green leafy vegetables. Mothers claim that the greens cause indigestion and diarrhoea because the infants' gut is immature. In contrast, older children in these same areas are not restricted in their intake of leafy vegetables as it is assumed that their digestive system is sufficiently mature to digest greens.

Most dietary restrictions on green leafy vegetables are limited to women of child-bearing years. In Java, leaves of sweet potatoes are restricted for young, unmarried girls, as are other species for adolescents of both sexes. In Telegana, India, most foods, including green leafy vegetables, are restricted 3 to 30 days post-partum but are then prescribed during lactation. In Hawaii, there are dietary restrictions for individual species of algae, but they were not detailed by the author.

Another concept of dietary restriction is encountered within the humoral classification of foods, the most well-documented being the "hot-cold" classification. The humoral theory of disease is based on the principle that diseases are caused by imbalance, so treatment is designed to restore the balance. Molony reports that a systematic coding system is used in assigning a classification to individual food items. These cultural classifications exhibit intracultural variation and are subject to rapid modification through culture contact and cultural diffusion. Latin American immigrants in the I United States generally classify greens as "cold", as do societies in Guatemala, China, and Malaysia. The implications of a "cold" classification relate to proscription during illness and certain seasons. In Malaysia it is thought that "cold" foods delay recovery from illness and that excess consumption can cause diarrhoea and fever. These foods are avoided during the rainy season, when the individual feels cold, and postpartum. In contrast, the certain species of greens, such as mustard greens, are classified as "hot" and are avoided by pregnant women. Excessive intake of these ' hot" species is thought to cause sore throat or fever.

In Zimbabwe and the Philippines, there are inadequate plant resources because of deforestation, a shift to an agricultural economy and monocropping, and overpopulation. This leads to a decrease in intake of green leafy vegetables without substitution of other vitamin A sources. In contrast, green leafy vegetables are abundant but are underutilized by populations in Liberia, India, and Papua New Guinea and among the Quechua in Peru and the Haustec in Mexico. Among nomadic tribes in Afghanistan, green leafy vegetables are eaten by children but are not an important dietary item for adults. Nomads in Iran do not eat them. Likewise, while edible algae are available, they is not eaten by the Seri of Mexico.

Members of the Jain religious group in south Rajasthan, India, do not eat wild greens during the rainy season despite their availability, because they believe that preparation/consumption of these greens would result in the religiously undesirable death of worms living on the plants (P. Sundaram, personal communication).

Seasonal Patterns

Most accounts of green leafy vegetable intake make reference to seasonal availability and consumption. The diversity of available edible species increases in the rainy season, as, for example. was documented in the Zambezian woodland. In regions of the Gambia, green leaves make an important contribution to total vitamin A intake during the non-mango season, which is between July and November. Among the Sandawe in Tanzania, greens are gathered during the December-to-April rainy season and then dried and stored for later use. Among the Oto and Twa in Zaire, while most species of wild greens are eaten during the rainy season, there is an increased consumption of cassava leaves during the dry season. In societies in which people buy their greens from the market, such as the urban populations in Iraq, there is also an increase in intake of green leafy vegetables during summer months when they are abundant and low in price. This fluctuation in the intake of greens does not occur in the United States, nor in the Twi-speaking regions of Ghana.

Economic Considerations

There are few accounts of green leafy vegetables having an important economic role, although they are often used during periods of food shortages and economic constraints. Reliance on gathered plant sources would allow for greater expenditures on other foods. The Bemba and Lamba tribes are said to have an important retail trade in cassava leaves. In at least one community in Ethiopia where there is no documented xerophthalmia and the average intake of greens among children is three times per week, the production and selling of leafy green vegetables is the responsibility of local prisoners. With extensive urban migration from the rural areas, certain species of greens are becoming important crops in urban markets in Guatemala, Kenya, and Tanzania. Shoots of the ostrich fern, commonly referred to as "fiddle-heads," are cooked or frozen for later use by some indigenous groups in Canada. However, they are gaining such popularity as a specialty food among non-indigenous groups that the wild population of this species is being depleted.

Most references to economic issues associated with leafy vegetables refer to social status. In Hyderabad, India, Swaziland, and the highlands of Mexico, while green leafy vegetables are part of the traditional economy, their consumption is associated with poverty. Therefore consumption of wild greens is inversely associated with economic prosperity. In Tanzania, vegetable intake, hence provitamin A intake, may be higher in the "lean" season than after the harvest, which reflects the inferior status associated with these plants. In contrast, in Iran there is higher consumption of green vegetables with increased economic status.

Fruits

Inclusion in the Diet

In Indonesia, mangoes and papayas are introduced early in the weaning process, with a positive correlation between intake and the absence of xerophthalmia. Among the Malays. fruit is eaten in substantial quantities by pregnant women. Wilson suggests that there is a global dietary belief that promotes the intake of those foods for which there are cravings during pregnancy, fruits being one of the more common food groups. When these cravings are not met, it is generally believed that marks will appear on the newborn that resemble the fruit not consumed.

There are numerous references to the popularity of fruit among children because of its sweet taste and soft texture. As fruits are often classified as food for children, there appears to be little competition with adult members of the household for them. In the

Taita Hills of Kenya, where xerophthalmia has not been documented, fruit is eaten as a snack or as a meal replacement, especially by children. In season, children eat fruit on an average of seven or more times per week, while adult women have an average weekly intake of one piece of fruit. Assignment to tasks outside the house allows the children to forage for these fruits, of which 97 species are classified as edible. Not all edible species are actually eaten; different species may be preferred by members of different ethnic groups within the same ecological region. The concept of fruit as "children's food" is also found among the Mbuti in eastern Zaire, in Swaziland, and in regions of Mali where treats purchased at markets for children include provitamin A-rich fruits such as mangoes and papayas.

Fruit use has apparently not been affected by deforestation in the Condo area of Zimbabwe, where fruit consumption is correlated with a shortage of cultivated resources and is not in synchrony with the fruiting season.

Among the Tiruray in the Philippines, immature papaya is used as a vegetable, whereas mature papaya is eaten as a fruit. Differential preference for ripeness in mangoes among Gambian women affects the nutrient intake since provitamin A activity varies with the stage of maturation.

The Seri of Mexico have numerous methods of preparing fruit for consumption, as described by Felger and Moser, although some species are consumed raw. In a Jivaro community in the Amazonas department of Peru, plantain is usually prepared by boiling or by roasting over coals. At least 17 varieties of bananas and plantain have been documented in the diet, and these fruits are introduced into the diet by one year of age. There are numerous reports of consumption of berries in the form of jam or jelly among indigenous groups in Canada. The Wood Cree eat cranberries raw, stewed, or served with fish and/or meat, or mix them with boiled fish eggs, liver, air bladders, and fat. There is frequent mention of plant foods being eaten with fat or oil, which is a suitable vehicle to increase the absorption of the provitamin A they contain.

In the Condo area of Zimbabwe, fruit is eaten for its perceived nutrient value (61"/o of those interviewed) and/or taste (52"/o). Among the Yoruba in Nigeria, plantain and papaya are perceived as being nutritious for pregnant women by 91% and 59%

respectively of women interviewed. In Tamil Nadu in India, green plantain is eaten by some at puberty for a strengthening effect, whereas it is avoided by others because it is believed to have a weakening effect.

Exclusion from the Diet

In lava, fruits are restricted for young unmarried girls, infants, and adolescents, and also for women during lactation because it is thought that negative effects will be passed through the breast milk to the infant. Among forest-dwelling tribes in Gujarat in India there is also some avoidance of fruits by lactating women for fear of gastrointestinal upset in the child, showing a similar concept of the transfer of the effect of the restricted food from the mother to the infant via the breast milk. Forest fruit is not given to infants in Gujarat for fear of choking the infant. In contrast, older children eat fruit to satiety, although these fruits are proscribed during illness.

Among the Yoruba in Nigeria, papaya is restricted for barren women because sterility is thought to be caused by worms, and papaya and other sweet fruits are considered to be delicacies for worms. Likewise, these fruits are restricted for individuals with helminthic infection. Papayas as well as mangoes are avoided during pregnancy in Tamil Nadu, India, where these fruits are classified as "hot" and thought to have the capacity to induce abortion. This has also been documented among the forest-dwelling tribes in Gujarat and among the Jain religious group in south Rajasthan, India (P. Sundaram, personal communication). In contrast, in Malaysia, papaya is classified as 'cold", and its intake is restricted because it is believed to aggravate illnesses classified as "cold," examples being malaria and xerophthalmia Among different ethnic groups interviewed in the United States, particularly those from northern Mexico, fruits are classified as "cold" and therefore are avoided during menses. Tomatoes are also avoided as they are believed to cause menstrual blood to congeal in the uterus, causing cancer. Chili is classified as a "hot" food in Malaysia and is considered a cause of stomach-ache, diarrhoea, fever, and sweating.

Seasonal Patterns

Most descriptions of fruit intake make reference to the seasonal availability that creates periods of variable risk of hypovitaminosis

A. The increase in provitamin A intake attributable to the mango season in regions of Brazil confounded the evaluation of the impact of a prophylaxis programme in the same region. In the Taita Hills in Kenya, papaya is available year-round, whereas most fruits are limited to the period between March and August. This is a pat tern similar to that observed in south-eastern regions of Ghana. Seasonal variation is also evident in the Gambia, where the mango season coincides with the season for red palm oil. In contrast, in the United States consumption of specific raw fruits is seasonal but the availability of canned and dried fruit allows for year-round consumption.

Economic Considerations

In Java, it has been observed that fruit intake is more frequent among women in higher income groups. Similarly, in Hyderabad, India, tomatoes are considered a prestige food and are eaten more frequently by the wealthier segments of the population. In Iran fruits are consumed in low quantities because of economic restraints. In contrast, children who gather wild fruits in the Taita Hills in Kenya are able to eat these as an alternative to the high-priced commercial snack foods available on the school compounds.

Plants with Vitamin A Stores

Inclusion in the Diet

Most roots and tubers are devoid of carotenoid activity, so it is very difficult to identify dietary beliefs and practices in the literature that affect provitamin A intake. Plant storage organs have classically been singled out in nutrition and anthropological studies for their dietary protein and energy contribution to the diet, with little emphasis on their potential contribution to provitamin A intake. In view of these limitations, dietary beliefs and practices related to plant storage organs are probably underrepresented in this literature review.

Plant storage organs are of importance to numerous African societies, and many different methods of preparation are observed. The most common methods of preparation among groups in the Zambezian woodland region are boiling and roasting over an open fire. In the New Guinea highlands, sweet potatoes are the staple food, but "strong" tasting species are not introduced into the diet of children until they are two years old. Species of the squash family are also documented dietary items, but they are seasonal in availability and consumption. In Hyderabad, India, tubers are the least consumed of all plant foods, but of these sweet potatoes are the most popular.

In the United States, carrots are ranked as the second largest contributor to total vitamin A intake. Likewise in Ethiopia, in communities where the prevalence of xerophthalmia is low, carrots make an important contribution to vitamin A intake in children. In Egypt, carrots are consumed in pickled form or are boiled and then eaten with potatoes because women argue that the crunchy texture presents difficulties, particularly for children (Wahba, personal communication). In contrast, carrots are usually eaten raw as a treat in Mali. This is problematic for infants, who are often denied this rich provitamin A source because mothers are concerned about possible damage to their teeth from the hard texture of carrots.

A questionnaire identifying dietary beliefs was used in a low-cost housing resettlement in Papua New Guinea. Of the households interviewed, 13% identified sweet potatoes as healthy for children and 12% also identified pumpkins as having health-promoting properties. During lactation, sweet potatoes were perceived as a healthy food (80% of all respondents), with 47% of the respondents stating that, in general, vitamin A-rich tubers were preferable food to plain rice.

Exclusion from the Diet

Wild roots and tubers are not widely consumed by the Luo in Kenya, which may be related to availability. They are not eaten at all by nomads in Iraq.

Dietary restrictions are documented, with emphasis on the classification of these foods as 'cold," as previously discussed. In Malaysia, the majority of green and yellow vegetables are classified as "cold," and consequently their intake is restricted because they are believed to aggravate illnesses like malaria and skin infections. This includes the squash family, members of which are classified as "windy". As 'windy" foods are thought to cause aching veins' weak legs and bones and rheumatism, they are generally limited in the diet. A similar classification exists among the Gujarat in India, although pumpkin is classified as "hot," and its consumption is therefore governed by the beliefs relating to "hot" foods. Likewise in Malaysia, tubers, including the sweet potato, are classified as "hot" and are only eaten during the rainy season, at night, or when the body feels cold. As a general rule, "hot" foods are restricted for pregnant women.

Seasonal Patterns

In the United States, sweet potatoes, carrots, and other vitamin A-rich vegetables are consumed yearround, with few if any seasonal fluctuations. In contrast, roots and tubers are reported to be seasonal in their availability and intake in Iran and Papua New Guinea.

Economic Considerations

We encountered little mention in the literature of the economic role plant storage organs may have for those societies consuming them. However, according to FAO food balance sheets, sweet potatoes are classified as a main staple food crop in Burundi, Kenya, Rwanda, Tanzania, and Uganda. In Iran. it has been noted that there is a lower intake of roots and tubers among the low-income groups. Likewise, their consumption is erratic in Ethiopia because of constraints on cash flow. It was found that the large inter-family variation in the intake of plant storage organs was explained in part by the family purchasing priority.

Plant Oils

Inclusion in the Diet

There is very little literature available on dietary beliefs surrounding the use of plant oils other than the documented use of red palm oil in certain regions of Africa. Given the small quantities that are used in the cooking process, they are particularly difficult to quantify in a dietary survey.

Among the Mbuti of eastern Zaire, red palm oil is used for cooking purposes whenever it is available. The Oto and the Twa use palm oil as a base for a sauce in which spiced cassava leaves are added. In those communities in Nigeria and Zambia where red palm oil is consumed regularly in the diet, xerophthalmia is not endemic. In the Yoruba tribe in Ghana and Nigeria, mothers are known to give one teaspoon (5 g) of palm oil as a treatment to infants with measles.

As discussed in the preceding paper, red palm and buriti palm oil are the richest known sources of provitamin A. While other plant oils have little if any vitamin A activity, their contribution to vitamin A intake is important for the absorption of this nutrient. Therefore, promotion of dietary fat should not be limited to those oils known to be rich in vitamin A activity, although the latter arguably would have the greatest impact on improving dietary vitamin A intake.

Exclusion from the Diet

We have found no documented cases of dietary restrictions relating to plant oils, although in several regions, including communities in Zambia and Liberia, red palm oil was available but not consumed.

Seasonal Patterns

In the Gambia, which has a well documented reliance on red palm oil for cooking purposes, it is seasonal in availability, coinciding with the mango season. During this period between April and June, the average intake of vitamin A and provitamin A is at its peak for the year.

Economic Considerations

Red palm oil is expensive in most regions because of the labour-intensive processing required for the final product. As a consequence its dietary use is often limited by price and availability. In India, when dietary fat in the form of ghee is prohibitive in cost, groundnut (peanut) oil is used as an alternative.

Milk, Milk Products, and Eggs

Inclusion in the Diet

Abrams states that all human cultures include some form of animal protein and fat in the diet. From a survey of 383 cultures represented in the Food Habits Survey of the Human Relations Area Files, of the two classifications of animal produce most commonly consumed, Abrams tabulated 363 societies consuming chicken meat and eggs, and 196 consuming cattle meat and milk.

Reports of egg consumption are few in the literature compared to the numerous dietary restrictions on eggs. In Tamil Nadu, India, eggs are prescribed at the age of menarche, as they are thought to increase fertility, although current economic constraints are limiting this belief. In Nigeria, only 14.5% of Yoruba women interviewed considered eggs a healthy food during pregnancy. In

Indonesia, eggs are the only preformed vitamin A source consumed significantly more by children who do not show signs of xerophthalmia than by their vitamin A-deficient peers. In China, preservation methods prolong the shelf life of duck or hen eggs without substantially reducing the preformed vitamin A content.

There is more documentation of the use of milk, particularly among nomadic groups. In Hyderabad, India, products used for the early supplementation of breast milk include cow milk, buffalo milk, and commercial milk preparations. In this same region, buttermilk is one of the few foods prescribed for adults during diarrhoeal attacks. In Ethiopia, milk makes an important contribution to the intake of preformed vitamin A among children. Both milk and boiled or fried eggs are consumed with more frequency by traditional hunter-gatherer groups in the Philippines than by their peasant counterparts.

Among nomadic groups, milk and its by-products have important dietary roles. Among nomads in Uganda, the milk from cows, goats, and sheep is consumed by the women and children who remain in permanent settlements. Milk is made sour by the addition of urine to facilitate storage. The use of sour milk has been documented elsewhere, including Iraq [SO]. Milk, yoghurt, and ghee are the only sources of vitamin A for the nomadic tribes in Iraq, and are mixed with bread or whole wheat. Casimir describes in detail the methods of utilizing milk observed among nomads in Afghanistan. Milk is not allowed to boil when heated prior to souring, and this is thought to preserve vitamins. Lactose-intolerant individuals consume fermented products like yoghurt. Among the Masai in Kenya, the traditional diet is cows' milk with maize meal, and milk is consumed fresh or in tea. Milk and butter are principle weaning foods, introduced between 18 and 24 months of age. Yoghurt is also consumed in large quantities among the Masai.

Exclusion from the Diet

Dietary restrictions relating to eggs are numerous, particulary for women of child-bearing age. In Tamil Nadu, there is a decrease in consumption of eggs during the third trimester of pregnancy as it is thought that they promote the growth of the foetus, thus creating a difficult delivery. A similar dietary restriction applies to milk in Hyderabad. Among certain tribes in the Gambia, Uganda, and Tanzania, eggs are restricted for women and girls as they are thought to cause sterility, and among certain groups in Zambia and Zimbabwe? eggs are restricted for children up to seven years old for fear of inducing convulsions. The Masai do not eat eggs under any circumstances, although this pattern has been changing recently among those who are becoming acculturated. Among the Tswana of Botswana, eggs from 13 species of wild birds are eaten by young males and occasionally by adult men, but are restricted for girls and women of child-bearing age.

In Iran, eggs are classified as "cold." so they are eaten less during warmer periods, sometimes being replaced by vegetable dishes. A survey of hunter-gatherer societies found restrictions on the consumption of eggs during pregnancy among the Walbiri (an Australian aboriginal society), during lactation among the Inuit, and at menarche among the Hare Indians. Among the Wamira in Papua New Guinea, eggs are restricted for those individuals who have the bird as their lineage totem.

Dettwyler and Fishman observed dietary prescription for eggs in two villages in Mali, where eggs were considered good for the foetus and the pregnant woman; but in another village eggs were restricted during pregnancy because they were believed to cause a difficult delivery. In this latter community, it was also believed that eggs are bad for children because they interfere with physical development. In Honduras, milk and eggs are restricted during gastrointestinal illness to "avoid contamination of the intestinal wound".

With respect to milk intake, Simoons offers three possible explanations as to why "non-milking" areas have emerged: lactose intolerance, a perception of milk as an unpleasant secretion, and a view that it is suitable only for feeding calves. In the Luapala Valley in Zambia, milk and other animal products are not available for consumption because of the presence of the tsetse fly. However, in some regions of Zimbabwe, goat milk is available but not consumed. In some regions of Uganda, it is argued that milk should not be mixed with any other foods, either in a dish or in the stomach, so several hours must pass between the ingestion of milk and other foods. Among the Masai, whole milk is not given to infants because it is thought that fat in the milk forms lumps that can choke the child if it vomits.

Seasonal Patterns

In the Gambia, milk and eggs are consumed only during the dry season. Among nomadic tribes, milk products are fermented and stored to augment the diet during the dry season, when milk production decreases. This has also been demonstrated among the Sandawe in Tanzania, where cattle struggle to survive during the dry season. Among the Masai, milk availability has seasonal fluctuations according to rainfall and the number of cattle owned by the individual. As permanent settlements are encouraged by the government, there is even more of a decrease in milk production during the dry season.

Economic Considerations

The prices of milk, milk products, and eggs have been cited as limiting factors in dietary intake. Eggs and milk are sold instead of being consumed at the local level in the Gambia, in Hyderabad. India, and in Amazonas, Peru. Among the Fula tribe in the Gambia, milk is often exchanged for grain and housing during the dry season.

Fish

Inclusion in the Diet

Among the Miskito of Nicaragua, dietary preferences used to determine the intensity and frequency of fishing expeditions. This ethnic group distinguishes high-quality animal flesh, which it terms 'meat," from lower quality 'flesh," which includes certain shellfish. "Meat" is used to fulfil kinship ties and obligations, and "flesh" is never served at important meals. The Tiruray hunter-gatherers in the Philippines eat numerous freshwater species of fish, whereas those shifting to a peasant lifestyle eat only purchased dried fish. Among the Wamiri of Papua New Guinea, fish are the most stable source of preformed vitamin A. Twenty species of freshwater fish, more than 50 species of saltwater fish, and numerous shellfish are included in the diet.

Methods of preparing fish vary among societies. Only boiled or roasted freshwater fish are consumed in the Luapala Valley in Zambia. As fish are eviscerated prior to preparation in some societies, most, if not all, of the preformed vitamin A is removed. In south-eastern regions of Ghana fish are prepared by similar methods.

In parts of Mali, some women believe that fish oil gives strength to the foetus. Among Chinese in Hong Kong, fish liver oil is used to treat baldness and bronchitis and to prevent coughs and asthma.

Exclusion from the Diet

Fish, being classified as an animal product, are proscribed for religous reasons among the Brahmin caste in Tamil Nadu, India, and among Buddists in Hong Kong. Likewise, fish are restricted at menarche in Tamil Nadu for non-vegetarian women. This has also been documented in Hyderabad, India.

Among the Nootka of western British Columbia, spring salmon, seal, bass, and whale are restricted during lactation and at menarche. Among the Kisarwe in Tanzania, catfish are restricted for women and girls of child-bearing age, with other fish species restricted for this group among the Busoga and the Buganda of Uganda.

Although many restrictions relating to fish are reported from Java, including one which associates fish intake with worm infestation in infants, only 20% of mothers interviewed reported knowledge or use of dietary restrictions. In contrast, Kahn gives a detailed description of dietary beliefs that relate to fish species, with some consumed exclusively by the elders of the community, others only by men. These dietary restrictions determine the fishing techniques and scheduling, which is both a female and male activity.

Species-specific dietary restrictions have also been observed among the Miskito of Nicaragua, while other ethnic groups in the region consume fish species rejected by the Miskito. Masai and Sambuni pastoralists in East Africa traditionally express a revulsion towards the consumption of fish.

Seasonal Patterns

Among the Sandawe in Tanzania, freshwater fish are caught in April and May and then are eaten in dried form when the rivers dry up. The Wamiri have an elaborate system of procuring fish in accordance with the seasons. River fishing by the women of the community is only practiced in the dry season, while shellfish are collected by women and children primarily during the rainy season. Ocean fishing, which is considered a male activity, is year-round.

Economic Considerations

The species of fish currently caught by the Miskito of Nicaragua no longer reflect the dietary preferences of the society. With developing commercial markets for different fish, the perception of what is valuable is determined by what can be sold. Likewise, in the Luapala province of Zambia, and among the Kigezi of Uganda, fishing is a successful industry, hut not enough fish reach the local level for consumption. Dettwyler and Fishman also found that in parts of Mali fish are often sold for cash to buy other foods or nonfood items.

Organ Meat and other Meat

Inclusion in the Diet

The few reports that we encountered that describe the consumption of wild game make no mention of which, if any, organs are eaten. For example, wild game is caught, albeit erratically, in the Papua New Guinea highlands, among the Tswana of Botswana (with some fowl species valued only by the elders), in Amazonas, Peru, and among the Ache in Paraguay. The viscera, particularly the liver, of chickens and other animals are consumed by groups in Malaysia as a treatment for night blindness, among the Tabora of Tanzania, and the Tiruray in the Philippines.

A review of the foods eaten by groups in the circumpolar area makes numerous references to the popularity of these vitamin A-rich foods, where raw seal liver is prescribed for adults during illness. However, many of the references cited are dated and do not reflect current economic and political pressures that are modifying the intake of traditional foods. The traditional dietary sources of preformed vitamin A in the Inuit diet are very high in vitamin A activity, leading at least one author to speculate that the form of hysteria known as "pibloktoq" is a manifestation of hypervitaminosis A. However, Doolan argues that the current shift to marketed foods among northern native populations results in an inadequate intake of vitamin A.

In some regions of Mali, pregnant women buy and eat grilled chicken and fish in the market because affordable quantities are too small to distribute among the entire household. Liver is eaten in very small quantities, and then only on market day. Children eat liver only with other foods.

Exclusion from the Diet

Among the Kisarawe in Tanzania, the consumption of viscera by pregnant women is restricted , as is the consumption of wild game among the Yoruba in Nigeria. Landy did not encounter dietary proscriptions among the Inuit, although there is mention of the Copper Inuit's rejecting kidney, considering it food for dogs. Among the Yoruba, chicken meat is proscribed for those diagnosed with sickle cell anaemia as it is believed that fowl bones intensify the aching associated with the disease.

Seasonal Patterns

Among the Masai in Kenya, meat consumption is seasonal. Two factors determining intake are the number of diseased or dead animals used for consumption and the timing of ceremonies. However, liver flukes, which are endemic in the region can make beef liver, at least, inedible.

Among the Baffin Inuit, consumption of ringed seal liver and other viscera is variable, both seasonally and from year to year.

Economic Considerations

No discussion of economic value or constraints on the consumption of organ meat was found in the literature.

Summary

1. The evidence strongly reinforces the significance of both intercultural and intracultural diversity with respect to dietary inclusions and exclusions. The same foods are subject to very different interpretations in different cultural settings. Thus, the selection and consumption of vitamin A-rich foods appears to be highly situation-specific, which points to the need for locally relevant data.
2. Dietary prescriptions and proscriptions are structured in relation both to normal physiological status and to the prevention and management of illness.
3. Seasonality in the utilization of vitamin A source foods appears to be significant in many, perhaps the majority, of geographical-cultural settings.
4. Economic restraints may be significant not only in relation to the relatively more costly preformed vitamin A from animal food sources, but also with respect to provitamin A from plant sources. Specific foods may be prohibitively costly, or they may be avoided because of their association with poverty.

Are Lifestyle Factors Good Predictors of Retinol and Vitamin C deficiency in Apparently Healthy Adults?

Adequate nutritional status of carotenoids and vitamin C has attained a greater importance during the past decade, as a protective role of vitamins due to their antioxidative action has been suggested in some health disorders. Major dietary sources of carotenoids and vitamin C for vegetarians are fruit and vegetables. Increased intake of fruit and vegetables has been associated with a reduced risk of various diseases including cancer and cardiovascular diseases.

Dietary levels of vitamins also depend on several other factors such as age and socioeconomic status (Hjartaker & Lund, 1998). In developing countries like India, socioeconomic factors and customary restrictions govern intake of foods rich in vitamin A and C (eg fruit, vegetables, animal foods, milk products). Assessment of vitamin status and identifying influencing factors in apparently healthy individuals from different socioeconomic and environmental background has significance for drafting preventive health measures against risk of vitamin deficiency.

There is a need therefore to explore interrelationships of dietary intakes, socioeconomic status and environment with plasma levels of these vitamins and identify influential factors.

Most of the studies reporting vitamin A status in Indians are done on pregnant women and children. Information on plasma levels of vitamin A and C in an apparently healthy vegetarian population is scarse. The present paper aims at (i) assessing the retinol and vitamin C status of an adult population, and (ii) examining risk of plasma retinol deficiency and plasma ascorbic acid deficiency using dietary intake, age, socioeconomic and environmental conditions as explanatory variables.

Methods

Study Design

The study was conducted in Maharashtra State, which is one of the major states in India having an area of 307 713 square kilometers and a population of around 100 million with 51.7% males and 48.3% females. Some 61.3% of the population is in rural areas and 38.6% in urban and semi-urban zones. Rural and tribal populations have agriculture as their main occupation, while semi-urban and urban areas included individuals from all socioeconomic classes having occupations like businessmen, industrial workers, employees of banks/offices/institutes, students, housewives, hawkers etc. Accordingly the urban population was divided into higher/middle/lower socioeconomic classes (HSE/ MSE/ LSE). Rural and tribal populations have to depend on the local food commodities, while semi-urban and urban populations have better access to a variety of foods in the market.

Subjects

Criteria for selection of subjects were: (l) not suffering from major illnesses like diabetes or hypertension; and (2) not taking medicines or vitamin-mineral supplements. A random sample of 500 individuals (20-45 y) was selected through several health camps organized by local voluntary organizations in different areas in Maharashtra state of Western India viz. rural, semi-urban and urban zones during February 1998 to June 2000. Out of these 500, 75 had a history of anaemia, while 32 were found to have joint problems/inflammation, or recurrent infections. Information on 71 could not be obtained because of inadequate blood samples, or incomplete questionnaires, although their general characteristics matched with the study group. Complete information was available for 322 individuals (214 men and 108 women) apparently healthy and non-anaemic, and these data have been reported in the present paper. An informed written consent was obtained from subjects towards voluntary participation. Subjects were asked to come in the morning at 8 am on an empty stomach and a fasting blood sample of 10 ml was collected by the doctor while doing a clinical examination. A food frequency questionnaire and proforma of socioeconomic, environmental information was filled in by interview method.

Cooked Food Frequency Questionnaire (FFQ) and Nutrient Intakes

A semi quantitative FFQ was designed to ask questions about usual dietary intake. The period of the FFQ was taken as 1 y to cover all seasonal fruit and vegetables. The FFQ covered 278 food items, traditionally consumed in India, which were classified under food categories: cereals, legumes, vegetables, fruit, milk, animal food, snacks, sweets and deserts. The questionnaire was administered by trained investigators by interview. The subjects were asked how often on average they had consumed each food item during the year, the frequency of consumption per day, and amount in terms of standard measures like cup, bowl, spoon etc. For example, for some food items, consumption may be seasonal or on festive occasions, while for others, like milk, consumption may be twice a day, one glass at a time. FFQ was standardized to get adequate information about food choices of different sections of population and to obtain suitable consumption categories.

Frequency for each food item was defined as never/once per month/once in two months/once a week/once per week/twice per week/three times per week/once a day/twice a day and so on. The response intervals were adjusted to the food item and in case of reversal items in one category, a weighted frequency was computed. Weights of the portion units were decided on the basis of average weight of each food item for that portion size collected from different households representing the sample. As the questionnaire was interview-administered, there were no blanks in the form. Subjects were asked about any multi-vitamin supplements.

Repeatability of the FFQ was tested by again administering the same FFQ to a random sample of 30 individuals after one month through an interview by the same trained investigator. The response to both the FFQ agreed well with respect to consumption of foods and computed intakes of energy and nutrients (value of test statistic ranged from 0.2 to 0.98. $P>0.1$ and Pearson's correlation coefficient from 0.79 to 0.96 for different nutrient and food intakes.

Daily food consumption in eight food groups was computed for every individual using the information in the FFQ about frequency and quantity. Fruit consumption was further classified into sweet fruit, eg banana or chiku, and non-sweet fruit like guava, orange or lime.

Measurements

Dietary intake of energy, protein, fat, -carotene and vitamin C was computed using nutrient values generated in our laboratory for individual cooked food items. The estimation of nutrient contents was done as per Raghuramulu *et al* (1983). Retinol and -contents were estimated for all the foods but retinol was detectable only in animal foods. Vitamin A intake was expressed as retinol equivalents per day. Height and weight recorded using measuring scale and weighing balance to the nearest 0.1 cm and 0.5 kg respectively. Subjects underwent a routine medical check-up, which included physical examination, blood pressure, and past and present health complaints by a medical doctor. Subjects having medical fitness were included in the analysis.

Education was asked as an open-ended question as illiterate, primary school, high school, graduate and postgraduate studies. The data was subsequently divided into four classes giving years of education: less than 4, 5-10, 11-15 and above 15, as per the existing educational system.

Information on age, environment and socioeconomic status were collected by the investigator through a separate questionnaire by interview. Income was asked for as total monthly income of the participant and the family, and family size. Per capita daily income was calculated and classified into four categories of income using the National Sample Survey (NSS, 1996) as the basis. Per capita per day income categories were: less than Rs20; Rs20-50; Rs.50-100; and Rs.100 and above. The average cost of 1 litre of milk during the period of survey was Rs.100 wheat Rs.100 per kg, rice Rs.100 per kg, vegetables Rs.12-30 per kg (cabbage, bottle gourd, cauliflower, beans) and fruit Rs.15-60 per kg (banana, guava, apple, cherries, strawberries), indicating the relative value of these income levels. Thus a person earning Rs.20/day having an average family size of four would find it difficult to spare money for milk/fruit/vegetables.

Environmental grading was considered as an explanatory variable. Under environmental conditions, factors such as type of housing, ventilation, surroundings, overcrowding, water supply, sewage system etc. were studied. Each of these factors was given a score on a 10-point scale. Scores of all the variables were added, the maximum score being 100. A pooled score above 70 was termed good, between 50 and 70 fair, 35-50 bad and less than 35 poor (NSS, 1996; Gokhale *et al*, 1993).

Blood Analysis

Fasting venous blood (10 ml) was collected in EDTA bulbs for every subject (not more than 12 h fasting). The samples were brought to the laboratory on the same day in ice bags within 2 h and centrifuged at 2000 rpm for 15 min. Plasma was separated and levels of retinol and ascorbic acid were estimated. Plasma retinol was estimated by photoflurometer (Raghuramulu *et al*,

1983) using excitation at 350 nm and fluorescence at 490 nm. Plasma ascorbic acid was estimated by spectrophotometer. Reduction of ascorbic acid to dehydro ascorbic acid by 2,6-dichlorophenol indophenol was estimated at 520 nm.

Haemoglobin was estimated by cyanmethaemoglobin method using standard kit (Qualigens Diagnostics, Glaxo India Ltd.).

Statstical Methods

Nutrient calculations were done by computer program in C and Microsoft Excel version MS-OFFICE 2000. Statistical analyses were done by SPSS version 7.5.2 for Windows 16 May, 1997). Results were considered significant at $P<0.05$. Parametric methods were used when analyzing anthropometric and socioeconomic variables, as these distributions were found to be normal by Kolmogorov-Smirnov test. The distributions of intake of food and nutrients were positively skewed; therefore non-parametric methods were used to test the differences between groups. Median values were reported for these variables. Univariate analyses were first carried out for the probable factors. Any factor with a probability of rejection less than 0.25 was considered as a candidate for the multivariate model along with all variables of known biological significance. Multiple logistic regression analyses were used to examine simultaneously the effect of food consumption, age, body mass index (BMI), education and socioeconomic status on the adequacy of plasma levels of retinol and vitamin C. A forward selection procedure was employed to include variables in the multivariate model. Importance of variables included in the model was verified by comparing each estimated coefficient with the coefficient from the univariate model containing that variable. All possible interactions of independent factors which were plausible, such as income and education, income and milk consumption, age and fruit-vegetable intakes etc., were entered in the model initially. However, no interaction terms remained in the final equation. To test adequacy of the model a small data set was set aside from the same survey. This was referred as the external data set. Goodness of fit of the model was tested by Hosmer-Lemshow test.

Results

Mean age ranged from 28.19±8.62 in urban LSE to 32.67±7.31 y in rural area in men. The age of the women ranged from 28.0±9.72

in urban MSE to 31.29±8.36 y in rural area. Mean BMI of the men and women was highest in the urban HSE (23.11±3.9, 21.55±3.3 kg/m^2, respectively) and lowest in the rural population (19.42±3.5, 18.15±3.2 kg/m^2).

For estimating marginal to severe retinol and vitamin C deficiency, the classification given by Matilainen *et al*, (1996) and Grusse & Watier (1993) was used. Plasma ascorbic acid level was within normal range for 24% of men and 33% of women. Only 12.8% of men and 14.8% of women showed normal plasma retinol status. With the cut-off of 20 μg/dl for deficient retinol concentration as per IVACG recommendations (Olson, 1990), 20.6% of men and 30.2% of women showed deficient levels.

Further examination of interrelationships among these characteristics was undertaken. Level of education was negatively associated with age (r=-0.23, P=0.0001) but positively linked with income (r=0.536, P=0.0001). Education was also positively correlated with plasma retinol (r=0.46, P=0.0001) and ascorbic acid. Plasma retinol and ascorbic acid were not correlated with age and BMI. Environment was positively correlated with plasma retinol (r=0.272, P=0.0001) and ascorbic acid (r=0.255, P=0.0001).

Median intake of cereals and legumes was below recommended dietary intakes for Indians (RDI; ICMR 1990) in case of men and women from different regions. Fruit intakes were below RDI in almost 44% of women and 34% of men from different regions. All the subjects consumed leafy vegetables and other vegetables in meager amounts. Animal food intakes were greatly below RDI in most of the subjects and a quarter of the subjects were not eating animal food at all. Intake of milk and milk products was adequate in only 34.6% of men and 25% of women, mainly from urban HSE and MSE classes.

Percentage of energy from fat was around 26-31% while that from protein was 9-11%. Median nutrient intakes for -carotene as retinol equivalent and ascorbic acid were lower than the RDA.

The intake of vitamin A as retinol equivalent showed a dose responsive behavior with plasma retinol. However such a marked dose response was not seen in intake of ascorbic acid and plasma ascorbic acid. Differences between rural population and urban HSE were highly significant in plasma retinol as well as in plasma ascorbic acid levels , but the differences between rural and semi urban sections were not significant nor those between different urban classes.

Intake of fruit, green leafy vegetables and milk products were significantly associated with plasma levels of retinol and ascorbic acid. Plasma ascorbic acid was more closely associated with non-sweet fruit intake. Age, education and income were strongly associated with fruit, vegetable intake and milk product consumption.

To investigate interrelationships of factors influencing plasma vitamin levels, multiple logistic regression analyses were carried out. In the univariate analyses, age, BMI, sex, consumption of other vegetables and Hb, were found not to be statistically significant ($P>0.25$). Hence in the multivariate model these factors were not included. Education level, environmental conditions, green leafy vegetables and milk product consumption were observed to be good predictors of plasma retinol, while education, non-sweet fruit consumption, and passive smoking were the influential factors for plasma ascorbic acid level. No interaction terms entered the model. By excluding smokers, the associations were the same, while exclusion of passive smokers reduced the coefficient of determination.

Discussion

The main aim of the present investigation was to model linkages between 19 dietary and non-dietary factors with plasma status of vitamin C and retinol. Although only a quarters of the study group was strictly vegetarian, the remaining population had very low and infrequent intakes of animal foods. The study population were consuming vegetarian foods for the majority of the days in the year. Our data refers to 322 men and women covering major sections of the society, viz. rural, tribal, semi-urban, and urban with economically three broad classes, higher, middle and lower. The entire data were collected under identical experimental conditions by the same team of investigators. Apart from nutritional, anthropometrical and socioeconomic status, many new factors like passive smoking, and non-sweet fruit intakes were considered as variables in the data analyses. Most of the studies reporting associations of fruit and vegetable intakes refer to cancer patients, cardiovascular patients, smokers or alcoholics (Willett, 1998). Our study reports such associations in apparently healthy individuals and therefore adds valuable information not known in the Indian subcontinent. This is an essential addition to the world database and further help in defining dietary modifications required for such at-risk populations. Moreover the data represents individuals not taking any vitamin-mineral supplements, thus avoiding confounding effect on linkages observed between vitamin status and other factors. Considering the diverse environmental exposures, these data with varied dietary patterns are important for understanding interrelationships.

Consumption of cereals, legumes, fruit, vegetables and milk in the present study matches national sample data reported for various regions (NNMB, 1991) indicating better representation of the population in the study group. A high correlation of education, income and intake of milk products, fruit and vegetables was observed in our data. Association of socioeconomic factors and consumption of fruit and vegetables has also been reported by studies in Western population.

The design of the FFQ enabled us to extract more detailed information on any specific parameters of interest. For example, association of fruit consumption with plasma ascorbic acid level has been reported in Western populations either as individual fruit or total fruit intake (Matilainen *et al*, 1996). Our data on sour and non-sweet fruit consumption showed a strong association with the plasma ascorbic acid level but a weak association with total fruit consumption. Association of vegetable intakes and plasma vitamin C concentrations was found to be weak in the present study. Our results agree well with those reported by Drewnowski *et al* (1997). Secondly, our data permitted us to assess the impact of green leafy vegetables and other vegetables separately. Results indicated that green leafy vegetables have a larger impact than other vegetables on plasma retinol. The influence of vegetables, as a single food group, on plasma vitamin A has been reported by other studies. Additionally milk consumption was also found to have a beneficial effect on plasma retinol. Considering the vegetarian eating habits in the Indian subcontinent and subnormal status of vitamin A, these results emphasize the greater need to increase consumption of green leafy vegetables and milk products.

The range of plasma vitamin C in our data was 0.2-0.6 mg/dl. Similar levels of plasma ascorbic acid have also been reported in the case of Russian men (0.21-0.57 mg/dl) and women (0.32-0.5

mg/dl; Spirichev *et al*, 1995). Mean plasma vitamin C levels in our data are 0.30 for men and 0.35 mg/dl for women, which is equivalent to 17-20μ mol/l. These are lower than the values in French adults (50±29 μmol/l for 407 men and women; Drewnowski, 1997) or values of plasma vitamin C in south Asians residing in England (37.4 μmol/l Ness *et al*, 1999). This may also be due to environmental pollution and absence of vitamin supplements. Further plasma ascorbic acid in women was reported to be significantly higher than in men (Matilainen *et al*, 1996). This is also true in our study, although not statistically significant. In one Indian study on 20 urban men (mean age 52 y), serum vitamin C was reported as 1.14±0.38 mg/dl (Sinha & Sharma, 1998). However their intakes of vitamin C are very high (110±69 mg/day) as against our intakes of 33.6-58.6 mg/day and reported average vitamin C intakes (NNMB, 37 mg/day).

Our values of plasma retinol ranged from 12.8 to 38.3 μg/dl in women and 12.3 to 40.8 μg/dl in men, which are lower than the reported Western data and Indian data on university students (Vijayalakshmi & Rema, 1994). However our intakes of beta-carotene as retinol equivalent (179-440 μg/day in men and women) are in agreement with the NNMB reports (294 μg/day retinol). Mean retinol intakes reported by Vijayalakshmi *et al*, were higher than this range (785 μg/day). Our data on retinol intake and plasma retinol levels of urban and rural groups match well with those reported by Sankhla *et al*, (1991) on 30 urban and 30 rural men (18-50 y) from North India (Agra district).

A dose-response relationship between computed retinol equivalent intakes and plasma retinol is in agreement with de Pee *et al* (1998). Since our calculation of vitamin A content was done on an individual food basis with our own laboratory estimates of nutrient contents, our values are more accurate than estimates based on a group level. Similar dose-response behaviour was not seen in the case of ascorbic acid. This may be because of the fact that vitamin A is fat-soluble and can be stored in the body. Therefore plasma vitamin A represents long-term status so also do the FFQ estimates, while ascorbic acid, being water-soluble, has limited stores. Cooking losses in ascorbic acid can vary depending upon the variations in cooking procedures.

The multiple logistic regression model for the chance of having a plasma vitamin level above or below the median of the population was based on the actual consumption of different foods rather than computed nutrient intakes.

This was felt to be necessary because of the fact that dietary intakes were computed from FFQ rather than the weighing method. Secondly, although nutrient contents of all recipes in FFQ were estimated in the laboratory, assumption of common recipes has to be made when converting FFQ data to nutrient intakes.

An interesting observation emerged from the study, that passive smoking had an adverse effect on plasma ascorbic acid level. The number of smokers was very small in the study population. However inquiry about any family member smoking revealed that passive smoking was a problem amongst the study group. There are a number of studies reporting the effect of smoking on blood parameters.

However effects of passive smoking have been documented clearly in the present study. This emphasizes the need for public health measures to strictly maintain a non-smoking atmosphere in places of work and at home.

Referring the to the above model, our data has given leads to possible linkage between low plasma status of vitamin A and C and dietary and socioenvironmental factors in normal individuals. Thus the importance to dietary inadequacy needs to be reconsidered in the case of aetiology of vitamin A or C deficiency. This has important implications in arresting the process of developing disease.

Considering the difficulties in estimating the biochemical parameters in field studies, our results on logistic regression can be utilized as guidelines for identifying groups at risk of deficiency. For example, information on green leafy vegetable intake, milk product intake, education and environmental conditions of a group of individuals can predict risks of vitamin deficiency.

In summary, our study population is leaner and has considerably lower intakes of vitamin A and C and lower levels of vitamin C than Western populations. Subnormal status of both vitamin A and C in apparently healthy individuals emphasizes the need for increasing consumption of fruit, green leafy vegetables and milk products, and literacy and pollution-free environments as well.

Calorie and Protein Intake and its Determinants Among Adolescent School Girls in Delhi

Adolescence is a crucial period in a woman's life. Health and nutritional status during this phase is critical for the physical maturity, which in turn influences the health of the offspring. It is seen that the rate of low birth weight, prematurity and neonatal and infant mortality is high among children born to malnourished adolescent girls. Adolescents constitute 21.2% of the total population of India. In India, malnutrition is an important public health problem among children and adolescents. Adequacy of dietary intake in terms of calorie and protein are important in order to improve the chances of child survival and safe motherhood. In this regard, it is pertinent to examine the factors that determine the calorie and protein consumption pattern of adolescent girls, in order to plan suitable intervention measures to correct the deficits in dietary intake. Therefore this study was conducted to assess the calorie and protein consumption and identify the factors influencing their consumption patterns among adolescent girls of Delhi.

Methodology

Dietary intake may be assessed by various method, as for example diet recall interview, food frequency questionnaire (FFQ), diet records etc. A food frequency questionnaire was designed, based on Willet's FFQ. A pilot survey was carried out among adolescents to identify the food items commonly eaten by them. The dietetics department of GTB Hospital was also consulted in this regard. Calorie and protein content of common Indian food items was calculated using tables on nutritive value of Indian foods. The FFQ was pilot tested on 20 adolescent girls and compared with 24 Hr. recall method. It showed an underreporting of calorie consumption by less than 3% and protein consumption by less than 1%, hence it was accepted as standard tool for data collection. A cross sectional study design was selected. In order to determine the factors influencing calorie and protein intake, it was decided to recruit adolescent girls from a government sponsored school. Such schools because of subsidized education are usually attended by adolescent girls from lower socio economic strata. Another privately owned school was selected for recruitement of students belonging to higher socio economic strata.

The sample size was calculated in order to find a difference in protein intake of 10% among the two group of adolescent girls at a significance level of 5%. The estimated sample size was 168 in each group. All students enrolled in VII to XII standard were offered to participate in the study, expected to be in the age range of 13 to 17 years. All students were explained the objectives of the study by one of the authors. An informed consent in writing was obtained from all those students who agreed to participate in the study. One hundred sixty students from the government school and one hundred sixty two students from the private school finally participated. The FFQs were analyzed to estimate the average calorie and protein consumption per day. The students with estimated calorie intake of less than 500 calories per day and more than 3000 calories per day were considered incorrect and excluded from the study. Similarly, students with estimated protein intake of less than 20 grams and more than 120 grams were also excluded. Thus calorie intake was analyzed for 153 government school and 148 private school students. Similarly protein intake was analyzed for 145 government school and 153 private school students.

Univariate analysis was performed using unpaired t-test and ANOVA. Multivariate analysis was performed using linear regression.

Seventy girls from government school and four girls from private school could not recollect their date of birth correctly, hence age could not be calculated.

Discussion

Of the 329 adolescent girls, who filled up the FFQ, the demographic profile suggest that there is fair representation of different socioeconomic group. It was observed that majority of students from the government school were from lower socioeconomic group because the education is almost free. The average family size of a private school student was significantly less than that of a government school student. A government school student was 3 times more likely to have three or more siblings compared to a private school student (OR = 2.96; 95% Cl = 1.84 - 4.76, $p > 0.000$). However no significant difference was observed with respect to gender of the siblings.

The mean protein intake of 298 students was 44.09 ± 20.9 grams. The protein intake on an average is 30% less than what is recommended by Indian Council of Medical Research (ICMR). The deficit was more pronounced in case of government school students (50%) then the private school students (5%). This could be attributed to poor economic status of the children studying in government schools. Predictably, the protein intakes showed a linear trend with respect to age of the students. However gross difference was observed regarding protein intake between government and private school students. Chugh et al in their study of dietary habits of affluent adolescent girls reported that protein and calorie intake was deficient in affluent girls of Delhi. In the study conducted by Nagi et al, there was no difference in calorie and protein intake in different income groups. Chaturvedi et al reported 23% to 32% less protein intake among adolescent girls in rural area of Rajasthan. To understand the influence of various factors on protein intake, a multivariate analysis was performed using linear regression. The two predictors for protein intake were income status and family size.

In order to further understand the protein intake pattern, the mean intake was calculated between government and privates school students after adjusting for other socio economic variables, viz. income, family size, birth order and number of siblings, the difference persisted throughout between the students of two schools. Thus suggesting that it is an important marker for protein intake among adolescent school girls. Regarding calorie intake, it was observed that overall calorie intake was quiet poor compared to the recommended values. The mean calorie intake for 301 adolescent school girls was 1155.9 ± 522.7 which is only 56% of recommended daily calorie intake. For the government and private schools, the values were 827.4 ± 191.2 and 1491.3 ± 541.0 respectively. In each weight and age category, the calorie intake was less compared to the recommendations of ICMR. Same are the observations of other researchers. The deficit in calorie intake in our study is 20% to 35% in various age groups of private school respondents and 55% to 64% in case of government school respondents. Inadequate calorie consumption among girls is also reported by Qamra et al among both higher and lower socio economic groups in Chandigarh. They found that 64% girls were consuming less than adequate calories. This difference was highly significant. In contrast. Mehta reported a higher calorie intake among 16 and 17 year old girls from a school of Delhi, which caters to higher socioeconomic group. However, the method used in her study was 24 Hour recall method. In the National Health and Nutrition Examination survey of the United states, the calorie intake among 16 to 19 year old girls was found to be 1965.61 calories. Similar findings are reported by Lluch et al. It makes us conclude that among the affluent class and in developed countries, the calorie intake is remarkably higher. However, the methodology used for assessment of calorie intake in these studies is different from that of ours.

The socioeconomic factors that significantly influenced calorie intake were income, number of siblings and weight of the students. This difference became more prominent, after adjusting for type of school i.e. government or private. However regression analysis showed that the only predictor variable was income of the family. Regression after adjusting for school type, showed that in case of government school, it was number of the siblings and for the private school, it was none.

Conclusion

The calorie and protein intake of the adolescent girls is much lower among the lower socio economic group adolescent girls. Even in the comparatively better economic status girls, the intake fell short of requirement. In our study, income and number of siblings emerged as predictor variables. It may be used to identify underfed adolescent girls and suitable interventions in the form of nutrition education and emphasis on improvement of food intake may be made in order to reduce the deficits.

The Relationship between Energy Intake and Diarrhoeal Disease in their effects on Child Growth: Biological Model, Evidence, and Implications for Public Health Policy

Although the effects of both inadequate energy intake and diarrhoeal disease in the aetiology of early childhood malnutrition have been well established, debate about their relative importance affects public health policies designed to improve child nutrition. Understanding the nature of the relationship among energy intake, diarrhoea, and child growth is important for identifying public health interventions most likely to result in improved nutrition status as well as the conditions under which specific interventions are likely to have the greatest benefit.

The positive effect of increased energy intake resulting from nutritional supplementation at 36 months is approximately 2 cm growth in length for Guatemalan and Colombian children. Calculated estimates of the cumulative effect of diarrhoea on length by the age of three years have ranged from 2.5 to 10 cm. The overall effect of energy intake on malnutrition is not independent of that of diarrhoea. however, because diarrhoea also affects intake, energy requirements, and the amount of energy available at the cellular level. Thus, we hypothesized that diarrhoea and inadequate energy intake are biologically interrelated in a synergistic fashion.

In their classic monograph. Scrimshaw et al. first described the synergistic relationship between malnutrition and infection on nutrition status. They stated: "The simultaneous presence of malnutrition and infection results in an interaction that is more serious for the host than would be expected from the combined effect of the two working independently." Statistically, synergism is described as an interaction that occurs when the effect of one independent variable on the dependent variable depends on the level of another independent variable such that their combined effects are greater than the sum of their individual effects.

A graphic representation of the model proposed by Lutter et al. is presented here. This model predicts that the biological relationship between the effects of inadequate energy intake and diarrhoea on nutrition status is synergistic.

Effects of the Variables

The Effect of Diarrhoea on Energy Balance

Diarrhoea, particularly when accompanied by fever, can compromise energy balance through three mechanisms: (1) reduced dietary intake ; (2) increased faecal loss because of malabsorption of micronutrients and macronutrients , decreased intestinal transit time, and loss of nutrients into the gut ; and (3) increased catabolism because of an acceleration in basal metabolic rate.

Each mechanism has a different effect on energy balance. For example, reduced intake leads to a decrease in energy ingested, and increased faecal loss results in reduced availability of ingested nutrients. The third mechanism, increased catabolism, results in increased requirements. Thus, the first two mechanisms cause a reduction in energy available at the cellular level at the same time that the third causes an increase in requirements. The overall effect can lead to an energy deficit during illness and, depending on the aetiology of illness, can extend for some time thereafter.

The Effect of Energy Intake and Diarrhoea on Nutrition Status

Inasmuch as troth inadequate energy intake and diarrhoea affect overall energy balance, the effect of either one on nutrition status is likely to depend on the level of the other. Thus, the positive effect of additional energy intake on child growth increases as the level of diarrhoea increases, and the negative effect of additional diarrhoea increases as the level of energy intake decreases. When nutrition status is not compromised because of inadequate energy intake relative to requirements, diarrhoea should not have a negative effect on growth, as has been observed among well-nourished children in the United States. However, where nutrition status is compromised because of inadequate energy intake relative to requirements, the negative effect of diarrhoea on growth will differ depending on the degree to which nutrition status is compromised.

The Model

The incremental effect of energy intake on nutrition status for children without diarrhoea is measured by the slope of the line segment ah relative to the Z axis; this slope is positive. The incremental effect of energy intake on nutrition status for children with the highest level of diarrhoea is measured by the slope of the line segment dc relative to the Z axis; this slope is positive (and greater than ab). The incremental effect of diarrhoea on nutrition status for the lowest level of energy intake is measured by the slope of the line segment ad relative to the X axis; this slope is negative. Finally, the incremental effect of diarrhoea on nutrition status for the highest level of energy intake is measured by the slope of the line segment bc relative to the X axis; this slope is zero in the figure. The synergism is shown by the greater slope of ad compared to bc, which reflects the greater negative incremental effect of diarrhoea for children with low energy intakes relative to those with high energy intakes. The surface abed represents estimated nutrition status for different combinations of energy intake and diarrhoea.

This biological synergism can be modelled for statistical estimation with the following equation: $Y=u+bD+cE+dDE+e$, where

Y is nutrition status, D is a measure of the level of diarrhoea, E is a measure of the level of energy intake, a, b, c and d are parameters to be estimated. and e is the error term.

Support for the Model

Results from three recent publications provide evidence for this underlying biological model.

Bogota, Colombia

In the context of evaluating the effect of nutritional supplementation on child growth, we first proposed that the relationship between energy intake and diarrhoea as it related to growth was synergistic: that the pernicious effect of diarrhoea would depend on the energy intake of the child, just as the effect of increased energy intake on growth would depend on the level of diarrhoea. We therefore tested the hypothesis that the positive effect of supplementation (resulting in a significant increase in energy intake) on growth would depend on the level of diarrhoea.

Length and diarrhoeal morbidity were compared at 36 months of age for two cohorts of urban Colombian children: supplemented from birth, and unsupplemented. Energy intakes were 1,329 ± 44 and 1,171 ± 45 kcal/day for unsupplemented children at 18 and 36 months of age respectively. Supplementation resulted in a significant increase of 220 and 253 kcal/ day respectively at these two ages. Although unsupplemented children were ill with diarrhoea a total of 83 days between birth and 36 months of age. compared to 73 days for supplemented children, this difference failed to reach statistical significance.

The effects of energy intake and diarrhoea on attained length at 36 months of age were assessed by linear regression, modelled mathematically as described above, except that energy intake was defined as a dichotomous variable and given a value of l for the children who were supplemented and 0 for those who were not. Diarrhoea was defined as the number of days of diarrhoea between birth and 36 months of age. Analysis of variance was also used to describe the results.

For the same prevalence of diarrhoea, significant differences were seen in the slopes of the regression equation but not in the intercepts for supplemented versus unsupplemented children. Lack of significant difference between the two intercepts indicates that in the absence of diarrhoea there was no difference in attained length between supplemented and unsupplemented children; both supplemented and unsupplemented children who experienced no diarrhoea had a mean length of 87.7 cm at 36 months. The slope for unsupplemented children, however, was significantly different from zero (-0.03 cm per day ill; p<.001), showing that each day with diarrhoea was associated with a reduction of 0.03 cm in attained length at the age of 36 months. The cumulative effect of this deficit for those unsupplemented children with the highest level of diarrhoea was 5 cm (87.7 - 78.7 cm). In contrast, the slope for supplemented children did not differ significantly from zero, showing that diarrhoea had no effect on attained length at 36 months. The mean length of these children was 87.7 cm at 36 months, regardless of the level of diarrhoea.

A dose response in the effectiveness of supplementation by quartile of diarrhoea was also shown by two-way analysis of variance. The difference in length between supplemented and unsupplemented children in the lowest quartile of diarrhoeal disease was small and not statistically significant. The differences became larger and their significance increased in the next three quartiles of diarrhoea, so that the difference in the highest quartile was nearly 5 cm.

Villages in Progreso, Guatemala

Two groups examined growth in length in rural Guatemalan children between 3 and 36 months of age in relation to the percentage of time ill with diarrhoea and supplemental energy from two traditional beverages: one with a high amount of energy (atole) and one with a low amount of energy (fresco). The interval of 3-36 months was used because Guatemalan infants were largely breast-fed until 3 months of age and experienced very little diarrhoea. Thus, the interval was that when the biological effect of increased energy intake (achieved through supplementation) and diarrhoea would be expected to occur.

Children supplemented with atole consumed significantly more supplemental energy than those supplemented with fresco: 124 + 85 versus 16 + 13 kcal/ day. Energy from the home diet did not differ significantly between the two groups: children supplemented with atole consumed 840 + 239 kcal/day at home compared to 889 + 291 kcal/day for those supplemented with fresco. The percentages of time ill with diarrhoea were 8.5 + 7.1 and 8.2 + 7.2 days respectively, which were not significantly different.

The effect of supplement type and diarrhoea, defined as the percentage of time ill, on growth in length between 3 and 36 months of age was examined using the same statistical model described above. Supplement type was described as a dichotomous variable and given the value of 1 for the children who were supplemented with atole and 0 for those supplemented with fresco.

The results of the regression equation showed significant differences in both the intercept and slopes. For children receiving atole, the percentage of time with diarrhoea did not have a statistically significant effect on growth. They grew 29.5 cm, regardless of the level of diarrhoea. For children receiving fresco, however, the percentage of time with diarrhoea was negatively and significantly related to growth. For this group the difference in growth between those with the highest and lowest levels of diarrhoea was 3.7 cm (28.0 - 24.3 cm). However, the differences in intercepts indicate that even at very low levels of diarrhoea the additional energy provided through supplementation positively and significantly affected

The results from the study in Colombia indicate the direction of the interaction between energy intake and diarrhoeal disease on growth, and therefore provide an a priori direction for hypothesis testing in the study from Guatemala.

Lima, Peru

The effects on weight gain of energy intake, proportion of energy from breast milk, diarrhoeal prevalence, and age were evaluated in poor urban Peruvian infants. Between I and 6 months of age, weight gain was positively associated with energy intake and the proportion of energy from breast milk, but was not associated with prevalence of diarrhoea. In contrast, between 6 and 12 months the interaction between energy intake and prevalence of diarrhoea on weight gain was found significant (p <.(X12). Among infants whose usual energy intake was greater than 75% of recommended amounts, no relationship between diarrhoeal prevalence and weight gain was found. However, among infants whose usual intake was less than 75% of the recommendation, a negative relationship was seen.

Discussion

Many studies have been undertaken to establish the direction of causality in the relationship between diarrhoea and nutrition status and these have recently been reviewed. However the biological model presented in this paper and supported with evidence from Colombia, Guatemala, and Peru argues that this relationship cannot be viewed in isolation from energy intake. The dissimilarities that were found among them result from differences in the amounts of energy ingested as well as the source of energy rather than differences in the underlying biological model.

Although the percentage of time ill with diarrhoea was roughly comparable in both the Colombian and Guatemalan populations, energy intakes differed remarkably. The unsupplemented Colombian children consumed almost twice as much energy as the Guatemalan children (1,329 versus 778 kcal/day), and the net increase from supplementation was approximately 230 kcal/day in Colombia compared to only 124 kcal/ day in Guatemala.

Thus, the finding in Guatemala of a supplement effect even at low levels of diarrhoea among children consuming the high-energy supplement can be attributed to the larger deficit in their energy intakes, such that even in the absence of diarrhoea both supplemented and unsupplemented children had inadequate energy intakes. This was not the case in Colombia, where additional energy from supplementation did not contribute to improved growth in the absence of diarrhoea, because in the absence of the energy cost of diarrhoea, home diets were sufficient to meet energy needs.

The study in Peru provides an example of how the source of energy affects the relationship between energy intake and diarrhoea on nutrition status. Numerous studies have confirmed the fact that breast-milk consumption is unchanged (or may be increased) during diarrhoea. In contrast, estimates of the reduction in energy intake from other food sources range from 15% to 20%. The overall energy cost resulting from reduced food intake during diarrhoea was hypothesized to depend on the proportion of energy coming from breast milk versus other sources. Also. although no data are available on the energy cost of faecal losses among breast-fed infants during diarrhoea, data do show that losses among non-breast-fed infants depend in part on the diet consumed. The overall energy cost of faecal loss during diarrhoea therefore also was hypothesized to depend on the proportion of energy coming from breast milk versus other foods.

Because breast milk represented the major source of energy for Peruvian infants between I and 6 months of age, diarrhoea did not affect their energy balance in the same way as for older infants receiving less of their total energy from that source. Among older infants receiving a smaller proportion of their total energy from breast milk, diarrhoea and energy intake had the same interactive effect on growth as was found among Colombian and Guatemalan children.

In Colombia and Guatemala the supplements provided not only additional energy but also protein, vitamins, and minerals. Therefore, the relative importance of energy intake versus that of overall improved dietary quality cannot be determined: both are likely to be important.

In the Peruvian study, the relationship between diarrhoea and growth varied with age and usual energy intake. In populations where breast-feeding is still prevalent, age is important because it serves as a proxy for the percentage of energy coming from breast milk.

Together, the results from these studies show that the relationship between inadequate energy intake and diarrhoea is synergistic and affects nutrition status in a manner far greater than the simple additive effects either one alone would predict. For example, Guatemalan children who consumed high amounts of the high-energy supplement (>100 kcal/day) and had high levels of diarrhoea (ill >10% of the time) grew approximately 3 cm more between 3 and 36 months than those who consumed the low-energy supplement but had comparable levels of diarrhoea. In Colombia, unsupplemented children in the highest quartile of disease were 5 cm shorter than unsupplemented children in the highest quartile of disease at 36 months of age. These differences are far greater than the 2 cm reported as the difference between supplemented versus unsupplemented Colombian and Guatemalan children at 36 months of age in these same studies.

The public health implications of these findings arc threefold:

First: an immediate strategy to improve child nutrition should focus on mechanisms to improve energy intake in general, and during and immediately after the diarrhoeal episode in particular. Because of anorexia it may he difficult to increase dietary intake during or immediately after a diarrhoeal episode. Research is needed to determine foods that are more readily accepted during illness and that could be used to maintain an energy source. There may also be a period after an episode when appetite is increased. To the extent that appropriate foods are available to meet this increased appetite, the negative effect of diarrhoea on energy balance may be offset. Research is necessary to determine whether this increase in appetite occurs and, if so, when.

Second: concurrently and as a long-term strategy, environmental conditions that put young children at risk for diarrhoea must be improved. This will include improvements in the infrastructure of water and sanitation, coupled with specific interventions to improve household food preparation and hygiene so as to lessen exposure to pathogens.

Third: breast-feeding has a special and previously unrecognized role in the relationship between energy intake and diarrhoea with respect to nutrition status. Its protective effect on risk of diarrhoea has long been recognized; however, it has only recently been demonstrated that when infants who are receiving a major proportion of their energy from breast milk do get diarrhoea, the illness does not have a negative effect on growth. Thus, efforts to promote increased energy intake among infants and young children should by coupled with efforts to promote exclusive breast-feeding through at least the first 4 months of infancy and partial breast-feeding through 24 months, when children arc most at risk for diarrhoea.

Determinants of Nutritional Behaviour: A Multitude of Levers for Successful Intervention?

For some decades, the identification of determinants of human nutrition behaviour has been a goal of many scientists of different disciplines. Among them, [Lewin, 1943 and Lewin, 1951] is regarded as a pioneer, who considered nutritional behaviour as a complex process involving cultural, social and psychological factors.

Up to now, many partial and holistic models have been published helping to understand and explain people's nutritional behaviour. "But we only know a small amount of what is to be known, and still cannot advise a parent about how to make his/her child like vegetables".

As the citation indicates, nutritional behaviour is not just studied for reasons of academic curiosity, but due to the unsatisfactory impact of many people's behaviour on their health. This, however, has already been true in the late 1970s, when in Germany a group of scientists interested in nutrition behaviour research organized themselves as a corresponding association called AGEV (i.e. 'Arbeitsgemeinschaft Ernährungsverhalten' which means 'Association for Nutritional Behaviour'). In 2002, AGEV celebrated its 25th anniversary within the scope of the 10th Food Choice Conference and held a symposium on 'Sensible policies for nutrition and life-style intervention'. The presentations given in that symposium are published in this issue of Appetite.

The aim of the present paper is to introduce into the topic of the AGEV-Symposium and to give insight into the objectives and activities of AGEV.

Determinants of Nutritional Behaviour

Nutritional behaviour is framed by a multilayer process including biological, anthropological, economic, psychological, socio-cultural, and home economics related determinants and it is shaped by the individual situation. In the following, a brief overview is given showing the impacts of a variety of determinants on nutritional behaviour.

Biological Determinants

The biological determinants of nutritional behaviour can be subdivided into the physiological, patho-physiological and genetic. Among these, physiology provides the most basic determinants of nutritional behaviour. Humans need energy and nutrients for their metabolism in order to survive. As Kass put it: "Show us an animal that is not turning over foodstuff and we shall pronounce him dead. To live is to metabolize."

From a metabolic point of view, humans simply are what they have ingested before ([Kass, 1994]). But they are unable to perceive their specific needs and react accordingly. They only know the general and non-specific feelings of hunger or satiety—results of complex physiological processes which still are not fully understood.

Humans' digestive physiology provides little restrictions to their food choices. They can select their food from a wide range of organic stuff, be it of plant origin or animal origin. Nevertheless, there are two important constraints that physiology imposes on nutritional behaviour, one referring to food quantity, the other to quality. Considering food quantity, it is obvious that the gastro-intestinal tract can only absorb a limited volume of food, even though the stomach is quite dilatable and can therefore serve as a food buffer. But this limitation forces humans to take up food--if possible—at least once a day, preferably more often. The quality related constraint that can be attributed to human physiology is caused by the fact that humans are monogastric. Thus, they can hardly make use of plants that have high fibre contents.

These nonetheless relatively soft physiological restrictions are intensified by a series of possible diseases, like infections (a simple flue, for instance, affecting the perception of the odour or taste of a food item), food intolerances or allergies, Crohn's disease or diabetes.

In recent years, nutritional genomics is increasingly discussed , but no significant gene related determinants of nutritional behaviour have yet been detected, except for the well known influence of gender, the sensory sensitivity to specific chemical substances like phenylthiocarbamide ([Schmid and Beauchamp, 1990]) and possibly certain taste preferences ([Davenport, 2001]).

Thus, biology determines humans' basic nutritional needs, but it hardly restricts their food choices.

Anthropological Determinants

The freedom in food choice that biology offers to man is a blessing as well as a curse. It helps to prevent starvation if a specific type of food is scarce, but it increases the occurrence of nutritional imbalances and intoxications.

In contrast to many animals, the nutrition behaviour of humans is hardly determined by instincts, except for the sucking reflex of newborns or a general preference for sweet tastes as well as an aversion towards bitter tastes. Their food choice and food intake, other than digestion and metabolism, are cognitively controlled using an open and extendible information system. In a process of trial and error man needed to learn which of the products provided by nature could serve as food and which not, sometimes with fatal consequences. But humans are quite well equipped to evaluate unknown stuff that might prove to be food: with their senses they can explore its colour and shape, its firmness or crispness, its odour and finally its taste and even its sound, and they are able to memorize these perceptions and recall them, if necessary.

The freedom of food choice puts man into a conflict of food neophobia and neophilia. The first prevents from intoxications, but almost unavoidably leads to nutrition imbalances; while the latter prevents from imbalances, but increases the chance of intoxications. Research on the extent of food neophobia and neophilia in various populations revealed still in our days significant interpersonal as well as cross-country variations.

Economic Determinants

Economists often assume that consumers are rational, "in that they pursue the best objectives for themselves subject to constraints of their environment". These restrictions primarily refer to the consumers' budget, the goods and corresponding information available to them, and finally the prices at which the goods are offered.

According to neoclassical microeconomic theory, the demands for goods are interrelated due to the generally limited budget and may therefore not be considered separated from each other. Generally, there are two types of relations between goods: goods are either complements (like marmalade and bread) or they are substitutes.

Based on these assumptions, the main interest of neoclassical consumption theory refers to the interrelationship of prices, income and expenses or consumption, respectively. It rather considers the impact of changes in prices or income on consumption than the absolute amounts of certain goods demanded by consumers. In most cases, market information available to the consumers is considered to be perfect and in cross-sectional studies prices are often regarded as constants. Therefore, both are often neglected, leaving income or the budget, respectively, as the only external variable explaining a specific demand.

Thus, neoclassical consumption theory is hardly able to deal with non-economic phenomena in the context of consumption sometimes leading to inconsistencies when theoretical expectations are confronted with empirical results. So [Deaton and Muellbauer,

1980], for instance, admitted that "there are important explanatory variables other than prices and total outlay."

The empirical importance of sociodemographic variables for the explanation of consumer behaviour, however, was already pointed out by early economists like [Allen and Bowley, 1935, Engel, 1857 and Sydenstricker and King, 1921], or [Prais and Houthakker, 1955]. But it took time for this knowledge to be generally recognized in economic theory. Now, it is quite common that socioeconomic and -demographic determinants of consumption (especially household composition) are taken into account, e.g. by means of consumer unit scales.

Quite a setback to supporters of the neoclassical consumption theory occurred in the early 1980s, when it was experimentally proven, that consumers' preferences depend on the way a decision problem is presented. This means that consumers are actually unable to make rational decisions, which disproves one of the fundamental assumptions in neoclassical theory. "The modern consumer has lost credibility as a rational agent in the eyes of food theorists". But these findings did not lead to a complete rejection of the theory—it can still be found in recent economic publications. Psychological aspects, however, got increasingly important in economic demand models.

Marketing approaches in consumer economics, generally discard most of the key assumptions of neoclassical theory and shifted economists' interests towards determinants of the demand for specific goods not just taking into account external factors (like prices, availability and certain marketing measures) but also internal ones (like socioeconomic, demographic or psychological characteristics of the consumers) ([Popkin and Haines, 1981]). In time series analyses of food demand, sometimes expectations (e.g. regarding future price and income levels) and desires (e.g. regarding demanded quantities) are also taken into account.

Psychological Determinants

From a psychological point of view, (nutrition) behaviour is traditionally explained by the S–O–R model. This means, there is a set of external and internal factors (=Stimuli S), which persons perceive and process mentally (=Organism O) before they finally react with a certain (nutrition) behaviour (=Reaction R). The mental processes involved are divided into activating ones (emotions, motives, attitudes) and cognitive ones (perceiving, thinking, learning).

Emotions partially promote a reaction by an individual (e.g. joy, interest), but partially also temper it (e.g. contentedness, sorrow) ([Bänsch, 1995]). In contrast to general consumer behaviour, however, nutrition has natural internal activating processes (hunger) and does not need external stimuli to initiate a reaction.

Motives are emotions with a certain orientation towards an action. They are needs, ambitions, wishes or yearnings that trigger a behaviour. There are plenty of motives that often compete when influencing people's food choice, e.g. enjoying taste, relieving hunger, expressing fellowship, representing social status, maintaining health or fitness, saving money and sticking to habits.

Finally, *attitudes* are a combination of motives and the assessment of the correspondence of certain objects with these motives. Closely related to the concept of attitudes are opinions, which are verbal expressions of attitudes. Attitudes used to be considered as important keys to understand people's behaviour. Now, however, it is disputed whether positive attitudes towards an object (like a certain food stuff) result in a corresponding object-related behaviour. Generally, attitudes were found to be only good predictors for cognitively well controlled behaviour , which usually is not true for nutrition.

Among the cognitive processes *perception* refers to the absorption, selection, organisation and interpretation of information. It provides a personal, non-objective image of the external reality. *Thinking*, the second cognitive process, means internal processing and mental generation of information. Other than perception, thinking is independent from external stimuli. Finally, *learning* is the process of mentally saving and retrieving information. Any behaviour that is not genetically determined is inescapably learnt, either by own experience or communications with trustworthy persons ([Bänsch, 1995]). In this context, an everyday activity like eating can be seen as a continuing process of learning. It is a recurring training by experiences with high frequency leading to a stable habitual behaviour.

On this conceptual basis, psychology of nutrition generally interprets a person's specific food choices as an individually optimized decision assessing all the advantages and disadvantages of motives or values relevant to the specific situation.

Socio-cultural Determinants

Nutrition has not yet received much recognition by sociologists, except for the aspect of food shortage and famine. Nevertheless, there is no doubt, that the social and cultural environment shapes (nutrition) behaviour ([Rozin, 1998]). Three types of groups influencing persons' behaviour can be distinguished:

- groups that persons belong to and in which they play their specific roles (e.g. the family and the circle of friends and colleagues)
- groups that persons do not belong to but where they would like to be accepted as members
- groups that persons do not want to be associated with, no matter whether they actually belong to or not.

Behaviour is influenced by the *norms* of these groups. Either one accepts the norms to be accepted as a member of the group (or at least be associated with the group) or one rejects the norms to be clearly dissociated from the group.

There are some obvious examples for the effect of group norms on nutrition behaviour. On the one hand, they explain the presence of collective aversions (e.g. in the Western culture towards the pleasure of insects as food) and on the other hand, these norms make understandable why many adults learnt to enjoy bitter tastes (like those of asparagus, beer or vermouth) even though they had a natural aversion against bitterness.

Often, socio-cultural and psychological determinants of nutritional behaviour are interrelated: the sociological view of the influence of norms can psychologically be interpreted as learning from models. Therefore, some authors assume, psychological and social components of behaviour interact in an undissolvable manner and thus should be referred to as psycho-social determinants.

The following examples of nutrition related motives are to demonstrate the interconnection between psychological and socio-cultural determinants of food choice :

1. *Identity*. Nutrition provides to oneself the impression of affiliation to a group which might for instance be defined by social stratum, regional provenance or nationality. Thus, a persistent retention of the dietary habits of migrants, for example, has often been observed.

2. *Communication*. Nutrition can serve as a means to express one's attitudes or one's membership of certain groups due to the symbolic meaning of many food stuffs. Caviar, for instance, is associated with affluence, champagne with festivity, wholegrain products with environmental and health consciousness, bread and water with asceticism, and bread and wine with Christianity.
3. *Community*. The earliest social rules known refer to the fair sharing of food which can be assured if the members of a group gather for common meals. As [Tremolieres, 1972] put it: "The oldest and highest taboo of human society is that a solitary enjoyment is a sin. Enjoyment must help towards communication and communion." The close relationship of community and nutrition is shown by the word `company' which is derived from the Latin words `con' and panis' meaning `bread partnership'.
4. *Spirituality*. Nutrition is a widely used field for spiritually motivated regimentations. Examples are the rules of kosher meal preparation for the Jews, the taboos of pork and any alcoholic beverages for the Muslims or the diverse fasting commandments in many religious communities.

Motives like the ones mentioned lead to the development and maintenance of cuisines—which are culturally defined bodies of regulations on how to properly prepare dishes and arrange them to meals. Cuisines generally narrow the set of theoretically edible material to what is considered food and thus moderate the neophobia versus neophilia conflict in nutrition. But cuisines can also be interpreted as 'institutionalized nutritional wisdom', i.e. they are partly results of a process of bio-cultural evolution developing cultural responses to biological needs. This, for instance, explains the alkali treatment of maize in American Indian societies. The technique improves the bioavailability of niacin and the amino acid quality of the digestible protein fraction of maize and thus influences significantly the 'nutritional efficacy of maize diets'.

Home Economics Velated Determinants

Traditionally, providing food is one of the main tasks of households. In this context, households are often only considered as units of consumption, but there are also plenty of producing activities. Food stuffs purchased often do not directly provide the utility consumers are seeking. In most cases, food is therefore processed, prepared, garnished and finally served before it is eaten.

Therefore, as long as food consumption does not completely take place away from home, nutrition behaviour is affected by several household characteristics like available means of transportation and kitchen equipment as well as the household members' know-how regarding food acquisition, transportation, storage and preparation. In this context, [Lewin, 1943] already emphasized the dominating role of the persons responsible for keeping the household whom he called 'gatekeepers'.

Even though these 'gatekeepers' play a major role in the process of food choice in households, they usually do not decide on their own. So, whenever food choice does not refer to a single person, conflicts arise concerning:

- individual food preferences
- symbolic meaning of union provided by common meals
- 'foodwork' (i.e. the work associated with meal preparation, including planning, purchasing, and cleaning up).

Therefore, observable food choices are often the results of formal or informal negotiations to mediate these conflicting motives.

Situation-related Determinants

Nutritional behaviour strongly depends on the individual situation which can be considered in a static or dynamic way. In the first case, an eating situation is regarded on its own independently of what happened before or might happen afterwards. In the second case, recent (eating) experiences and expectations concerning future events are also taken into account.

The main concern of a static approach to eating situations is availability which has several aspects influencing nutritional behaviour.

Firstly and most obviously, there is the availability of *food*, which depends on factors like season, climate, or economic development. Thus, the eating habits on vacation, for instance, almost inevitably differ from those of everyday life, especially if one is abroad, simply due to the availability of new foods and dishes associated with a lack of availability of usual ones.

Yet food is not the only important aspect of availability. Nutrition does not just mean the consumption of food and dishes– it is also associated with the use of the scarce good of *time*. Thus, nutritional behaviour is influenced by time budgets—one's own as well as the ones of the persons who are to prepare the meal or with whom one intends to share the meal.

Still another aspect of availability in the context of nutrition refers to '*infrastructure*' which means that some very simple properties of a situation like the presence of some kind of a stove or a table or the availability of crockery or cutlery may determine what is appropriate to be eaten or not.

With a dynamic approach to eating situations the aspects of satiation (quantitative aspect) and alternation (qualitative aspect) deserve specific attention. Regarding satiation makes clear that the amount of food one eats at a meal is influenced one's actual status of satiety which depends on the amount that one had with the previous meal. But there is also an impacts from the expectations concerning the next meal: the more food one expects to have for that meal the less will be chosen for the actual one and vice versa. Closely related to this aspect of satiation is the period of time between the meals. The influence of alternation is derived from the fact that people tend to avoid having the same or a similar kind of food or dish for two consecutive meals. So the recent experience of enjoying a sweet dish, for instance, favours the selection of a spicy dish for the next meal and the expectation of having a spicy dish for the next meal will bias the actual food choice towards a sweet one.

AGEV—A German Association for Nutritional Behaviour

From a public health point of view, the determinants of nutritional behaviour have often led to unsatisfactory results (like the epidemic of obesity) which is not just true in the populations of Europe or North America, but increasingly also in developing countries like India. This causes preventable cases of nutrition related diseases associated with avoidable suffering for the affected and their relatives as well as costs in the health services that could be saved.

Facing this situation, a group of scientist interested in nutrition behaviour research met in Münster (Germany) on January 15th, 1977, and later formed AGEV—a German association for nutritional behaviour. The association has an interdisciplinary orientation, which means it is not just interested in physiological or biochemical aspects of nutrition, but also in anthropological, psychological, sociological, economic, cultural or historical ones. Furthermore, despite of the fact that most of the AGEV members are Germans, the association is not just focussing on Germany, but has also an international perspective.

The activities of AGEV are aimed at accumulating knowledge on all aspects of human nutrition behaviour supporting the scientific exchange in nutrition research between natural, social and cultural sciences identifying innovative research areas and initiate corresponding work bridging the gap between science and practice.

These aims are pursued mainly by the organisation of regular (i.e. annual) scientific meetings and the publication of their outcomes. Now, AGEV can look back to a history of 25 meetings, with four of them held in an international context. Most recently AGEV dealt with topics like 'Spatial (i.e. regional or ethnic) aspects of food habits' or 'Research, development and consumer acceptance of functional food'. One of the last such activities was a cooperation with the organizers of the 10th Food Choice Conference in Wageningen, the Netherlands , which gave AGEV the chance to celebrate its 25th anniversary by holding a plenary session on 'Sensible policies for nutrition and life-style intervention.'

Index

□□□